Atheism After Christendom

Disbelief in an Age of Encounter

Simon Perry

Paternoster:
thinking faith

26 25 24 23 22 21 20 19 18 17 16 15   12 11 10 9 8 7 6 5 4 3 2 1

First published 2015 by Paternoster
Paternoster is an imprint of Authentic Media Limited
52 Presley Way, Crownhill, Milton Keynes, MK8 0ES.
www.authenticmedia.co.uk

British Library Cataloguing in Publication Data

A catalogue record for this book is available from the British Library

ISBN 978-1-84227-829-1
978-1-78078-078-8 (e-book)

Cover Design by David McNeill (www.revocreative.co.uk)
Printed and bound by CPI Group (UK) Ltd., Croydon, CR0 4YY

Contents

Contents

Series Preface: *After Christendom*

Christendom was a historical era, a geographical region, a political arrangement, a sacral culture and an ideology. For many centuries Europeans have lived in a society that was nominally Christian. Church and state have been the pillars of a remarkable civilisation that can be traced back to the decision of the emperor Constantine I early in the fourth century to replace paganism with Christianity as the imperial religion.

Christendom, a brilliant but brutal culture, flourished in the Middle Ages, fragmented in the reformation of the sixteenth century, but persisted despite the onslaught of modernity. While exporting its values and practices to other parts of the world, however, it has been slowly declining during the past three centuries. In the twenty-first century Christendom is unravelling.

What will emerge from the demise of Christendom is not yet clear, but we can now describe much of western culture as 'post-Christendom'.

Post-Christendom is the culture that emerges as the Christian faith loses coherence within a society that has been definitively shaped by the Christian story and as the institutions that have been developed to express Christian convictions decline in influence.

This definition, proposed and unpacked in *Post-Christendom**, the first book in the 'After Christendom' series, has gained widespread acceptance. *Post-Christendom* investigated the Christendom legacy and raised numerous issues that are explored in the rest of the series. The authors of this series, who write from within the Anabaptist tradition, see the current challenges facing the church not as the loss of a golden age but as opportunities to recover a more biblical and more Christian way of being God's people in God's world.

The series addresses a wide range of issues, including social and political engagement, how we read Scripture, youth work, mission, worship and the shape and ethos of the church after Christendom.

Books already published:

Stuart Murray: *Post-Christendom*
Stuart Murray: *Church after Christendom*
Jonathan Bartley: *Faith and Politics after Christendom*
Jo & Nigel Pimlott: *Youth Work after Christendom*
Alan & Eleanor Kreider: *Worship and Mission after Christendom*
Lloyd Pietersen: *Reading the Bible after Christendom*
Andrew Francis: *Hospitality and Community after Christendom*

These books are not intended to be the last word on the subjects they address, but an invitation to discussion and further exploration. Additional material, including extracts from published books and information about future volumes, can be found at anabaptistnetwork.com/After-Christendom.

Stuart Murray

---

* Stuart Murray: *Post-Christendom; church and mission in a strange new world* (Carlisle: Paternoster, 2004), 19.

Acknowledgements

George Steiner, whose book *Real Presences* has thwarted my every attempt to become a modern atheist, once asked, 'What worthwhile book after the Pentateuch has been written by a committee?'

Those with an active role in bringing this essay to life are certainly numerous. The book echoes with voices that are not my own, whether they have shaped the substructure of my thought (like Steiner), assured me the book was worth writing at all (Rev Dr Ruth Gouldbourne), or constantly encouraged me to march into territory far beyond the competency of my own back yard (Dr Edwige Moyroud). The staff at Paternoster of course, have laboured patiently at the text and significantly improved my crude manuscripts, so thanks to Mike Parsons and Mollie Barker, and to Peter Little.

The privilege of working at a Cambridge College has multiplied the number of voices in the text, and the fellows and students of Robinson College have helped to shape the final form of the manuscript. Many have taken great interest in this project, and some have read and critiqued draft chapters that drew upon their field of expertise. In particular, I would like to express gratitude to Professor Myles Burnyeat (Emeritus Professor of Ancient Philosophy), who sifted through my philosophy chapter and helped with my interpretations of Plato and Augustine. Dr Mark Hayes (Director of Studies in Economics) read an early draft of my economics chapter and corrected some mis-readings of Adam Smith and John Maynard Keynes. Dr Kevin Chalut (Royal Society Research Fellow in Physics) steered me around some of the pitfalls in my reading of modern physics. Mr Ross Reason (the Bursar), highlighted weak points in my engagement with Peter Singer. Miss Lotte Reinbold (Post Graduate student reading for a PhD in history) read the first few chapters and offered invaluable insight on both the contents and the style. In particular, I would like to thank two fellows who have read the entire manuscript: Dr Steve Trudgill (Emeritus Fellow in Geography) and Professor Morna Hooker (Lady Margaret's Professor Emerita) have both brought generous critique and embody the open-minded engagement with otherness that I have tried to articulate and encourage throughout this work.

Numerous students and fellows have also debated and discussed the issues raised in this book, and helped to sharpen the text at several key points; amongst whom Dr Brian Sloane, Dr Mary Stewart, Professor Robin Kirkpatrick, Professor Judith Lieu and Professor Twink Allen have been great encouragers, as have visiting fellows, Michael and Anita Hadley and Professor Leonard Conolly. Over the dinner table, at the bar, rowing a boat or wearing boxing gloves, several students have also been more influential than they know. Especially worthy of my gratitude are Matt Simpson, Henry Tozer, Ewan McGregor, Jenni Mills, Ros Old, Sam Holmes, Kathryn Mansfield, Kate Honey, Katie Reid, Max Maher, Jonathan Yip, and imposters Fingal Plumpton and James Whitehead.

Of course, the many voices here do not constitute a committee – and the majority of them would struggle to affirm every claim the book makes. But I am deeply conscious that in writing this book, I have been dependent upon the guidance, scrutiny and encouragement of many people – not least my four children. A thousand miles per month of car journeys have given them more opportunity than they may have wanted to hear and discuss simplified versions of this book and so it is dedicated to Alice May, Stefan Thomas, Lewis Edward and Willem James.

Introduction:

Atheism in an Age of Encounter

There are as many atheisms as there are Christianities. This is hardly surprising, since both have long and complex histories. As a vague and slippery category, those who identify themselves as 'atheist' in a secular society thereby tell us nothing about who they are. Some atheists have taken courageous, often traumatic steps to abandon the religious faith from which they once drew comfort. Others are atheist not by conscious decision, but in docile compliance with the hidden ideologies of their culture. Some are atheist because they dare to stand against the dehumanizing beliefs of their age. Others are atheist in unwitting submission to the subtle mythologies that shape our understanding of the universe. Some are atheist because they are thinkers; others, because they are not. Atheism can generate great acts of compassion and political love, and it can endorse severe prejudice and incite acts of violence. While some atheisms set themselves against religion in any form, other strands of atheist conviction run in deep and natural harmony with core strands of Christian belief. The burden of this book is to show how such harmony is found by only the most radical traditions of both atheism and Christianity. Radical, in the literal sense that their truest convictions are not superficial claims, but grow 'from roots' (*radicalis*) running deep into the fibre of their being and the depths of their heritage.

In all that follows, I will distinguish – in the broadest of brushstrokes – between *radical* versions of atheism and Christianity on the one hand, and their *creedal* counterparts on the other. By 'creedal', I refer not to specific Christian denominations, but to any who treasure convictions they are force-fed, either overtly by an ecclesiastical Big Brother, or covertly by an authoritarian regime masquerading as a democracy. Those who recite the Christian creeds are not necessarily creedal in this sense, while many secularists and atheists who denounce creeds of any sort may subconsciously adopt unwritten, unselfconscious creeds without realizing it. Nevertheless, creeds as traditionally understood have their origin in Christian history – in particular with the establishment of the era known as Christendom.

For Stuart Murray, Christendom was at once, 'a historical era, a geographical region, a political arrangement, a sacral culture and an ideology.'[1] At its core, I will argue, is commitment to a dubious power dynamic: firstly, obtain power so that, secondly, you may use that power to help others. Christendom is the name of any attempt to fuse Christian belief with this power dynamic. One result is a widespread conviction that if the church is to have any significant influence in the world, it must first learn to ride piggyback upon the reigning political power of its day. It is hardly surprising, now the Christendom era is ending, that secular Europe is left with a bad taste in its mouth. Murray has thus spearheaded a series of provocative reflections upon what the passing of Christendom means for contemporary church and society, the subject of the After Christendom project in which this book offers one voice.

Understanding the extent to which we live in a post-Christendom world is complicated by the disintegration of Christendom from a single solid entity into a dust cloud. Where once Christendom was virtually synonymous with the Catholic Church in Western Europe, the Reformations of the sixteenth century split the church into the mini-Christendoms that gradually settled along regional boundaries. With the growing religious liberty of the Enlightenment, mini-Christendoms turned into micro-Christendoms among different denominations and organizations, and even into the atomic-Christendoms of individual communities. This is why Christendom cannot be associated directly with any specific church tradition. The spirit of its power dynamic can thrive in the smallest, most independent of cell churches. Even these communities can function as atomic-Christendoms in which big fish may dominate small ponds with coercive power: while the authority may not be the God of Rome with the Pope as his spokesperson, no less problematic is the image of the Bible as God's Word and the preacher as its official mediator. Neither the village preacher nor the Pope of Rome is immune to the power games that characterize natural human life. In the pages below I use the term 'Christendom' in three main senses: historical Christendom (which has clearly passed), regional Christendoms (which have now almost dwindled out of existence), and contemporary Christendom (in which churches and Christians still seek secular forms of power as a prerequisite for doing God's will on earth).

My purpose here is by no means to condemn Christendom, but rather to highlight the fact that, despite its historical dominance, it has never been the *only* nor even the *truest* model of Christianity. Prior to Constantine the Great (c. AD 272–337), Christians had been an active force across the Roman Empire for almost three centuries. Throughout the medieval era, pockets of Christian resistance objected to the ideals and practices of the Christian order. In modern times, alternative Christian communities have slowly become free to find their voice. And today, as regional Christendom enters a state of advanced disintegration, Christians who seek to live by an alternative framework of belief have an ancient, colourful and largely unheard heritage from which to draw.

This view, of course, is at odds with the stance taken by many creedal atheists, who refuse to recognize the validity of any form of Christian belief that does not assent to the crudest Christendom ideal. Chief among today's creedal atheists are the representatives of the so-called 'New Atheism'. I make no attempt to offer a systematic rebuttal of their arguments. After all, such debates tend to be saved from tedious predictability only by the aggression or wit of an author's style. Even so, the writings offered by the 'four horsemen' of New Atheism (Richard Dawkins, Sam Harris, Daniel Dennett and the late Christopher Hitchens) exemplify how *the more militant forms of modern atheism are simply not atheist enough to be of any benefit to humanity*. This may sound drastically nonsensical, but much of what I argue here is designed to present atheism not simply as an intellectual or theoretical pursuit, but as a diverse collection of movements that are fundamentally political and social. When viewed through these lenses, the merits and shortfalls of various atheisms appear in a new light.

The first half of the book focuses upon the historical realities and ideas from which atheisms emerge, exploring ancient atheism (chapter 1), revolutionary atheism (chapter 2), philosophy (chapter 3) and the Bible (chapter 4). After an interlude on resurrection, the second half of the book engages atheist approaches to science (chapter 5), ethics (chapter 6), economics (chapter 7) and culture (chapter 8). My purpose here is to construct a positive case for radical atheism that is profoundly compatible with Christian Scripture.

The point of convergence between atheism and Christianity, I propose, is found by relating well with the *otherness* (or in biblical terms, 'holiness') of other people, which – in turn – is inseparable from the way we relate to the otherness of the world as we experience it, and the otherness of the world beyond our knowledge and experience. Recent decades have brought us into ever-closer encounter with the otherness of those whose strange religion, colour, language, class, culture or subculture we could previously ignore. In a digital, globalized and increasingly interconnected world, the disturbing *other* confronts us, countering us at the deepest level, challenging us into radical encounter. Their very existence hangs a question mark over the assumed supremacy of our own worldview, the legitimacy of our inherited privilege over them, the security of the social, material and ideological comforts we enjoy. Are we more likely to welcome or to reject this disruptive other?

The Christian doctrine of the incarnation upholds the conviction that, in Jesus of Nazareth, the Almighty God who created the multiverse and set the furthest galaxies swirling becomes a 'chav'. The Lord of Hosts, the Director General of heaven and earth, becomes 'trailer trash', a demonized nobody from a feral underclass.[2] This outsider-Christ has remained virtually invisible to creedal forms of Christianity and atheism, but his quiet, persistent presence through history simply will not go away. My underlying assumption is that this troublesome, awkward, embodiment of otherness is worthy of some attention.

1.

Atheism Before Modernity

The Imperial Cult

The fastest-growing religion in the first century AD revolved around a man who was widely considered divine. He was, after all, the Son of God. He offered salvation to the whole earth, brought peace and established true justice. Beginning in the eastern provinces of the Roman Empire, this new religion was a grass-roots movement, slowly gathering momentum and gradually extending its reach westwards until eventually it penetrated Rome itself. Across all strata of society, throughout almost every region of the empire, the coming of the Son of God would be 'good news' for all people. This 'Son of God', the man who came to be worshipped in all corners of the Roman world, was none other than Caesar.

From Augustus (27 BC – AD 14) to Constantine (AD 306–37), Rome's expanding imperial cult was 'the most important type of worship.'[1] Such worship, being so thoroughly intertwined with political concerns and social realities, kept the massive imperial machine running smoothly. Far from being a secondary issue for rulers and subjects, worship constructed what historian Simon Price has described as a 'cognitive system'. It formed a lens through which Roman subjects made sense of their world. 'The imperial cult,' he concludes, 'along with politics and diplomacy, constructed the reality of the Roman empire.'[2]

This cult had a complex genesis, its history rooted in the ruler cults of the Greek city-states. For the inhabitants of ancient Greece, there was no international law, Geneva Convention or United Nations. No coloured maps that fixed national boundaries with relative stability. Inhabitants of these cities – like all other ancient peoples – lived with a profound fear of violence which could, at any instant, sweep through cities and lives, bringing devastation. Most modern westerners can only guess at how daily life would feel when lived in the knowledge that the crops you sowed might be reaped by future invaders at whose hands your achievements, your family and your life could be torn away at any moment. In such a context, any leader who brought lasting military security brought life itself.

For citizens anxious about attacks from expansionist war-bands, what better way to show allegiance to a ruthless and powerful warlord than to establish a shrine in his honour? What better way to guarantee the protection of a powerful king than to ensure he is honoured at your city's shrines and temples? For a king, what better way to maintain obedience and loyalty in your cities than to have their inhabitants worshipping at your shrine? In reality, kings themselves were rarely worshipped as gods, but were viewed merely as 'temple-sharing gods', and usually the cults that emerged were only 'city cults'. However, when Caesar Augustus burst onto the pages of history, it was entire provinces rather than individual cities that established ruler-cults, and those cults were less cautious about pronouncing certain emperors 'divine'. Rome had, after all, performed many of the feats associated only with the action of the gods: establishing not simply peace, but an environment in which peace was the norm that allowed justice to flourish. So much so that some thought to base their entire calendar upon Augustus' coming into the world.[3] The widespread recognition of Augustus' divine achievements is carved into the stonework that embodied Rome's authority across the empire. Price notes, however, that although Roman authority was embodied in marble, 'the widespread imperial temples and imperial statues did not form the cold grandeur of alien authority.'[4] Worshipping in this cult included not only sacrifices, but games and festivals, performances, and feasts of bread and wine, all of which fed off and fed into the glory of Rome. These acts of worship were not simply religious events attended by those who would otherwise have been rolling their thumbs, waiting for someone to invent television. The lives and livelihoods of citizens were, by these acts of worship, 'glued in' socially, politically and economically to the overarching authority of Rome.

This was reflected in the developing theology of the cult. In about AD 175, the Platonic philosopher Celsus wrote a tract outlining the 'soft' monotheism of the cult. The gods of conquered people were invited to bask in Rome's higher glory, placing the religious customs and beliefs of conquered people into the Roman context. Rome's gods did not so much conquer other tribal deities as welcome them into the pantheon. But here the polytheism ended. 'Celsus was a religious and social conservative who believed that the interests of a multicultural empire would best be served if the various subject peoples worshipped according to their own traditions, so long as they were willing to subscribe to a myth that all such worship was offered ultimately to the supreme God, or intellect, who oversaw the security and destiny of the empire.'[5] Rome's imperial cult gently conditioned conquered people to behave as such.

But there was one people-group whose members had proven themselves gloriously incapable of behaving as though they were conquered. By the time of Augustus, the Jewish people were spread across the empire, and – no doubt thanks to a genetic, dogged resistance to alien ideologies – were granted special concessions. There was no image of their god in the Pantheon, and their men were exempted from military service. Although Celsus had little respect for Jewish belief, its sheer antiquity alone forced him to accept it as a valid religion.[6] While Rome could tolerate Jewish monotheism, there were sub-groups within Judaism that were not granted the status of *religio licita*, legal religion.

From the Roman rulers' perspective, maintaining order, stability and peace is no easy task and must always entail – as recent wars in the Middle East have shown – a battle for 'hearts and minds'. This, by and large, was the function of the imperial cult. Conquered gods would be brought to stand in the Pantheon, where they were honoured but relativized, where their divinity was placed into a specific context: the all-pervasive power of Rome. With everyone worshipping the emperor, the empire itself was much easier to police, its order, stability and justice easier to maintain. But throughout the period of the Roman imperial cult, there operated a troublesome underground movement spawned by Jewish monotheism. Its adherents met in secret, in tiny cells across the empire, and, despite Rome's best efforts to crush them, their numbers continued to grow. The empire described this group as 'atheists' because they did not recognize the authority of the state's gods. These atheists (known also by other derogatory terms such as Nazarenes, Galileans or Christians) had a particular way of life that was bound to bring them into confrontation with the imperial cult.

Unlike the private religious cults who – across the empire – worshipped various household deities, the atheists worshipped a god whose existence posed a threat to the smooth running of the empire. This was a deity emerging from the Jewish belief in only one God, a God personified in the leader of a failed revolutionary movement, Jesus of Nazareth. Those who worshipped this Jesus refused to acknowledge Caesar as lord and, in so doing, brought down upon their own heads the full weight of Roman fury. This had little to do with any personal offence an emperor might feel at not being worshipped – no emperor would seriously have considered himself divine in any case. It was rather that the day-to-day running of the empire depended upon acknowledging the lordship of Caesar, and those who refused were thereby challenging the legitimacy not only of the emperor, but of the entire ideological, economic, political, social, ethical ordering of the world. Ultimately, the imperial machine, though run by an emperor, was based upon the worship of greater gods rooted deep in the psyche of Roman history and culture. To run an empire well, an emperor needed to show that he enjoyed their blessing.

Mars, Venus and the Founding of an Empire

After the civil wars of Rome, Augustus (63 BC – AD 14) had united the warring factions of the republic, brought peace (the *pax Augusta*) and ushered in the new era of empire. The religious backing for his endeavour was to be found in his divine ancestry. Drawing together the maternal, nurturing and caring nature of Venus, and the militaristic paternal strength of Mars, Augustus could claim all the credentials required of an emperor. Augustus broadcast the divine harmony of his genes through the most effective technology available: the architecture of the Roman Forum.

Surrounded by Aeneas, Romulus and the *summi viri*, the Caryatids, and the statues of Mars and Venus, the seminal point of the Forum of Augustus, placed centrally within the projecting forecourt, was a statue of the emperor himself . . . Here . . . Augustus served as the formative point of mediation between his divine ancestors Mars and Venus. Their divine child was Harmonia, Augustus was the creator of the *pax Augusta*.[7]

Imperial Rome thus combined (and was seen to combine) the military ferocity of Mars with the economic allure of Venus. Strength and beauty, aggression (against others) and nourishment (for one's own) were written into the marble heart of the world's capital. The emperor presented himself as genetic heir to these divine attributes, both of which were necessary for running an empire. As the imperial cult took root throughout the conquered realms, worship of the emperor necessarily implied worship of Mars and Venus whose attributes he wielded so successfully. So long as Roman citizens benefited from the imperial political machine, Mars and Venus were worthy gods. But the gods of Rome did not bestow their gifts upon every inhabitant of the empire. Countless folk living out in the provinces did not benefit from the status quo, and may well have experienced Mars and Venus as demons rather than gods. Early Christians, though apparently acknowledging the divine power of these gods, refused to worship them, and were properly deemed as atheist.

But were these proto-atheists in defiance of any creed? Prior to Constantine the Romans certainly had no written documents concerning religious conformity. But in order to defend such a view, it is assumed that words as 'communicative acts' are the only 'communicative acts' in circulation. In a world of widespread illiteracy, the power of image and symbol, of art and architecture, was used to maximum effect. At the most basic level, statues of imperial leaders were found in all major centres of trade and commerce across the empire, rarely in the temples but frequently in the marketplaces where they would personify the deities of Mars and Venus. The coins by which goods were bought and sold carried images of Rome's military might and functioned as the first-century equivalent of a live Twitter feed. Those lucky enough to be literate would read the inscriptions on the coins: 'Caesar is the Son of God'; 'Caesars: our Lords'; 'Mars, the Pacifier'; 'Heavenly Venus', etc. Worship, trade and military might were mutually inseparable. One need only consider the layout of the typical Roman settlement, as one historian has pointed out: 'Roman cities had always had a sacred geography of temple, forum, circus, palace or theatre proclaiming the links between public and religious life.'[8] The statues of imperial families, erected in marketplaces and public arenas throughout the empire, silently proclaimed several key articles of faith which would have included:

- Your economic wellbeing depends upon the emperor's Venus genes.
- Your wellbeing will be defended by the unassailable might of the emperor's Mars genes.
- This is the natural order of the universe.

For those towards the centre of Rome's empire, its citizens and those who benefit from the imperial regime, this is 'good news'. However, this wordless creed also carries an implicit warning for those on the periphery of the empire, less likely to benefit from its goods and more likely to be unhappy with their plight:

- Any thought of economic, military or religious rebellion against Rome will meet with an undefeatable, divinely ordained military power.[9]

To be atheist, in such a context, was a dangerous and defiant rejection of the gods of the age. This was not a rejection of divinity, as such, so much as a rejection of a regime that claimed its authority and actions were unquestionable because they were divine. In what follows, I will argue that this political defiance lies at the heart of what it means to be atheist. It is this defiance that earned the earliest atheists their reputation and is articulated in their writings. As the atheists' movement gathered momentum in the first century, they disseminated their alternative religio-political convictions through means of a variety of literary genres, preserved today in books of the New Testament.

Though the interpretive lenses of Christendom and the Enlightenment (both discussed below) have painstakingly filtered out the politically explosive nature of these documents, contemporary biblical scholarship is highlighting this long-neglected dimension. Early in the fourth century, the emperor Diocletian engaged in a programme of systematic persecution of these atheists which included the public burning of their texts.[10] That he deemed this tactic to be as necessary to the downfall of the movement as the destruction of its buildings and the removal of its leaders shows the political force these documents carried. Had they been harmless, mythological writings concerned only with the spiritual wellbeing of gullible myth-victims, their destruction would hardly have been necessary. In varying degrees, the gospels and the letters articulate their defiance against the Roman gods, but nowhere is it as explicit as in the text widely known as Revelation.

Any Roman official unschooled in the nature and function of Jewish apocalyptic traditions would be as baffled as any modern-day reader about the contents of this text. Its author is traditionally supposed to be a political prisoner by the name of John, incarcerated on the Greek island of Patmos, seeking a way to smuggle his atheist dogma beneath the radar of Roman censorship. John is deliberately antagonistic towards the corrupt and corrupting power of the empire. As Richard Bauckham notes, 'Revelation advances a thorough-going prophetic critique of the system of Roman power. It is a critique which makes Revelation the most powerful piece of political resistance literature from the period of the early empire.'[11]

Bauckham and others have rightly seen that two principal images surfacing at various points throughout the text refer directly to the ideology of the imperial cult. The picture of the Beast represents the hard imperialism as manifest in the exercise of political and particularly military power. But military power alone is not enough to run an empire, as successive governments knew well enough. The battle for 'hearts and minds', what we might call a 'soft' imperialism, is fought on the level of the promise of prosperity and economic gain. To critique this wing of the cult, John uses the picture of the Whore of Babylon. While alluring and attractive, the prosperity she offers is bought with the blood of innocent victims. The management of any empire requires highly visible military supremacy (embodied in the god Mars) and a highly seductive economic attraction (embodied in the goddess

Venus). John's portrayal of the Beast and the Whore may well be a deliberate parody of Mars and Venus. The author of Revelation, like those who penned the other documents of the New Testament, calls his readers to an atheistic way of life.

The Empire's Reaction

Those for whom the dictionary determines (rather than describes) our use of words will, in all likelihood, be hyperventilating that my definition of atheism is not *real* atheism. To describe Christians as atheists may seem curious or even unfounded. The Christian apologist Justin Martyr (AD 100–65), shared this concern: '... Hence are we called atheists. And we confess that we are atheists, so far as gods of this sort [wicked and impious demons] are concerned, but not with respect to the most true God, the Father of righteousness and temperance and the other virtues, who is free from all impurity.'[12]

Regardless of what may later be argued about theoretical atheism, a deep-seated, rebellious strain runs through many divergent strands of atheist conviction, and its strongest roots are to be found within the experience of the ancient Judeo-Christian movements as they laboured under the oppressive imperial regimes. However, in his defence of Christians, Justin is able to cite Socrates, who was executed for atheism: 'And when Socrates endeavoured, by true reason and examination, to ... deliver men from the demons, then the demons themselves, by means of men who rejoiced in iniquity, compassed his death, as an atheist and a profane person, on the charge that he was introducing new divinities.'[13]

The real substance of the charge against Socrates had little to do with his personal convictions regarding divine being, but with the fact that he was leading the young men of Athens astray, and by the time of his death had amassed a significant following. 'Young men' in fourth-century BC Athens had very different societal roles from men of equivalent age in contemporary western society. Athenian young men (aged 15–18) were on the brink of becoming citizens who formed the backbone of this fledgling democracy. When life expectancy was 26 years of age, when the citizens of

Athens (comprising less than 5 per cent of the Athenian population once women, children and, above all, slaves are taken out of the equation) were the only ones to vote, when military effectiveness relied upon their commitment to the city-state, to divert crowds of 'young men' away from unquestioning devotion to the state was a potential source of major political disruption. Since the next decade of Athenian life was in the fragile hands of these young men whom Socrates was busy intoxicating, the authorities' dismay is hardly surprising, especially given the external turmoil the city faced at the end of the fifth century. As Bettany Hughes notes:

> the idea that he [Socrates] was somehow captivating the strong young men in the gym with his endless, radical chat, diverting them from the path of good Athenian citizenship, was, to fifth- and fourth-century minds, very troubling . . . Young men were trained to speak persuasively . . . in order to conform rather than rebel. They were not raised to challenge, but to buttress the status quo – that finely woven net of family, tribal, democratic and religious loyalties that held the city-state together – and so the anxiety about Socrates' influence over young men ran deep.[14]

The charge of atheism on which Socrates was executed was in no conceivable sense a primarily religious charge. The death of Socrates was the execution of an ideological terrorist who was perceived to undermine devotion to the state, to threaten the social order and to destabilize the security upon which Athenian welfare depended. It was these crimes that rendered Socrates atheist. Similarly, as we have seen, the charge of atheism was levelled at Christians in the Roman Empire not because of their private, mystical beliefs. The Roman authorities were happy to leave those intact, provided that they did not foster sedition or have an adverse effect upon morality.[15] But as the New Testament documents have shown, Christianity was gathering momentum and could certainly be construed as having a negative effect upon the wellbeing of the empire.

Throughout the first three centuries after the formation of this movement, the persecution exacted upon these Christian communities varied in intensity. Nevertheless, it forced them underground, to meet in secret, with no temples or images to display. It is hardly surprising, then, that irate pagans should accuse them of cannibalism (eating the body and blood of Christ) and incest (at love-feasts with brothers and sisters in Christ). The bloody vengeance exacted upon these atheists did not succeed in stamping the movement out. Exasperated officials were thus further inflamed by the Christians' lack of respect even for their own lives. Christian movements continued to expand across the empire, despite the universal veneration of the imperial cult.

From the time of Nero's first persecution (as Rome burned in AD 64), until the Edict of Milan (311), whenever the empire, its status or its stability were under threat, the cannons turned upon the Christians. Whenever the Whore was troubled, the Beast would come to her aid and the persecution of Christians intensified. The Christian apologist Tertullian (AD 160–225) had famously claimed that, 'We multiply whenever we are mown down by you; the blood of Christians is seed.'[16] In the early years of the fourth century, Tertullian's logic underwent the ultimate test. The 'Great Persecution' which took place under the emperor Diocletian (284–305) was the last explicit attempt to destroy Christianity, which – according to Eusebius[17] – had now penetrated every level of society and government. It failed. According to Eusebius, Christians had God fighting on their side. Such divine aid, for Eusebius, eventually became incarnate in the person of Constantine the Great.

Constantine

By the time Constantine followed his father to become emperor (AD 306), the empire had been divided into its four regions, two in the West (ruled by himself and Maxentius) and two in the East (ruled by Licinius and Galerius). Now that Constantine had become one of four emperors, he set about unifying the title. Taking his war machine to the gates of Rome, he claimed to have witnessed a vision of the sign of a cross en route. Constantine believed he had been instructed in a subsequent dream, on the eve of battle, to take this symbol as his war banner. Outnumbered and strategically disadvantaged by his position, Constantine was nevertheless victorious and attributed his success to aid from the God of the Christians. Having defeated Maxentius, he now dominated the West. Before long, he would ally himself with Licinius against Maximinus (Galerius' successor) and ultimately defeat Licinius himself to seize control of the entire empire. One empire, one emperor, one God. The divine representative upon earth is, of course, Constantine himself.

However, Constantine – like his predecessors – knew that unifying the empire would take more than military victories. He needed social cohesion, and the most effective means of providing this was the rapidly expanded grass-roots movement, Christianity. Not only did the persecution of Christians cease, but as Constantine's career progressed, Christians found themselves increasingly favoured by the empire. Whether Constantine had genuinely converted to Christianity is an area of ongoing debate for some historians. But more important than the emperor's personal convictions are the effects of his actions.

The imperial cult in its current format had clearly failed to prevent this enormous empire from disintegration. Its basis, anyway, was not so much the crude belief that a particular human being could be divine, but that this particular human being could implement policy with divine authority. The most efficient method of achieving this end was no longer to be drawn from within the traditions and particular belief structures of the archaic, traditional gods of ancient Rome. Alistair Kee has argued this point with some force. 'It is not true Constantine gave up all idea of an imperial cult in favour of Christianity. Rather, a transformed Christianity became the imperial cult by any other name.'[18]

The basis of the imperial cult was not so much the crude belief that a man could be divine, but the universal acceptance that the policies he implemented were divinely sanctioned, and as such embodied an authority that was absolute and unquestionable. As Kee argued, above his great military prowess, and over against the supposed blundering ignorance often attributed to him by those who simply saw him as an ill-informed Christian convert, Constantine's greatest conquest was ecclesiological: 'He conquered the Christian Church . . . Without a threat or a blow, and all unsuspecting, the Christians were led into captivity and their religion transformed into a new imperial cult . . . But this achievement, unheralded then, unrecognized now, represents Constantine's greatest conquest, the one which has persisted largely unchallenged through the centuries in Europe and wherever European Christianity has spread.'[19]

This achievement was aided largely by the establishment of a creed. Having succeeded in defeating the three other 'emperors' within the ancient Roman 'tetrarchy', Constantine had made himself sole governor over a sprawling empire, vulnerable to disintegration. But if the Christian communities were to provide the social glue that would help to unify the empire, the churches themselves must embody a unity that would serve this purpose. The early fourth-century church, however, was a multifaceted and disparate collection of communities that would need to be straightened out if they were to be of service to the emperor.

For this reason, in 325 Constantine assembled a large council of bishops at Nicea. The end result was the Nicene Creed, a universally applicable statement of right Christian belief that would help to end the potentially destructive theological disputes within the church. However, although there is nothing in the creed that contradicts Scripture, the elements it chose to include and exclude resulted in a document which – if taken as a summary of Christian faith – is wildly at odds with Christian scriptures. The most glaring and largely unacknowledged blunder is that the creed emphasizes the judgement of God but remains silent about the love of God. Nor do the problems end there. The Jesus who proclaimed a God whose power is expressed in weakness, whose presence subverts the top-down dynamic of wealth and politics, who welcomed the 'nobodies' and demanded that the powerful be held to account, is quietly ignored by the Imperial Creed. The character of the God who sides with the poor, who welcomes the outsider, who reveals himself in self-giving love, is beyond the interest of the very creed that claims to outline true belief. Between his birth and death, Jesus – according to the creed – neither said nor did anything crucial for the Christian faith. As Luke Timothy Johnson concedes, the creed is 'soteriological' in its approach[20] – that is, it focuses simply upon the issue of 'salvation'. Hardly surprising that the result is a depoliticized view of God, casting him as a divinity who is happy to leave the business of politics to others while he focuses upon salvation. While salvation itself had long been a political issue – with Roman emperors hailed as bringing salvation – the creed pushes salvation away from real life and towards the afterlife so it could become a series of spiritual transactions partitioned off from the real world.

Had this creed simply been a local, time-bound statement that simply affirmed certain core Christian convictions over against contradicting views, then the critique offered above would be of limited value. For sure, Christian communities across the empire had often adopted creedal statements for such purposes. However, it is the universal application of this creed, both in terms of time and space, that raises concerns for its critics. A text which is the product of specific historical accident has largely defined Christianity for the medieval era and beyond, as well as shaping atheistic responses to Christianity.

Medieval Christendom

By the time Rome was overrun in the late fifth century, Christian belief was deeply rooted. Bishops and later popes enjoyed increasing shares of power, as various political authorities adopted Christendom models of government. As Stuart Murray concludes, the mutual development of scriptural interpretation, church authority and mission wove together a tightly bonded and near impregnable system of belief. 'The Christendom shift represented a recasting of the Christian story and different perspectives on the fundamental beliefs and practices of the churches. This inter-connectedness made it difficult to challenge a system widely regarded as permanent and simply "the way things are". Medieval Christendom was monolithic, totalitarian and seemingly impervious to critique.'[21]

Throughout the entire Christendom era, however, a number of Christian communities resisted the injustices that were inevitably brought to bear upon the wider population. While a comprehensive survey is beyond the scope of my argument, it is sufficient simply to recognize the existence of some of these groups. Here, I shall restrict my overview to the subversive groups Murray lists as offering an alternative set of Christian belief and practice to that offered by the state religion. While that official state religion was a Christianized version of the imperial cult, movements that sought to remain faithful to the documents of the New Testament found themselves – like the earliest Christian communities – thrust into a context of conflict and persecution. It is hardly surprising that each of the groups listed below had the charge of atheism levelled against them:

Donatism was a fourth-century movement in North Africa, emerging from the controversy that arose after former Christian leaders who had renounced their faith under persecution were reappointed as leaders once toleration was granted. As such they were largely purists, and found themselves in conflict with Rome. They were the first victims of persecution at the hands of other Christians, as Emperor Constantine considered them heretics. However, the Donatists refused to recant, and survived in Africa until the Arab invasions of the sixth century.

Waldensians were named after a twelfth-century businessman, Valdes. The Frenchman had scriptures translated, and gathered others from across the social spectrum to join him in the life of simplicity, poverty and preaching. While not anti-institutional, their actions invited opposition from the institutional church and they found themselves condemned as heretics. The movement continued for centuries, until the time of the Reformation (see next chapter), when their tradition flowed into what today is called the Waldensian Church.

Lollards were originally followers of John Wycliffe (c.1328–84), famous for an early translation of biblical texts into common English so it would no longer be mediated through an officially authorized clergy. His followers were largely peasants, whose preaching and theology were disparaged as 'mumbling' – thought to be the origin of the derogatory term 'lollard'. Their concern was to reform the English clergy with a renewed focus upon the teachings of Scripture. Their efforts were not appreciated by the authorities, especially when they became implicated in peasant revolts against the abuses of those with wealth and power.

Anabaptists were, literally, those who 'baptized again'. In sixteenth-century Europe, this was a dangerous move, and an implicit act of sedition. After all, everyone had been baptized as infants into church and society. To be baptized again was to dismiss the validity of one's first baptism, and with it the entire system that was built around the nominal Christianity of Western

Europe. Again, this was a movement driven underground by Catholics as well as Protestants.

The importance of these and other groups should not be underestimated. These are not the minor exceptions of an otherwise shallow-minded and weak-willed Christian religion. Rather, they show that the abuses of Christendom were recognized by many as being at odds with the Christ they experienced in Scripture. What was more, the individuals belonging to each of these groups were willing to face persecution for the sake of their beliefs – not because of a mindless faith that made them devalue their own lives. Rather, it was their affirmation of life in the face of Christendom's authorities that inspired many members of these groups to undergo the kind of suffering they identified in the Christ they encountered in Scripture. Each movement, of course, was flawed and in different ways could hardly be celebrated as perfect examples of Christian belief. Nor could they bring a clearly articulated set of policies to solve all of Christendom's problems. Nevertheless, Murray recognizes the significance and influence of such movements:

> It is difficult for persecuted and marginalised groups to develop a positive agenda for a society from which they are excluded and which they cannot influence by normal means. Many critics are wedded to top-down strategies and Christendom-style social and political engagement. They fail to appreciate dissident groups were modelling alternative social, economic and political options. Certainly their persecutors found their activities extremely threatening, fearing their nonconformist behaviour and message could undermine the social and political system.[22]

As stated above, the empire continued to brand those who unsettled the political and ideological status quo as 'atheists'. But which gods are the Donatists, the Waldensians, the Lollards and the Anabaptists rejecting? Who are the gods of Christendom?

The answer is less straightforward than it might have been for Imperial Rome. It is complicated not only by the genuine Christian faith adopted by many bishops and popes, particularly in the earlier centuries of the Christendom era. Neither can we point the finger at even the most corrupted popes of the Middle Ages as though they enjoyed the sovereign power of a figure like Augustus or Constantine. The Christendom era saw alliances between bishops and princes, popes and emperors, between church and state – dynamics that fluctuated across time and space. Nevertheless, the imperial power dynamic remained in force: the hierarchical power structures; the privileging of those at the centre at the expense of those on the periphery; the economic gravity of Rome that drew wealth from the provinces; the need for military means of achieving political ends; the appeal to religion to endorse the status quo; the brutal imposition of this religion upon the masses. In sum, Christendom was the era in which the old Roman gods Mars and Venus remained in power by disguising themselves in Christian fancy dress.

Conclusion

Prior to the modern era, atheism was, by and large, a term used by tyrants to suppress those who threatened them. For those in power, atheism was not an outright rejection of all gods so much as a rejection of *our* gods, and since *our* gods uphold *our* regime, atheism is a rejection of *us*. In ancient Rome, atheism was a critique of Mars and Venus, a critique of the emperor who carried their genes, and a critique of the empire as a whole. Atheists were enemies of the state. Under Constantine, however, heaven was subjected to regime change as the state adopted the religion of the atheists. Which gods, then, were in power throughout the Christendom era?

While this chapter has argued that Constantine did not Christianize the empire so much as dupe Christians into endorsing the empire, it does not necessarily follow that the Christendom shift was disastrous or lamentable. On the one hand, this chapter has been implicitly critical of the compromises that shaped Christendom. Under Constantine, churches became 'the church', Christianity became a creed, mission became conquest. As Kee noted (borrowing the term from Nietzsche), Constantine achieved across the empire 'the trans-valuation of all values' which have filtered into the psyche of the Christendom mindset. Under his rule, the forceful imposition of Roman ideology upon the subjects of the empire continued as ever it had. Constantine had simply issued the Beast with a police uniform and adorned the Whore with an evening dress. Whatever imperial Christianity was, it remained a religion of and for the empire, and as such was drained of its subversive, prophetic lifeblood.

Compared to the older versions of the imperial cult, the new Constantinian version was distinctly flavoured by values distilled from the dynamic of Christian faith. For instance, in ancient Rome and Greece, exposing unwanted infants to the elements, leaving them to die at the roadside or dumping them at the rubbish tip was common practice. Officially, the notion was that the unprotected child was thrust into the arms of the gods. Romulus and Remus, the mythological founders of Rome, had themselves been abandoned as infants. The Christian practice of rescuing these unwanted babies represented an attitude that would eventually be adopted empire-wide. This practice was not simply the addition of a Christian moral code as though former pagans were now expected to refrain from drinking, smoking, swearing and committing infanticide. It is a practice that offers a window into this 'trans-valuation of values'. The practice is based upon the recognition that even the most humble, pathetic human life carries unspeakable value. Had Constantine not enlisted the support of the Christian God, it is questionable whether the entire Christendom tradition (and the modern western culture that flowed from it) would value human life in precisely the way it does.

For instance, a truly post-Christendom ethics is identifiable in the writings of contemporary thinkers like Joseph Fletcher, James Rachels and Peter Singer. As a well-informed and well-meaning ethicist with a genuine desire for justice, Singer offers an ethics more closely akin to that of pre-Christendom Rome. His endorsement of parental rights for termination of defective infants is precisely a return to the ancient pagan practice, arising not from some malicious defect in his moral character, but from a genuinely post-Christendom understanding of what it means to be good and what it means to be human. On this subject Singer achieves a trans-valuation of values, an escape from what Nietzsche saw as Christendom's pitiful obsession with caring for the weak and the vulnerable.[23] Those secular westerners who feel it 'unnatural' to terminate newborns do so because Christendom's ethical mindset is more deeply rooted in the western psyche than many dare to realize. Compromised though it was, Christendom established deeply rooted values that today are mistaken as natural, timeless or unquestionable. Of course. these are complex questions, but any criticism of Christendom that fails to take such questions into account is destined to be partial at best. My point here is simply that, in the wake of the Constantinian revolution, even the grounds upon which we attempt to assess vices and virtues of Christendom are themselves – to a great extent – the very legacy of Christendom. Atheists who would throw stones at Christendom are in danger of hitting their own children.

The cessation of certain pagan practices heralded by Constantine's new order, the value of human life affirmed by his new religion – when considered in fourth-century context – were tremendous feats, consistent with the worldview affirmed by the earliest Christians and their scriptures. However, although some of the ethical norms that shaped this new empire were to be welcomed, the manner in which the empire functioned, the means by which it retained power, accumulated wealth, exerted strength and maintained its ideology, were little different from all that preceded. Mars and Venus, though their identity was now concealed, continue to function as ever they had. In other words, even throughout the height of the Christendom era, those Christian believers charged with atheism (including the Donatists, Waldensians, Lollards and Anabaptists) were atheist because they rejected the real gods of their age, namely Mars and Venus. With this in mind, any history of atheism which fails to credit these subversive Christian groups fails to appreciate the full weight of the atheist heritage. Here we reach the central claim of this book: that the principal strand of the atheist heritage is political subversion against those who claim divine sanction for their oppressive action in the world.

2.

Revolutionary Atheism

During the Middle Ages, although a complex vocabulary had expanded to describe a vast array of intricate religious heresies, there was no word to describe simple non-belief in any form of deity. The standard explanation for this lack is that if you did not believe in God but did value your own life, it was safest to conceal your unbelief. After all, under the Christendom regime those who would not fully assent to the Christian creeds might find themselves subjected to severe persecution. However, it remains highly questionable whether, in the pre-modern era, there were any whose unbelief would be remotely compatible with that represented by modern atheism. As chapter 3 will show, modernity (and the atheisms to which it gives birth) did not conjure up non-belief out of a void, but was based upon a set of positive (if subconscious) claims about the nature of the universe and our place within it. Modern unbelief has little in common with pre-modern atheism. As shown in the last chapter, prior to modernity the term 'atheist' was employed principally as a criminal charge. However, in the early sixteenth century, the Reformation tore its way across Europe, splintering the church of Christendom that had been largely unified for a thousand years. Christian communities split into various warring factions, and the word 'atheist' became a term of abuse, a rhetorical weapon for criticizing the living daylights out of those who held alternative Christian beliefs.

The Reformation, like all other historical epochs, did not come about solely because of the genius and energy of enlightened individuals, as if by their own gargantuan effort they conjured up a brand new worldview like a rabbit from a hat. A series of factors combined to ensure the end of Rome's dominance: the growing trade wealth of the Italian city-states and the renaissance in arts and sciences; the increased power of German princes who would support Martin Luther; exposure to new worlds and new civilizations that were no less humane than Christendom's; the desire of nation-states to assert national independence; the ever-advancing decay of papal moral integrity; and, of course, the ongoing underground activity of subversive Christian groups (outlined in chapter 1). As Christendom disintegrated into mini-Christendoms, losing its grip on European religion, atheism was destined to become a badge of honour rather than a criminal charge.

In what follows, I lean heavily upon the work of two heavyweight scholars of atheism: Gavin Hyman and Michael J. Buckley. Both figures recognize that the huge cultural shift that followed the Reformation was channelled through the work of many key thinkers, writers, leaders and philosophers, but they identify four figures of particular interest. A focus upon these figures (Descartes, Newton, Diderot and d'Holbach) offers a glimpse into the most crucial developments that shaped modern atheist convictions.

Descartes (1596–1650)

René Descartes is widely recognized as ushering in the new era that was to become known as 'modernity'. While he was by no means an atheist, Descartes played a major role in railroading Europe from medieval feudalism into the unwitting and all-pervasive cultural atheism of modernity. Writing at a time when Europe was in chaos, Christendom was disintegrating, when battles for religious truth were waged along tribal boundaries within and between nations, Descartes packaged a rare and treasured commodity: certainty. To a Europe convulsed by the chaos of civil and ideological wars, confused, shaken and hesitant, the prospect of a grounded and defensible sense of certainty was an understandably precious goal. To this world, Descartes offered not a blind certainty that required thinkers to ignore alternative truth claims, but a certainty that could only be attained by undergoing radical, earth-shattering doubt. The identity of a God in heaven remained a matter of fierce debate, but as the authority of distant

Rome began to fade, the stability of emerging nation-states and national churches was, as yet, far from secure. Descartes presented Europe with the reassuring certainty of a new worldview, one based upon placing the individual, thinking human subject at the centre of the universe.

Descartes chose to doubt everything, as thoroughly and as radically as he could. According to his philosophy, everything you think you know could be a dream; your mind could be the playground of an omnipotent and malicious demon. All knowledge and all experience, everything and everyone (including yourself), was to be doubted. But even amid this exercise in severe doubt, one thing could not be doubted: namely, that you are in the process of thinking. Hence his famous phrase, *cogito ergo sum*, 'I think; therefore, I am.' Whatever else is happening around me, says Descartes, there is no doubt that I myself am thinking. From this position of individual, isolated thought, an entire new worldview could be constructed amid the rubble of an obliterated Christendom.

Hyman spells out the significance of Descartes' radical programme of *demolition* of the ruins of the old order and *reconstruction* of a modern world. During the Christendom era, one's experience of the world was filtered through the lens of radical dependence upon a God who is both original Creator and an ongoing, sustaining presence. Descartes had reconstructed the world around the individual, and while God and others still existed, they now become 'objects', out there, separate from me, the 'subject'. No longer do we need a church or nation-state to dictate religious truth to us; instead, our own reasoning capacities provide us with the true foundation for knowing what the world really is.[1] Descartes still argued for belief in the God with whom Christian Europe was familiar, but this God was no longer a *foundation for* belief, but an *object of* belief.

Where once God the Creator was at the centre of everything, and humans understood themselves in relation to him, now the human individual took centre-stage and God became a beloved creation of human thought. Whereas once it was a belief in God that shaped human experience of the world, now the human experience of the world would shape one's belief in God. Once it was humans who existed at the caprice of the Creator; now the tables were turned and the Creator existed at the caprice of the creature. In sum, the God of Scripture was turned into a fantasy destined to vanish in a puff of incense the moment people ceased to believe in him. With the establishment of a 'me-centred' world, it was only a matter of time.

The notion of a 'me-centred' world need not be taken negatively. It is simply a culture-wide view of the world where everything outside me – other people, the world, the universe, and any deity or absence of deity – is an object of belief filtered through *my* imagination, *my* reasoning capacities, and *my* ability to think, feel and act. The god of this new age, however, was not the god of Christendom, still less the deity found in Jewish and Christian scriptures. Regardless of the myriad of particular beliefs about the new god of this new modern era, overarching them all was the grander narrative in which the thinking individual would reign supreme. *Man is the measure of all things.*[2] Enter Newton.

Newton (1642–1727)

Isaac Newton was a theologian and alchemist, whose attempts to make sense of the universe led to monumental breakthroughs in physics, mathematics and optics. 'Newton was not the first of the age of reason,' said John Maynard Keynes. 'He was the last of the magicians.'[3] This was no slur, however. Alchemy (the art of turning base metals into gold) was not simply a medieval pursuit for those who sought a supernatural short cut to wealth. Newton was captivated by the possibility of transforming matter, of unveiling the secrets of the God-given world by means of rational thought, observation and experimentation. It was this approach that led to key discoveries in the fields of gravity and optics, paving the way towards the modern worldview. It was what enabled this notoriously unadventurous English gentleman to identify laws that were obeyed in the furthest reaches of the universe without ever setting foot out of eastern England.

Even the whiff of 'received truth' was repulsive to Newton, who lived in an era when some wings of the church still clung to power and regarded themselves as custodians of truth. Since this was also an age in which religious, scientific and political truths were mutually inseparable, the consequences of his breakthrough in physics were bound to have far-reaching consequences. Galileo, for instance, had believed that the skies above were governed by different natural laws from those by which everything on the earth was bound. This worked well for a hierarchical view of society, with God himself on his throne, whose heavens were by no means subject to the rules of mere mortals. But Newton discovered the unifying force of gravity, obliterating distinctions between the earthly and heavenly bodies. By irrefutable reason and experimentation, Newton had shown that the planets in the skies behaved no differently from the pebble in your hand. But this was not merely a revolution in physics. The gravity that Newton discovered would not only pull apples down from their trees, but would wrench bishops down from their seats, would drag kings down from their thrones, and ultimately, would pull God himself down from his heavens. If Descartes had mapped out a worldview in which 'man is the measure of all things', Newton (though opposing his French forerunner on certain specific points) consolidated it. If the medieval worldview had been principally theocentric (or 'god-centred'), then the modern world was becoming more anthropocentric (or 'human-centred').

This shift in worldview is worthy of reflection, since it contradicts a view that still dominates popular thought – that as science progressed, the human ego faced an onslaught of humiliating demotions. Firstly, we discover that the earth is not the centre of the universe, but revolves around the sun. We discover that we are part of a solar system among countless others, within a galaxy among countless others, and now – according to many theoretical physicists – within a universe among countless others. Often, an anti-religious polemic is smuggled into such a narrative, as though religions in general and Christianity in particular endorsed this increasingly discredited 'me-centred' view of the world.[4] Even figures as insightful as Simon Schaffer, Martin Rees and Max Tegmark are among those who perpetuate the claim that the ego-centred universe is a view drawn from Christian Scripture. There is no hint of evidence for this claim, and plenty of evidence to the contrary. Nothing in Jewish or Christian Scripture promotes the view that humanity is at the centre of the universe, nor that planet earth lies at the centre (a view actually offered by Aristotle).

On the other hand, the primal Christian virtue throughout Scripture is humility – the Bible at times appeals to humanity's abysmal irrelevance to the mechanics of the universe as a source of wonder.[5]

It is historical coincidence, to say the least, that, as humanity learns more about the unimaginable vastness of the universe and the hideous insignificance of our place within it, we promote ourselves as masters of that universe – marvelling at the supremacy of our own rationality and the sheer enormity of our (bafflingly minuscule) range of knowledge. In this light, modernity looks like a cultural form of 'small man syndrome' where, having been robbed of our central importance, we compensate by celebrating our achievements and placing human thought and rationality on centre-stage. Modernity is not the story of humanity's demotion so much as God's. Humanity promotes itself at God's expense. This was certainly not the intent of either Descartes or Newton, but it was a quest ruthlessly pursued by some of their followers.

Diderot (1713–84)

Denis Diderot was a philosopher, widely known for editing the *Encyclopedie*, an early version of the modern encyclopaedia in which knowledge is systematically arranged and widely accessible. Though he had studied at a Jesuit school, his writing and thinking gradually moved away from the received truths of Christian orthodoxy, towards an explicitly atheistic tone. By 1749 he had been arrested for his subversive writings, released after three months on the condition that he 'do nothing in future which is in any way contrary to religion or morality.'[6] It may be for this reason that many of his atheistic writings were not published until after his death. Nevertheless, Diderot made the first moves towards turning atheism into a virtue rather than an insult.

Diderot had studied Descartes and Newton, finding himself in agreement with their methods but not their findings. Both figures, according to Diderot, were prevented from pursuing their own best insights because they were unable to shake their accursed belief in God. In Diderot's eyes, Descartes made huge leaps of assumption in his reasoning that were wildly inconsistent with his own ruthless methods and worldview. Descartes had succeeded in obliterating the boundary between the human and the divine, promoting the view that the universe was a single, physical system. Newton, likewise, had revolutionized the human understanding of the universe, subjecting the heavens to the same laws that governed the earth, but smuggling divine action into the causes that still eluded him. Diderot, in his view, took Descartes and Newton more seriously than they took themselves, helping to ensure that the revolutionary aspect of their thought became actual rather than potential.

'In many ways,' says Buckley, 'Diderot is the first of the atheists, not simply in chronological reckoning but as an initial and premier advocate and influence. He argued his case not by repudiating the mathematical physics of Descartes or the universal mechanics of Newton but by bringing them, as he contended, to fulfilment.'[7] In this sense, Diderot carries the flame kindled by these figures of a bygone era to ignite the dawning age of Enlightenment. Diderot himself, however, cannot simply be cast as an enemy of God and an icon of atheism. Apart from the fact that his own writings always retain an elusive quality, he does not leave the impression that his ultimate aim is to destroy belief in God. His revulsion at the doctrines of the church, his disdain for Christian orthodoxy, and even his dismissal of the Christian God were secondary to another overriding concern. As Peter France notes, 'his own concerns go far beyond this negative anti-Christianity.'[8] Diderot, like Descartes and Newton, simply will not tolerate any form of received truth. When that truth is received from a church that bases its own authority upon uncertain and untestable assumption, abuses that authority with reckless disregard for human suffering, and defends that authority by physical force rather than human reason, the time has come to subvert that authority. It is hardly surprising, then, that Diderot (quoting Jean Meslier) declared that he would not be happy until 'the last king has been strangled in the entrails of the last priest.'[9] In other words, Diderot's prime concern was to undermine Christendom, to steal its power and to destroy its deity. This was a concern shared and pursued further still by Diderot's friend, the Baron d'Holbach.

D'Holbach (1723–89)

D'Holbach is widely regarded as the first unambiguously self-professed atheist in the modern West.[10] A Swiss aristocrat, d'Holbach famously ran a *salon* in Paris which attracted leading thinkers of the Enlightenment, including Diderot and Rousseau, Adam Smith and David Hume, Edward Gibbon and Benjamin Franklin. Eighteenth-century Paris had a variety of such salons, an upper-class invitation-only wine bar akin to the Gentlemen's Clubs that emerged in London later in the century. Elite members of society would meet in such clubs to debate intellectual and political trends. In an age when atheism was still barely acceptable, the Scottish philosopher David Hume, on visiting the Parisian salon, is reported to have told d'Holbach he had never met an atheist. D'Holbach gestured around the room and replied that Hume was in the company of seventeen.[11]

Nevertheless, d'Holbach continued to write under pseudonyms as he articulated a new view of nature devoid of any dependence upon the God of Christianity. For d'Holbach, matter itself was not motionless and lifeless until moved by a divine Creator. Instead, matter – like human beings – had a life and energy of its own. There was no need for the plate-spinning god of Newton to keep the universe running smoothly. The insights of Newton and Descartes come to fruition only when divested of their associations with divinity, a sentiment that generated d'Holbach's most famous work, *The System of Nature* (1770). His writing style at times is simply unsupported but eloquent assertion; at other times, he uses careful and sustained reasoning. It is anti-religious polemic of the highest order, which – like the writing of Diderot – is subconsciously levelled at the abuses of Christendom. Attacking the religion of his day with all the venom, eloquence and intelligence of an eighteenth-century Dawkins, *The System of Nature* is clearly the work of a fanatic. As Ira Wade concludes, 'D'Holbach is really fanatical against the idea of God. He returns to it over and over, and with the same trite arguments, but with a vehemence which betrays a kind of obsession. It is, however, the obsession of a lucid person, who has apparently been exasperated by the arguments of those who are obsessed in exactly the opposite way.'[12]

The System of Nature remained the foremost articulation of atheist conviction until Bertrand Russell in the twentieth century, and offers three main arguments against religion. Firstly, religion offers no basis for morality. Secondly, religion is at odds with the findings of new scientific breakthroughs. Thirdly, and most importantly, religion upholds and endorses an unjust social order, drawing attention away from the horrors of the present to a blissful post-mortem existence. A more satisfactory morality would require us to rid ourselves of any authority imposed upon us by a repressive church:

> The author concludes that there can be no morality without consulting the nature of man and his relationships with his fellow man. There can be no fixed principles of conduct by basing it upon unjust, capricious, wicked Gods, no firm politics without consulting the nature of man, living in society in order to insure his happiness and satisfy his needs. No good government can be established on the notion of a despotic Deity. No laws will ever be just without consulting the nature and goals of society. No jurisprudence can ever benefit nations if it is founded on the passions of tyrants. No education will be reasonable unless it is established on reasonableness rather than prejudices.[13]

As would be the case with many of those who followed d'Holbach (up to and including Russell), the vast majority of his writings can be affirmed by believers in a post-Christendom era, whose understanding of church, Scripture, politics and justice is not rooted in the ideals of the Christendom power dynamic.

Later Modernity

Channelled through the likes of Diderot and d'Holbach, the insights of Descartes and Newton became truly revolutionary, in the fullest political sense. In France itself, the Revolution (1789) brought to fruition much of what d'Holbach had sought. Both king and priesthood were brought down, church and state comprehensively separated. Atheism was, in some circles, becoming less an insult and more a compliment. Across the Atlantic, as Hyman notes, although the American Revolution (1775–83) similarly saw church and state separated, this was for the sake of religious toleration rather than to promote the religious intolerance that would mark the early years of the French Revolution. In North America, church and state were separated in order to avoid privileging one form of religion over another, since the Founding Fathers saw that separating church from state did not require separating religion from politics.

In Britain, it would be another hundred years before atheism became socially and intellectually acceptable. Atheism was an ideology still largely associated with political revolution, for which there was little taste in Victorian Britain. As late as 1880 it took six years for the atheist politician Charles Bradlaugh to battle his way legally from being elected as the Member of Parliament for Northampton to taking his seat at the House of Commons, which continued to regard itself as a religious institution. By the time of the great Darwin controversy of the late nineteenth century, Thomas Huxley (1825–95) – also known as 'Darwin's Bulldog' – refused to identify himself with atheism. This was largely because he believed that atheists, in denying the existence of God so fiercely, were, like their creationist opponents, making metaphysical claims that could never be tested. But this was not the only reason. Hyman notes, 'One of the reasons for the continuing stigma that attached to atheism was its connection with violent revolutionary politics, which had been vividly displayed by the French Revolution . . . Not only would atheism be tainted with blood, violence and revolution, but also Christianity came to be regarded as inherently conservative and reactionary, an upholder of the status quo.'[14]

Bertrand Russell (1872–1970) is widely recognized as the most influential British atheist and philosopher of the twentieth century. Though coming from a background of privilege (his father had been a Member of Parliament and his two grandfathers held the title of 'Lord'), he remained a subversive figure. Throughout his life Russell was a tireless campaigner for social justice and faced constant harassment as a result. His campaign against the First World War saw him thrown out of Trinity College, Cambridge. His writings in the US saw him thrown out of the university system and unable to publish. His campaigning against nuclear war saw him imprisoned at the age of 89. In an interview in 1959, he spoke with great passion about why he campaigned against war in general and nuclear war in particular: 'I can't bear the thought of many hundreds of millions of people dying in agony only and solely because the rulers of the world are stupid and wicked, and I can't bear it.'[15] This drive for justice, and the deep sense of human compassion from which it clearly arose, seemed central also to his opposition to Christianity. Any theologically astute reader of Russell's classic lecture, 'Why I Am Not a Christian', cannot help but notice that the vast majority of his energy is invested in debunking the dehumanizing myths of Christendom, not the heart of Christian belief. This is a theme to be explored further in a later chapter. But for now, we note that Russell's greatest virtue as an atheist is that his atheism was rooted in a practical drive to make the world a better place.

As modernity flourished, it brought with it a worldview that was more Cartesian than Descartes himself, and more Newtonian than Newton ever intended.

- Descartes displaced the old theocentric worldview with an anthropocentric (or more precisely, an egocentric) view of the world. God became an *object of* belief rather than the *grounds for* belief.
- Newton consolidated this new worldview, making God unnecessary for the movement of planets in the heavens and apples on the earth. God took a backseat role in running the universe.
- Diderot accepted the new insights of Descartes and Newton, but went further to describe a natural world in which God had no part.
- D'Holbach, the first avowed atheist, used new scientific views of the universe to launch a relentless and vicious attack upon the god who upheld an unjust, repressive church.

In chapter 1 it was shown that pre-modern atheism was a rejection of the gods of the age, and as such had a subversive strain woven through its DNA. With the advent of the modern era and the collapse of Christendom as a single entity, atheism changed shape as the gods of the age began to change their form. Nevertheless, the earliest modern atheists, like Diderot and d'Holbach, were driven by that same quest for a better world, a quest that unsettled those in power who sought to maintain order. This subversive strand could be readily identified by atheists throughout this era, up to and including Bertrand Russell in the twentieth century. Of course, all that is offered here is a brief overview, but these figures are by no means cherry-picked in order to make a case. The historical context is such that any in the early modern era regarded as atheist are destined thereby to find themselves in trouble with those in authority: Christopher Marlowe (1563–93), the Elizabethan playwright, died mysteriously while awaiting trial, supposedly for his atheism; Thomas Hobbes (1588–1679), the philosopher, found himself in trouble with the authorities since it was feared his *Leviathan* relativized the church's authority and encouraged atheism; 'Aikenhead the Atheist' (1676–97) was the last person in Britain executed for blasphemy – the sentence actually warranting his death climaxing with the charge of arguing against 'the providence of God in the Government of the world.'[16] From d'Holbach to Bertrand Russell, the writings of avowed atheists are not simply anti-Christian, but more specifically critical of the oppressive church associated with Christendom.

The Domestication of Atheism

The late twentieth century saw a revolution in atheism, not dissimilar to the Constantinian revolution in Christianity. Its roots lay in the advent of modernity, the era in which an 'anthropocentric' view of the universe gradually displaced a 'theocentric' view. However, there are many forms of both the god-centred and human-centred belief systems and the two are not as easily distinguished as may be apparent at first glance. If, as John's gospel states, God himself has become human; if 'the Word became flesh' so that loving God entails loving one's neighbour, and vice versa, then the distinction between being god-centred and human-centred is blurred. Similarly, if the gods of any regime exist solely to uphold those humans in power, whether they are the gods of Rome or the Christ of Christendom, then the theocentric world was only ever anthropocentric in any case. This chapter has so far argued that modernity is not simply the displacement of a god-centred view with a human-centred one. It is, more specifically, the 'me-centred' rather than the 'human-centred' worldview that has taken root, a view which we have traced all the way back to Descartes' famous declaration, 'I think; therefore, I am.' There is nothing necessarily immoral or selfish in this me-centredness, since this is a human focus that – if anything – requires enormous personal, moral responsibility. *Received wisdom* (which short-circuits a person's critical faculties) is rightly an affront to the modern mind, and any tradition (Christian or otherwise) content to trade in such nuggets of second-hand truth, be it by coercion, manipulation or faulty reasoning, is fundamentally dehumanizing. The highest ideals of modernity expose the sheer lunacy of any who seek to bypass the individual, thinking, human self.

The sovereignty of the Self succeeded the sovereignty of God. As the age of modernity blossomed, unbelief in God became not only acceptable but increasingly respectable. *What then, does it mean to be atheist when atheism becomes the modern cultural norm? What happens to the subversive dimension of atheism when there is nothing to subvert?* Atheism needed a worthy enemy, but by the end of the twentieth century the god of Christendom had been reduced to an odd cultural leftover from a romantic but ignorant past. The passing of Christendom had robbed atheism of its nemesis.

As argued in chapter 1, atheism is – at root – a rejection of the gods of one's own age. Those gods were once the gods of Greece, gods whom Socrates opposed and was hence executed on the charge of 'atheism'. Those gods were once Roman emperors, gods whom Jews and Christians resisted and were hence persecuted as 'atheists'. Those gods then became the pseudo-Christian god of Christendom, against whom Christian groups like Donatists and Waldensians, Lollards and Anabaptists rebelled and were outlawed as 'atheists'. The god of Christendom was eventually pronounced dead by Friedrich Nietzsche. Since then, however, atheists have continued to rebel against this dated and defunct god. This does not prevent New Atheists from thinking it requires great moral courage to rebel against this aged and decrepit divinity. Dennett, for instance, salutes his own bravery as he declares, 'I risk a fist to the face, or even worse. Yet I persist.'[17] Commenting on the self-proclaimed courage of Dawkins and Dennett, Alvin

Plantinga observes, 'Apparently atheism has its own heroes of the faith – at any rate its own self-styled heroes. Here it's not easy to take them seriously; religion-bashing in the current Western academy is about as dangerous as endorsing the party's candidate at a Republican rally.'[18]

The impetus for the New Atheism is drawn from the events of 2001 in which wild acts of terrorism obliterated any notion of religion as politically irrelevant in the modern world. Prior to this, says Dawkins, 'Many of us saw religion as harmless nonsense. Beliefs might lack all supporting evidence but, we thought, if people needed a crutch for consolation, where's the harm? September 11th changed all that.'[19]

However, it was not simply the motivation of the attacks upon the Trade Towers in New York and the Pentagon in Washington that can be deemed religious. While religion no doubt played its part in their execution, any serious consideration of these atrocities will find their genesis not merely in religious beliefs, but in a complex history of political action in which 'religion' is one of several key factors. Religion certainly played no lesser role in generating the secular western response to these attacks. Nowhere on the globe is the god Mars so unambiguously enshrined as in the Pentagon.[20] Nowhere was the goddess Venus so fully incarnate as in the Trade Towers. The reaction of Mars and Venus (outlined in the chapters that follow) is an assertion of their unassailable power in the world. The twin features associated with Mars and Venus (i.e. the visibility of military superiority and the adoption of economic ideology) are crucial to maintaining an empire in any era. The gods of our age – this book will argue – are alive and well in the form of Mars and Venus.

Since it was the mobilization of the empire in the wake of the 9/11 attacks that gave rise to the New Atheist movement, it is worth exploring the relationship between the 'four horsemen' and the gods who dominate the western world of the twenty-first century. If atheism has a tradition of subverting the gods of the age when those gods prove oppressive, the New Atheism offers ideological support for those gods. A thinker as intellectually and ethically attuned as Russell, for instance, would be horrified at the rhetoric of Harris and Hitchens in particular. As argued below, these figures have become what Terry Eagleton has described as 'the intellectual wing of the war on terror.'[21]

In sum, in a world that has now become largely secularized, the social role of the atheist has shifted radically. No longer are atheists deemed any kind of political threat to the social order – the West is, after all, dominated by a secular social order. Rather, the New Atheists serve as secular priests and prophets for the power structures that now have largely displaced those of Christendom. There is an ironic parallel that runs in line here with the struggles that beset the Christendom era: as argued in chapter 1, the beating heart of Christian belief and practice was thrown out with the Christendom shift. Precisely the same is true in the New Atheist movement: *while its core beliefs appear to be the same as those of other atheists throughout post-Enlightenment history, their renewed context puts them at the service of the very oppressive authorities their atheistic ancestors opposed.* If Russell, for instance, invested his life in opposing war, and faced opposition and persecution as a result, the New Atheists stir their admirers to support war. It is for this reason that Noam Chomsky regards these figures as religious fanatics, worshippers of state religion. This raises the question of whether it is possible for avowedly secular states to become objects of worship.

Religion and Politics

One of the core narratives of the modern worldview is the myth that religion and politics can be mutually separated. Modernity has been largely concerned with removing Christendom's god from the pragmatic concerns of daily life, promoting him out of the universe, privatizing him behind the closed doors of personal choice, banishing him as a divine troublemaker, dismissing him as an irrelevance and spiritualizing him out of material existence. Underlying this endeavour is the belief that the various (Christian) religions that began to multiply across post-Reformation Europe should all be kept separate from the down-to-earth business of politics. And so emerged widespread belief in the existence of a transcendent entity called 'religion', a dangerous, divisive leftover from a less civilized age that could be contained and perhaps one day even exterminated by the unstoppable progress of scientific and rational knowledge. The nation-states that found their voice after the disintegration of Christendom would be 'secular' as opposed to 'religious', and religion became a 'thing' tidily distinct from politics, economics and social order. Although there is no such thing as religion (if a 'thing' is a material object in the real world), its existence remains necessary as a scapegoat for all the shortcomings of the secularist worldview. One need only consider random truths about 'religion' traded by today's purveyors in pop wisdom:

- 'With or without religion, you would have good people doing good things and evil people doing evil things. But for good people to do evil things, that takes religion.'[22]
- '[M]ore wars have been waged, more people killed, and . . . more evil perpetrated in the name of religion than by any other institutional force in human history.'[23]
- 'One of the things that is wrong with religion is that it teaches us to be satisfied with answers which are not really answers at all.'[24]

Such aphorisms offer a comforting diversion from thinking seriously about the myths that modernity has drilled into the cultural psyche. While there have always been religions, prior to the modern era there was no essential 'religion' contrasted with a world that was non-religious. The cultures of ancient Greece, Egypt and Israel had no word for religion because worship was enmeshed in the daily reality of what the world is. The Romans did, but it had little in common with modern attempts to define the word. *Religio*, in ancient Rome, was a 'binding obligation' or deeply rooted devotion that was by no means restricted to belief in a supernatural deity. In the citations above, it would be instructive to replace the word 'religion' with the word 'devotion' to highlight the true substance of such received truth.

Unfortunately, 'religion' cannot simply be dismissed as an abstraction of questionable value. The belief that 'religion is dangerous' is itself a dangerous belief employed to justify mass violence. In his incisive study, *The Myth of Religious Violence*,[25] William T. Cavanaugh has explored this issue rigorously. Cavanaugh notes the sheer impossibility of defining 'religion' either by examining the beliefs and practices of specific world religions (substantivism) or the practical effects of a system of belief (functionalism). In either case, religion is regarded as a timeless essence that finds local, particular expression in this or that context. As such it serves as a shape-shifting term of contempt destined to elude definition: any definition too loosely worded will not condemn all that a modern atheist may wish to condemn; the only definition of religion broad enough for such a task will end up including all humanity and thereby obliterate the distinction between the religious and the non-religious. It is for this reason Cavanaugh notes our understanding of religion tends to be mythological, that is, it locates modern westerners inside a narrative designed to make certain courses of action feel natural:

> The attempt to say that there is a transhistorical and transcultural concept of religion that is separable from secular phenomena *is itself* part of a particular configuration of power, that of the modern, liberal nation-state as it developed in the West. In this context, religion is constructed as transhistorical, transcultural, essentially interior, and essentially distinct from public, secular rationality. To construe Christianity as a religion, therefore, helps to separate loyalty to God from one's public loyalty to the nation-state.[26]

Cavanaugh's point is most clearly made in his public lectures where he asks two pernicious questions:

1. Would you be willing to kill another person for Jesus?
2. Would you be willing to kill another person for your country?

Regardless of our answer to either question, it is clearly only the latter that any sophisticated westerner could ask with a straight face. The underlying question here is our primitive readiness to kill for the sake of those closest to us, those with whom we self-identify. In a post-Christendom world, the nation-state has replaced the church as demanding our *binding obligation*. Cavanaugh makes no attempt to whitewash history, pretending that religious impulses have had no negative effects, nor does he shift the crimes of history to political or social causes, nor even does he deny the existence of religion. Instead he deconstructs the supposed separability of the religious from the secular, a distinction used to justify secular violence, particularly in our own day against parts of the Islamic world. To do so requires that 'a strong contrast is drawn between religious and secular violence. Violence that is labelled religious is always particularly virulent and reprehensible. But violence that is labelled secular hardly counts as violence at all, since it is inherently peace-making. Secular violence [so the logic runs] is often necessary and sometimes praiseworthy, especially when it is used to quell the inherent violence of religion.'[27] Cavanaugh's painstaking research helps to clarify just how 'religion' is a category that helps to divide a rational, enlightened, peace-loving 'us' from an irrational, ignorant, bloodthirsty 'them'. The very existence of the meaningless category of 'religion' is a post-Christendom political necessity.

In all that follows, I try to avoid the language of religion and speak rather in terms of worship. While it is impossible to speak in any meaningful sense about religion, worship can be much more straightforwardly conceived as a core dimension of all human life. At the most basic level, worship has no 'religious' connotation and refers simply to those things that we value, i.e. the things to which we attach worth. This is the root of the English word, i.e. worth-ship, but a vague notion of 'worth' does not take us very far. A spoon, for instance, is worthy if it is worth using. While we may not consciously worship a spoon, the fact that we use it repeatedly demonstrates our faith that it will serve its purpose. Our implicit, unacknowledged trust in it declares its worthiness. Human life is based upon countless trivial, subconscious acts of trust: the alarm clock that awakens us, the food that nourishes us, the transport that carries us, and so on. On a daily basis, we invest our trust in objects that are worthy because they support our lifestyle. Worship is the spoon's journey from the bowl to the mouth.

Of course, not everyone will structure their lives around a spoon. There are degrees of 'worth' we are prepared to attach to an object. There are people, ideologies, even gods, whose 'worth' we acknowledge and who exert formative power over us, shaping our identity. The question is not whether these entities objectively exist but how their character is revealed through the effects they have on our lives. This is consistent with the New Testament's Greek conception of *leitourgos*, from which we derive our word 'liturgy'. Traditionally, the word is translated as 'public service', although its roots are a combination of *laos* (people/public/social) and *ergos* (work/action). In essence, this word refers to the way those things that we inwardly treasure are outwardly manifested in our day-to-day living. Liturgy is what happens to energy when it is spent.

Since humans structure their lives around the things they value, worship is located at the heart of human life. Further, politics – at root – refers to the way that people structure their lives around the things they value. In this light, politics is always and invariably based upon worship, and worship will always manifest itself politically. This is not to say that worship necessarily entails a relationship with a powerful divine entity, but simply that worship describes the core motives driving the human spirit. To be human is to be a worshipper. *If, as Aristotle claimed, human beings are political animals it is only because they were already worshipping animals.*

From this perspective, the history of the term 'atheism' is worth summarizing again.

- Prior to Christendom, *atheism* was a criminal charge levelled at those who undermined the stability of the ruling powers.
- Under Christendom, *atheism* remained a criminal charge, levelled at Christians whose belief in a subversive Christ threatened those eager to defend the status quo.
- During the European Reformations, Christendom split into various smaller mini-Christendoms, and new religious groups sprang up. Here, *atheism* became a term of abuse, for accusing one's enemies of not being truly Christian.
- In the early modern period, *atheism* grew in respectability as the church's power dwindled further.
- By the end of the twentieth century, *atheism* looked set to become the natural state in western society.
- After the events of 9/11, *atheism* underwent a new cultural shift, gathering renewed support in opposing religion, with key leaders of the New Atheism serving the interests of those in power.
- As such, the radical militancy of many atheists means that *atheism* has all the hallmarks of an aggressive if unselfconscious religion.

So long as this unselfconsciously new state religion does not entail the veneration of a supernatural deity, so long as it avoids trading in 'received truth' or peddling in myth, this new religion may not appear to be religious at all. Much of what remains in this book will argue, however, that unwitting reliance upon supernatural intervention, received truth and unhistorical myth are central hallmarks of New Atheism. Here we follow Hyman's belief that atheism is rooted in the me-centred belief system of modernity – and in many ways, the sun is setting on modernity.

Conclusion

In the wake of Descartes and Newton, the individual took pride of place in understanding, ushering in a new era with a new world-view. Where Christendom – for better or worse – proclaimed the sovereignty of God, modernity displaced this view with the sovereignty of the Self. By the late twentieth century, confidence in the Sovereign Self faced a mounting crisis: two world wars, a new 'cold war' and the growing threat of oblivion at the hands of nuclear technology undermined the conviction that progress was a universal human good; capitalism – as chapter 7 will show – was the economic dimension of modernity, but the bright future it promised began to appear as a growing darkness; ecological disaster began to reveal itself as the fruit of technological progress; new discoveries in quantum physics undermined belief that we understand how the world really works at the most basic level; election campaigns (and Christian evangelism) turned into marketing exercises based upon rival bids for power rather than truth; suspicion of authority displaced trust in our leaders; empires collapsed; markets crashed. Voices that once were ignored and marginalized began to offer alternative perspectives on the world: the old certainties of modernity were gradually undermined; everything was doubted – even the notion 'I think; therefore, I am' was exposed to severe doubt.[28] The certainties so treasured by Descartes and Newton began to disintegrate. The only certainty left was that certainty had always been a myth designed to provide security in a universe that was infinitely chaotic, violent and unsympathetic now that God had been forced into exile.

Having scaled the Olympian heights to gain a god's eye view of the world, the Sovereign Self has learned that Olympus is the home of many gods with competing views, interests and claims. Some philosophers increasingly lamented the woes of modernity, and heralded the advent of postmodernity. As the next chapter will show, postmodern thinkers (Jacques Derrida, Stanley Fish, et al.) offered a variety of strategies for undermining the sovereignty of the Self. The success of their strategies will be considered in due course, but the entire validity of their attempts to dethrone the Sovereign Self itself is fiercely opposed by the vast majority of New Atheists. Their universal repugnance at postmodernity is understandable, since – as this chapter has argued – their atheism is dependent upon the modern worldview which is slowly but surely disintegrating. In this sense, we may regard the New Atheist cause as an unwitting but ferocious traditionalism, clinging in vain to the comforts, securities and certainties of a passing age. Such traditionalism casts its spell upon its adherents, blinding them to the traditional nature of their conviction by branding it radical, cutting-edge and 'new'.

Traditionally, atheism is understood simply as a rejection of any form of divinity from beyond the material world, not as a political movement. Atheism, for many, is simply the belief that anyone who exercises the power of reason to observe clear evidence will reject the possibility of God's existence. This, however, is a secondary dimension of modern atheism, a consequence of prior convictions. So far, this book has explored the subversive political roots of atheism, describing these as a central and necessary feature, and this chapter has followed the work of Hyman and Buckley, showing that modern atheism is the outworking of the victory of the cult of the Self. In other words, a new worldview based upon the centrality of the individual ego resulted in, but was not based upon, the denial of God's existence.

Postmodernity, however, represents a cultural rebellion against modernity's Sovereign Self. In this light, the most promising strategy offered by postmodernity involves consideration of the 'other'. Emmanuel Levinas (1906–95) coined the phrase 'otherness' to destabilize the reign of the Self. The very existence of the 'other', as the next chapter will show, challenges all the hard-won and treasured beliefs and the certainties of the Self. If Feuerbach and Nietzsche had seen that God was simply a figment of the Self's imagination, then the non-existence of God is no less imaginary. The question of how the Self relates to the world beyond all that is familiar haunts every claim about God's existence or otherwise. Modernity, as I have described it, has enabled us to construct an ideological fortress, securing for humanity a set of certainties, facts, principles, values and morals in the midst of a wild, chaotic and dangerous universe that is objectively aimless, meaningless and godless. But the fortress is crumbling, forcing us to consider afresh our relation to the disturbing, disruptive and terrifying reality of that which is genuinely other.

3.

Philosophical Traditions and Otherness

The question of how human beings get along with 'others' has risen to prominence in the so-called 'postmodern' era of philosophy, and has slowly gathered momentum from the 1970s onwards. The question of how we relate to the 'other', and how we engage with the 'otherness' they embody, remains high on the agenda of many contemporary philosophers. Definitions of the 'other' vary, but two key features can usually be identified. Another person, especially one from another culture, already represents an alternative way of understanding the world. My reaction to their presence will be somewhere on a scale between two extremes. At one end, I may feel threatened by them and retreat into my own worldview where I need not listen to this 'other' or take them seriously. Content with my own way of understanding the world, to be confronted with this other may prove to be disruptive, discomforting, too thought-provoking. At the other end of the spectrum, I may wish to welcome this other, to embrace their otherness, as I seek to listen, to understand, and to be exposed to a radically alternative way of encountering the world. I may not, in the end, agree with this other – but seeking to understand them well may cast the shadow of relativity over my own understanding of the world. In the twenty-first century, most westerners would like to consider themselves towards this latter end of the scale.

But otherness does not only signify interaction between persons. The sheer otherness of the world beyond that with which I am familiar may be as disturbing to me as the presence of another living person. Otherness refers, no less, to the cold realities of the universe, as it can evoke fear, wonder and frustration at the monstrous insignificance of my place within it: the sheer vastness of history – human, global and cosmic; the infinite expanse of potential scientific knowledge when compared with how little we know and how tentatively we know it; the possible existence of entities which may, by their nature, lie forever beyond the scope of 'science', as science is currently conceived.

Again, our reaction to such realities can be on a scale between extremes. At one end of the spectrum is the refusal to entertain the reality of anything with which I am not already familiar. Those who adhere either to religious certainties, or to scientific imperialism (considered fully in chapter 5) both represent a worldview that excuses individuals from engaging seriously with anything that might pull the rug from under their feet. Bible-thumping Christians, for instance, often claim a degree of certainty about the universe that the Bible never offered; scientific imperialists, similarly, seek to reduce the mysteries of the universe to the field in which they happen to consider themselves expert. Both mindsets operate on the basis of a closed universe, protecting its inhabitants from the reality of an otherness that may unsettle their worldview. At the other end of the spectrum are those whose worldview is based upon a readiness to encounter the world in such a way as to have their previous convictions called into question. This, of course, is how true science progresses. It is also the embodiment of Christianity's most long-neglected but fundamental virtue: humility. Again, most modern westerners would like to picture themselves at the latter end of this scale, preferring openness to arrogance.

The otherness of other people, and the otherness (and inherent unknowable-ness) of the material universe, have always been a preoccupation of philosophers. Whether these forms of otherness threaten all we hold dear, or whether they invite us into a richer experience of life, the two dimensions belong together. From the perspective of the thinking individual, the capacity to be transformed by the otherness encountered in people or in the world remains a single underlying quality. Though ancient philosophers may not have used the grammar of otherness this way, the dual focus – both upon the dry facts of the universe on the one hand, and upon the nature of human beings on the other – is to be found in the work of those we consider classical philosophers.

This chapter will offer a brief overview of how 'otherness' has been welcomed in the western history of philosophy, though of course, in so doing it can barely scratch the surface of each thinker considered. My intention is not to summarize any philosopher's thought – a dubious exercise in any case. The great thinkers of history are best heard not simply in order to be summarized or assimilated, but so that their living voices may echo across history to address contemporary concerns. My focus in this chapter is upon those whose thought had a notable impact upon the Christendom and modernist mindset.[1] The readings offered here are mostly mainstream interpretations of figures of towering intellect (and Jean-Paul Sartre), and are certainly not intended as any kind of summary of the immense depth and complexity of their thought. Indeed, the emphasis here is not necessarily on accessing the depths of their philosophy, but on offering instead an overview of the philosophies *attributed to* these individual thinkers and their effects upon the world as it is.

Classical Antiquity (Pre-Fifth Century AD)

Plato serves as a good starting-point in this respect. Reacting to those philosophers who believed the universe could be explained solely by the movements of physical, material entities (the 'materialists'), Plato offered a means of understanding the universe that also took serious account of human behaviour and institutions. To emphasize the fragility of human thought, Plato communicated his philosophy in the form of dialogues, usually involving a literary reincarnation of his teacher, Socrates. This mischievous, playful character pursues endless lines of questioning, and often proves himself capable of abandoning his own long-cherished views if they are shown to be mistaken. It is this frequent line of questioning in the Platonic dialogues that demonstrates, in ancient philosophy, a concern to engage well with otherness.

Whether Plato achieved this is another question. For him, *generalities* always take precedence over the *particular* situations and dilemmas one may face in the here and now. It is easy to see how some interpreters of Plato saw him downplay the importance of everyday experience. Many see in his philosophy a retreat from the everyday world to an ideal, non-material world. While we may want to question whether these are fair readings of Plato, it is certainly true that this interpretation had enormous influence throughout the later Roman world in general and for the formation of Christianity in particular. However, that influence is not mediated through Saint Paul, as is sometimes supposed. The apostle Paul, though clearly influenced by Platonic thought, was certainly not captivated by it. The thrust of Paul's letters, therefore, is not the primary means by which Plato shaped the Christian church. It was not until the third century AD that so-called Neo-Platonism began to assert itself over Christian self-understanding. Here, it is Plotinus (204–70) who becomes a catalyst for Platonizing Christian identity.

The third century saw the Roman Empire undergo a period of severe political and economic crisis. Senior military figures with armies at their disposal could effectively sell the emperorship to the highest bidder, before murdering them to make a new sale. Germanic and Persian tribes exploited to the full the weaknesses that opened up along the frontiers as a result of the empire's introversion. In addition, disease had reduced the population of the empire by up to a third, leading to economic chaos and social disruption seizing many key cities. These troubles are manifest in Plotinus' work in a peculiar way: they simply do not feature. Rather than explicitly tackling the worldly troubles by which he was surrounded, Plotinus promoted a philosophy of withdrawal to quiet inner reflection. If the *particular* situations of the daily world were too horrific to contemplate, refuge can thankfully be found in the *generalities* of Plato's ideal world.

Had the emperor of the day (with whom Plotinus was personally acquainted) submitted a request for a bespoke, practical philosophy to serve his political purpose, it would very closely resemble what Plotinus offered. Plotinus' thought was devoid of pragmatic engagement with the world of politics. He found in Plato an escape from the disintegration and decay of the ugly world of humans, into the serenity of otherworldly self-reflection. To a world of unrest and rebellion, Plotinus offered a philosophical sedative, where beauty, truth and justice are to be sought via the mind – not via political action. Such a philosophy is certainly in tune with the wishes of an emperor keen to maintain order and stability.

One resounding political critique of Christianity finds its roots in this Neo-Platonism. Namely that those who suffer in this world should be content with their lot, and find consolation for their troubles in the assurance of a future, blissful, eternal but post-mortem existence in another world. This is one of the means by which major strands of Christian belief were interpreted into their exact opposite. For instance, the kingdom of God – which in the gospels is a highly charged, disruptive form of government – once interpreted in Platonic terms is domesticated into a retreat from the quest for actual justice in the everyday world, into a spiritual, politically sterile, otherworldly reality which eventually became equated with a realm called heaven, the supposed final destination of the tediously well-behaved. Here, philosophical influence fundamentally defused the explosive charge carried by early Christian beliefs, as the Christian's attention is diverted from the ugliness of earth to the beauty of heaven. Plotinus is a thinker who both reflects the mood of his age and helps to shape a version of Christianity that would soon prove useful for Constantine. This led Bertrand Russell to conclude that, 'Plotinus is both an end and a beginning – an end as regards the Greeks, a beginning as regards Christendom.'[2]

The Medieval Era (Fifth to Fifteenth Century)

The Romans were happy to tolerate a multitude of religions, so long as those religions did not undermine the political, economic and social foundations of the empire. The reason that the early Christians were branded atheist and subjected to persecution was precisely that their beliefs posed a direct threat to the internal stability of the empire. These Christians recognized the human value not only of Roman citizens, but of each and every human being, including slaves and barbarians, women and infants, all of whom were believed to have been created and loved by God. This led to the formation of political communities (today we would call them churches) whose ways of living together undermined the strictly hierarchical values of the Roman household where one life would out-value another. By holding this belief in the dignity of *all* human life, Christians did not thereby simply adopt an alternative set of family values. They embodied a politics that threatened to destabilize the hierarchical value system on which the entirety of Roman civilization was founded. Worse still, these political communities were taking root at all levels of society, and in every corner of the empire. However, with the rise of Constantine and the so-called Christendom settlement, a Christian-friendly emperor paved the way for a new form of Christianity: a religion that was – in all but name – a new imperial cult, complete with doctrines, commandments, authority structures and, above all, empire-wide uniformity. Though this reconfigured version of Christian belief retained the language and some of the spiritual contents of its ancient counterpart, its earthly, political dynamics were jettisoned if they hindered the smooth running of the imperial machine.

Saint Augustine (354–430) was heir to this philosophical tradition of Plato (interpreted largely through Plotinus), and interpreted Christianity in Platonic terms. Augustine's prolific writings set the tone for the theology and philosophy that dominated Christendom for eight centuries. This is not to say that Augustine was uncritical of Platonism. In fact, he devotes books 8–10 of his *City of God* to a critical engagement with Platonic thought. But while he sought to weigh the writings of the Platonists against the Christian Scriptures, the substructure of his thought rests again upon the otherworldliness already to be identified in Plotinus. Like Plotinus, Augustine wrote in an era when the Roman Empire faced disintegration and insecurity. His most famous work, the *Confessions*, though offering a beautiful series of theological and philosophical self-reflections, can read like a subconscious withdrawal from all that is nasty and wrong with the world. Augustine's world is a horrible place, human existence is an imperfect and hopelessly doomed enterprise, and this pessimism leads to a theology of withdrawal from the otherness of other people and the world at large – to reflect upon a greater, spiritual otherness. This is stated clearly in his *City of God*, a reminder that – though the Roman Empire is falling and civilization is clearly failing – there is a greater, perfect, heavenly city towards which the people should lift their gaze. Of course, this is a simplification of Augustine, but there is little doubt either that this otherworldly mindset underpins the whole sweep of his writings, or that this is how his writings have been widely understood. Augustine endorsed the Platonic worldview at the expense of the subversive, politically engaged, pre-Christendom forms of Christian belief.

Taking stock at this point, we see the concept of otherness develop in a particular direction:

- Otherness is to be encountered both in human beings and in the universe.
- Platonic traditions drove the experience of otherness away from the actual world, to a supposed otherworldly reality.
- This was convenient for the Roman Empire and for Christendom. Keeping the eyes of the masses turned away from the unpleasantness of daily life, towards a blissful afterlife and heavenly existence, makes it easier to maintain order, peace and social stability.
- Augustine gave Christendom a sophisticated philosophy that helped to maintain the status quo.

Here, rather than engaging the otherness we might encounter in human beings and the world, we are invited away from the horizontal axis of pragmatic belief, towards a vertical, spiritual world of ideals. In a tradition that lingers into the twenty-first century, ethics is conceived of in private and personal, apolitical terms. As Russell pointed out, 'It is strange that the last men of intellectual eminence before the dark ages were concerned, not with saving civilization or expelling the barbarians or reforming the abuses of the administration, but with preaching the merit of virginity and the damnation of un-baptized infants.'[3] Augustine wrote a theological philosophy that served Christendom for eight centuries.

The Roman Empire, however, would not last so long. Augustine died as the Vandals besieged the town of Hippo where he was bishop. The empire had split into a Greek-speaking East (with its capital at Byzantium) and the Latin-speaking West. In the centuries that followed, all frontiers found themselves under threat. Islam had arisen in the East, eventually overpowering what remained of the empire. In the West, Nordic and Germanic tribes swept from the north, displacing Christian with pagan beliefs in many corners of Europe. Although Christendom had grown deep roots, Christian thinkers found themselves at pains to preserve their heritage. It is for this reason that many see the entire sweep of medieval philosophy as preservative, lacking any impetus of its own but clinging desperately to dated Christian philosophy in the light of pagan onslaught. But it was not only to Plato that they clung. Plato's principal student was Aristotle, a figure whose thought – though largely in tune with that of his teacher – challenged it at several key points.

Aristotle's works had long been preserved in the East, and when Islam became dominant, his works continued to be treasured by Muslim scholars. By the thirteenth century, crusades to the Holy Land had brought to light a flood of Aristotelian literature, including commentaries – most notably by the figure of Averroes (the Latin name of a Muslim scholar, Ibn Rushd). These works were translated, sometimes from Arabic, sometimes directly from Greek, into Latin. Pope Gregory IX lost little time condemning Aristotle's works, interpreted as they were through Islamic sources. But among the Dominican order of monks was a young student from Aquino in Italy, whose insatiable curiosity led him to reflect in depth upon these ancient, forbidden writings. Thomas Aquinas (1225–74) conscripted Aristotle for service in Christian theology, just as Augustine had conscripted Plato.

In contrast to Plato's otherworldliness, Aristotle offered to a society slowly emerging from feudalism a more scientific, pragmatic philosophy. The ancient Greek thought that was spreading again across Europe brought with it a welcome emphasis upon reason and science. In fact, the structure of Aquinas' principal work, *Contra Gentiles*, proceeds on the basis of step-by-step reasoning, only to discover, at the end of the process, that the findings happen to be consistent with the truths of divine revelation. Nevertheless, despite the flawed findings obvious in some of Aristotle's (and Aquinas') own reasoning, it was the process itself that was to be treasured. At this point, one might imagine that Christendom was on the brink of an era in which the otherness of the everyday world was to be treasured, and the otherworldly flight from down-to-earth philosophy was finally to be abandoned.

Unfortunately, those in power were not about to distinguish between the value of Aristotle's method (intended to be enduring) and the value of his findings (which were to have been open to revision). While Aristotle would no doubt have been content to sacrifice the latter for the sake of increased knowledge yielding itself to reason, the church was not so open. Aristotelian scientific findings quickly acquired near infallible status, putting the handbrake upon scientific progress that is now almost universally lamented. Aquinas, though his teaching was initially condemned by the universities of Paris and Oxford, was later made a saint (1323) and Aristotle heralded as '*the* Philosopher'. Both were thereby robbed of the capacity to be wrong and, by their infallibility, Christendom secured itself against any form of scientific otherness that might pose a threat. For sure, the 'Thomism' that took root in the Catholic Church has long remained in force, and by the Council of Trent (1545–63) Aquinas' authority became a measure of Christian orthodoxy. But by then, other forces were at work.

The Reformation (Sixteenth Century)

The political machinery of Europe was steadily being upgraded. The power of successive popes had gradually diminished, leaving them ever more dependent upon the growing powers of rival regional princes. In Britain and France particularly, the emergence of national monarchies relativized papal supremacy. In Italy, the Renaissance came about as the late fifteenth-century 'rebirth' of Greek thinking combined with the trade-wealth of the Italian city-states to furnish ruling classes with cultural and scientific awareness. Meanwhile, the mounting corruption of the papacy fed a growing reluctance to see national funds transferred to distant lands to line clerical pockets. By the sixteenth century, the increasing complexity of societal structures (including a new middle class), the widespread ability to read what rolled off the newly invented printing press, and the growing power of German princes paved the way for the European Reformation.

In 1517 Martin Luther, a young Augustinian monk, began a universal reform that visited a splintering blow upon the unity of Christendom. Where there had been one true church because there was one true faith, Luther offered a radically alternative way of being Christian from which various new ways of 'being church' emerged. Displacing papal authority with his appeal to the authority of Scripture, and focusing upon the necessity of baptism for the individual, Luther highlighted the importance of 'justification by faith'. In so doing, he tore the vitality of the Christian life (and in this period, the value of life as a whole) out of the hands of Rome, straight into the hands of individuals. These individuals, however, were still subject to the authority of secular kings and princes – and it was ultimately into their hands that Luther transferred power. So began a violent chain reaction that spelt the end of Christendom as a single, unified whole.

Under a single, unified Christendom, the political, human otherness beyond its boundaries had been a relatively simple matter. Once it had fragmented into rival nations, differing manifestations of corporate human otherness were found threatening from everywhere. How did these 'mini-Christendoms' cope with this otherness when it came to their doorstep? War. Few historians interpret the so-called religious wars as anything other than nationalistic exploits with religious pretexts. This is not to say, however, that religious allegiances had no role. Here, it seems, divine otherness was invoked to crush the human otherness that stood in the way of sound Christian belief. But the bishops who blessed weapons of warfare were themselves willing instruments of these wars whose causes lay in national self-assertion. The most infamous of these religious conflicts was the Thirty Years' War, which brought widespread devastation to central Europe. It was a veteran of that war whose philosophy sank a tranquillizer into the wounded but still dangerous animal that was Christendom.

The Modern Era (Seventeenth to Twentieth Century)

The previous chapter showed that the modern world has its roots in the thinking of René Descartes, who had waved his philosophical wand and turned the great and powerful Yahweh into the fragile and mischievous Tinkerbell. In a context of growing distrust in the 'otherness' of the Pope's authority, in which nations began to assert their own religious identities, Descartes (1596–1650) helped the world to disengage from the spiritual authority of Rome. He had witnessed at close hand the devastation that religious wars had wrought across northern Europe, and – like his philosophical predecessors – advocated withdrawal. This he did by means of radical self-reflection.

In a world that was in chaos, he promoted a profound level of conscious doubt. What could be trusted? Other people might not be trusted. Their existence, as well as your own, may be an object of your own imagination. You may be dreaming. In fact, your entire existence may be the construct of some deceptive, malevolent spirit, forcing you to exist in the world of your imagination – where all who are dear to you are nothing but illusions. But if one doubts everything it is possible to doubt, there is still one thing that remains beyond reach: the thought process of doubting is itself an *activity* in which I am undoubtedly engaged. Hence, the fact that I am thinking is itself proof that I do exist after all. This, at root, is known as Cartesian doubt – although Descartes was not the first to doubt this way. Augustine had said almost precisely the same in the fifth century. But Augustine wrote in an era when Christendom was being established, and such doubt was far less conducive to the political authorities than it would be in the era when Christendom was being dismantled. As it happened, then, Descartes' form of doubt was not some humility-driven end in itself; it was a hubristic starting point for a brave new world that existed beyond the confines of Christendom.

Descartes set about constructing a positive, trustworthy worldview in which others do exist after all, in which I serve a nation, worship God, and listen to wise folk. This became the foundation of the modern worldview – but no longer was this a worldview informed by that which is beyond myself. Descartes' world is the world of my own making. The modern worldview is founded upon this Cartesian doubt – that of the thinking, isolated, detached, human individual. Descartes demolished everything outside of me, and then rebuilt it on my own terms. While God existed as an object of my thought, no longer was he at the centre of the universe, but rather somewhere out there on the periphery of human thought. The modern world is built on the sure foundation of the human individual, but such an understanding of the world is vulnerable. Otherness, on the Cartesian model of modernity, is simply a projection of the individual onto a universal screen. In other words, it is unwittingly suppressed.

It was with the backdrop of this post-Cartesian worldview that David Hume (1711–76) expressed his ruthless scepticism. All that we know about others and about our universe comes to us through the vulnerable apparatus of our human attempts to make sense of the world. Can our human capacity for knowledge be trusted as a way of grasping what the world really is? No, says Hume, it cannot, thus justifying widespread rejection of philosophy and theology, to the point at which Hume is still cited by sceptics well into the twenty-first century. Scepticism, however, was not the last word of the eighteenth century. Immanuel Kant (1724–1804) wrote in an era of Enlightenment, in which the newly established invention of a thinking, fallible *subject* experienced a world outside itself, comprised of *objects*. While Hume was happy to accept the reality of the *objective* world as it is, he contended that – since it is always, only, ever known *subjectively* – all knowledge is profoundly insecure. Since Hume is often regarded as a boundary marker whose writing was to awaken Kant from his 'dogmatic slumber', another recap may prove useful at this point.

- Aquinas introduced to the medieval era a scientific way of engaging with the world. Unfortunately, not only his thoroughgoing methods but also his flawed findings gained infallible status in the church of Christendom, leaving the handbrake on scientific progress.
- The stranglehold of Christendom, however, was broken when Martin Luther shattered Christendom into various 'mini-Christendoms'.
- The results were the so-called 'religious wars' of the sixteenth and seventeenth centuries, tearing across western Europe and bringing widespread devastation, misery and suffering. Nations disengaged from Rome and asserted their national, religious independence.
- A new way of thinking emerged, one in which the focal point of thought was not religion as mediated by Rome, but independent thought channelled through the individual, human subject. The human Self became sovereign: this is modernity.
- Though Descartes had centred philosophy and science around the individual subject, Hume had highlighted the unreliable

nature of the individual human subject. We could now be sure of nothing; philosophy was dead.

Thus the problem that beset Kant was precisely the conflict between how we understand the world and how we understand everyday human life: Kant sought a unified understanding of the different strands of existence. Writing in the wake of Newton's findings in the world of physics, Kant believed the universe was governed by laws and that everything in the physical world happened, and could only have happened that way, because of prior causes. However, to claim that universal laws govern human behaviour (ethics) is to deny individuals any moral freedom to act this or that way – if all that I do, good or bad, is predetermined by laws of cause and effect. How can there be individual responsibility if we are helpless victims of a cold universe that compels us to act one way or another?

Kant's solution is found in a 'deontological' or 'duty-based' form of ethics. My own motives must be considered in the light of universal principles of reason, since only when my actions obey universal laws can they be deemed moral. This he calls the 'categorical imperative': 'Act only according to that maxim by which you can at the same time will that it should become a universal law.' Any attempt to make oneself a 'special case', for Kant, is highly suspect. Hence, in the modern world, the basis for ethics is no longer rooted in any religious or relational belief structure, but with the alternative – duty. In a world where religion was divisive, and opposing views of God resulted in bloodshed, the surest guide to right behaviour became the scientific, universal, timeless notion of duty.

It was one of Kant's followers, G.W.F. Hegel (1770–1831) who brought some form of 'God' back into the daily experience of humanity. He developed what has become known as 'Hegelian dialectic', where one begins with an idea (thesis), encounters a contradictory idea (anti-thesis), and develops a fusion between the two (syn-thesis). This synthesis, once established, then becomes a new thesis, which itself will face a new antithesis and so on. Applying this dialectic to history, Hegel (as he is traditionally interpreted) offers a theory of how humanity progresses, and this in fact forms the basis of modern belief in the so-called 'myth of progress'. This is not a randomly generated progress, but one which is ever-evolving under the guidance of the ambiguous being known as Spirit. There is a divine causality that works within this Hegelian view of history that has proven immensely popular since it was first produced.

Some, however, have seen the popular application of Hegel's thought as dehumanizing. This is not simply because he was a proponent of early German nationalism, nor because he considered his own thought as the glorious pinnacle of all history's philosophy. Rather, it is how progress and modernity intertwine. Otherness, in this system, is absorbed into the world of the familiar before a new form of otherness is encountered. Given that Hegel is the last (and possibly the greatest) towering intellect moving within the spirit of modernity, much of his thinking helps to make sense of the world as it is today. From here, we arrive at the twentieth century with little modification. Hence, examples of his dialectic may still strike a chord:

Thesis:	The American Dream
Antithesis:	The dangerous world 'out there' that is not America
Synthesis:	Disneyworld ('Sample the culture and cuisine of fifty different countries!')

More seriously:

Thesis:	A strong German nation
Antithesis:	The Jewish problem
Synthesis:	The final solution

Perhaps, as a consequence:

Thesis:	Outrage at the suffering inflicted during the Holocaust
Antithesis:	Treasuring the comfort that rests upon the suffering of others
Synthesis:	Systems of banking, warfare, politics and media that blind us to the horrific consequences of our actions upon others

In fact it was the Jewish scholar Zygmunt Bauman who viewed the Holocaust as the inevitable result, not of anti-Semitism, but of modernity. For Bauman, modernity as a whole is structured around hostility towards the 'other'. The world that is strange, beyond that with which we are familiar, i.e. the world 'out there', invokes wonder and curiosity. However, it also invokes fear and suspicion, because the stranger, the other, cannot be categorized and brought under rational control. The 'other' is therefore perceived as a threat, a potential thief, mugger or terrorist. That which is from 'beyond' the world we have ordered for ourselves is a potential source of disorder, a threat to our security. How are we to deal with such a threat? Bauman's *Modernity and the Holocaust* argues that the Holocaust is not an unfortunate exception to the otherwise civilized progress of modernity, but the final goal to which modernity leads: over-categorization of things and people (in this particular instance, Jews); rational pragmatism eclipsing human concerns; ethics based not upon relationships but upon following perceived rules. Modernity, according to Bauman, leads finally to the expulsion of the 'other'. But Bauman was not alone, and certainly not the first to stand against the overall flow of modernity.

The Anti-Modernists

Romanticism

The first movement associated with rebellion against the forces of modernity was that of the Romantics. The term, a little misleading, might best be understood today as Romanesque, referring to the great architectural ruins of ancient civilizations which speak of a transcendent glory that has no reference to the Christian God. The Romantic era (from the late eighteenth to mid-nineteenth century) spanned the French Revolution and the Industrial Revolution in Britain. The former was an earth-shattering event, in which the ruling classes and their god and their laws were defied and overcome. The latter saw a world that dehumanized peasant populations, drawing them to cities, cramming them into mills and workhouses, mines and chimneys. Why not, after all, since human beings – according to Enlightenment thought – were little more than rational machines?

The Romantics were mainly poets, writers and artists, who offered a different view of humanity. Now that Christendom was entering an advanced state of decay, a new set of rules for human behaviour had to be invented. But the Kantian ideas of duty lacked emotion and sensibility. Rather than looking beyond the self to a world 'out there', the Romantic vision is one of self-realization. The ego is paramount: emotional expression – regardless of what action it leads to – is a sufficient basis for ethics. This approach is borne out by Keats' tragic poetry, Mary Shelley's chilling portrayal of humanity in *Frankenstein*, and Lord Byron's own recklessly self-indulgent life.

But if modernity is the era which celebrates the sovereignty of the human self, then the Romantic movement – as generally understood – must be seen as a strand *within* rather than a serious critique *of* the modern world. In the absence of Christendom's tyrannical God, the Romantics offered an alternative modern ethics, based upon radical egotism. Emotion, here, is mistaken for its delusional counterpart, sensibility. Terry Eagleton's critique of the movement's great philanthropists and literary figures focuses upon this point: that the help given to an other is given not for the other's sake, but for the sake of my own ego. Here there is no relational emotion, where I am exposed to the otherness of the other person. An ethics based on radical egotism can only result in the violent clash of coming into contact with other egos – and, ultimately, the silencing of the other.

Existentialism

Running parallel with the Romantic movement was one that came to be known as 'existentialism'. Its initial proponent was Søren Kierkegaard (1813–55), a Danish philosopher who set himself against Hegelianism and against the state church. For Kierkegaard, the Spirit of the Age was like a prison. Members of mass societies were confined within a herd mentality that would shape their thinking, their living and their fate. Like the Romantics, Kierkegaard knew that humans were more than simply rational creatures, but had spiritual, emotional, relational dimensions that shaped and gave expression to their being. If humans were hope-lessly brainwashed by the spirit of their age, then Kierkegaard would call them to 'stand out' (or in Heideggerian Greek, to 'ek-sist'). This societal defiance has formed the narrative substruc-ture of several box office successes, from the children's story *Babe* to the science fiction phenomenon *The Matrix*. In both stories the main character defies the world of convention: Babe is the pig that thinks he's a dog, and finds his purpose in life herding sheep; Neo escapes the 'Matrix', an artificial world designed to devolve human beings into human resources. Having escaped, Neo finds his purpose liberating others from that dehumanizing world. Both movies carry an implicit challenge for the audience to defy the world of convention, to ek-sist.

To exist, then, is to stand out of the herd mentality by means of individual self-assertion, to defy reason, custom, even law. The following century witnessed increasing awareness of human identity being hopelessly submerged in mass society, and exis-tentialism became widely celebrated. Rudolf Bultmann rightly perceived aspects of existential belief in the writings of the New Testament.[4] His friend (and colleague at Marburg University), Martin Heidegger, also produced a philosophy that contained a strong existentialist element. However, it was Jean-Paul Sartre who popularized the movement in the period after the Second World War. Having feasted on an intellectual diet of existential thought, what Sartre digested and then strained to squeeze out through his pen spilled into a collection of writings by which Heidegger and others were repulsed. For Sartre, it was no longer a tyrannical politics, an oppressive church, or a shallow cultural philosophy, but otherness as a whole from which the existentialist would stand out – a move which has since rendered the move-ment notoriously difficult to define. Sartre's infamous declaration, 'Hell is other people',[5] expresses a deep appreciation of the diabol-ical threat of the otherness of the other.

The existentialism associated with Sartre finally advocates, yet again, withdrawal from otherness. However we choose to contour the concerns of existentialists, the sheer individualism of existen-tial passions invites the same critique offered to the Romantics; namely, that (taken on its own) it remains egotistic, unconstrained by serious consideration of the other. For instance, existentialism requires that we summon up our moral, social and intellectual energies to 'defy convention'. At the time of writing, this phrase appears as a tagline for three television advertising campaigns enticing potential consumers to buy mass-produced motor vehicles[6] – i.e. appealing to individual delusions of *defiance*, but relying on those individuals' subconscious *compliance* with convention. This highlights the insufficiency of existentialism as a stand-alone philosophy, begging the prior questions of precisely what we defy and with what we comply.

Nietzsche

A third anti-modern movement is to be found in the gargantuan thought of one man, a thoroughgoing atheist and the Abraham of postmodernity, namely, Friedrich Wilhelm Nietzsche (1844–1900). His famous declaration that 'God is dead' is not a belief he had reasoned towards but an observation that his philosophy was structured around. Unlike all modern advocates of the New Atheism, Nietzsche understood Christianity and the effects that it had had upon the world. The god of Christendom was dead, but Nietzsche was under no illusion about the enormity of his effects upon history.

As I argued in the previous chapter, the values treasured by most modern westerners are indeed Christian in origin. Values based upon compassion, caring for the weak and the vulnerable, though upheld with varying degrees of success in the Christendom era, were Christian innovations. They displaced the notions of society treasured by Romans, where slaves were worthless, freemen were slightly more valuable, citizens were more privileged, and the ruling aristocracy enjoyed immense worth. A civilization in which unwanted babies were dumped on rubbish tips but emperors were worshipped as divine was a civilization in which compassion was not an officially treasured virtue. Only with the advent of Christianity did it become so. This is not to argue that Christians had a monopoly on compassion. Even the Romans could show compassion to their peers, as could any primitive people group. But universal human compassion (the readiness to 'suffer with' another) is not a universal human virtue. However, with the advent of Christendom, compassion officially became – in theory at least – a universally recognized quality. Christendom is perhaps the major reason we regard qualities like compassion as good. There is no objective reason we should.

Nietzsche knew this well enough, and knew that if the era of Christendom were to be surpassed in any meaningful sense, then its deeply rooted values would need to be torn out. It is for this reason that much of Nietzsche's writings seemed so out of sync with what we imagine to be good. He was attempting what he called the 'trans-valuation of all values'. For Nietzsche, Christianity has inflicted a wound upon humanity, an open wound that still bleeds with compassion for others and with worship of God. If only we can stop the bleeding, i.e. cease engaging with otherness, then we can conserve our resources to lift us to a higher plane of humanity. Moral and metaphysical otherness are to be abandoned altogether. In managing to think so comprehensively and brilliantly beyond his own context (most notably in his *Thus Spake Zarathustra*) his work naturally inspired late twentieth-century writers who were attempting to effect a so-called 'paradigm shift'. Before turning to the champions of postmodernity, the modernity they try to supersede is worth re-sketching.

Postmodernity? (Late Twentieth Century to the Present)

- **Kant** categorized life, the universe and everything into laws that must be obeyed, and, in the case of ethics, rules that must be universal.
- **Hegel** systematized the progress of human life, applying his dialectic method (of thesis, antithesis, synthesis) to human history.
- **Romantics** detested the subjection of humanity to cold laws, and emphasized freedom of choice, emotional expression, albeit in an egotistical way.
- **Existentialists:** Kierkegaard and his followers similarly emphasized emotion, and personal individual decision, as humans are invited to 'stand out' (or 'ek-sist') from the herd mentality of the day.
- **Nietzsche** understood that the human self can only be raised to a higher way of life, no longer by worshipping God and

showing compassion, but by re-imagining human values altogether.

At the root of modernity lay a strong belief in 'the sovereignty of
the Self'. While in practice state churches continued to exist, phil-
osophically all belief in God was marginalized from mainstream
public life. But in the late twentieth century, it was becoming
increasingly clear that modernity was not working. As we have
seen, both Romanticism and existentialism remained thoroughly
modern, based as they were on the conviction that the individual human self is still sovereign. Postmodernists, as the name
suggests, sought to move beyond modernity by dethroning the
Sovereign Self. Three of its key characteristics offer a window into
the dynamics of the movement.

Relativism

'Truth is relative,' says the postmodernist. The desire to congrat-
ulate or assure ourselves that we are right, that certain facts are
unquestionable and that our worldview is the natural one, betrays
a quiet arrogance in the modern mindset. The relativist reminds
us that all of our claims, beliefs and certainties are filtered through
our human, time-bound, culture-bound, earth-bound fallibility.
Relativists note that all truths are more precisely 'truth claims',
and who is to decide whether one person's view is more valid
than another? There is no overarching, great single 'truth' that can
be used to measure competing truth claims.

Postmodernity says that principles, values, foundations, rights
and duties, long thought to be eternal, unchanging absolutes, are
little more than a modernist dream conjured up to make us feel secure
in a violent and godless universe. Whatever we decide to do, whatever is useful for us to believe, whatever it is expedient to argue, our
appeal to eternal, absolute truth comes late in the day. These appeals
to some great absolute, objective force of reason serve as a useful
justification for decisions we have made for entirely subjective,
selfish reasons. For the postmodernist, there is, then, no 'meta-nar-
rative', no great single overarching truth about life, the universe and
everything. The standard modern response to relativism is to point
out that, if 'truth is relative', then so too is the very truth that truth is

relative. Those who claim 'truth is relative' are making an absolute claim that is universal, unquestionable fact – thereby defeating their own case. But this is not the last word on relativism.

Neo-Pragmatism

Contemporary pragmatist thinkers attempted to dethrone the Sovereign Self by emphasizing that the individual human self is simply the product of his or her 'interpretive community'. Stanley Fish has shown that we learn to become who we are only within some context, and we cannot climb out of that context to experience anyone who is genuinely 'other'. Although there are many contexts that shape many communities, says Fish, the community that shapes *our* view is an *absolute* authority for us. Our truth is indeed theoretically 'relative' to others, and yet within our communities (from which we can never escape) we can make absolute truth claims without contradiction. Unfortunately, this way of thinking fundamentally excludes the other.

The moment someone 'other' becomes comprehensible to us, the moment we understand them, it can only be because they are now 'one of us' and are thereby no longer 'other'. For Fish, anything and anyone from beyond my interpretive community is thereby unintelligible. As one critic has pointed out:

> With typical American parochialism and self-obsession, Fish's book is silent about famine, forced migration, revolutionary nationalism, military aggression, the depredations of capital, the inequities of world trade, the disintegration of whole communities. Yet these have been the consequences of the system of which the United States is the linchpin for many perched on the unmetaphysical outside of it. Being unable to leap out of your own cultural skin seems to mean in Fish's case having no grasp of how your country is helping to wreak havoc in that inscrutable place known as abroad. One has the indelible impression that Fish does not think a great deal of abroad, and would be quite happy to see it abolished.[7]

Ultimately, for Fish, the other is there to be conquered. 'Might is right,' he declares of whole communities. The question of how I encounter others within the community of which I form a part is a question that Fish never once raises, despite writing hundreds upon hundreds of pages celebrating such communities. In the kind of community Fish describes, the individual is quietly reaffirmed and celebrated. The sovereignty of the Self remains intact, and there is nothing '*post*modern' about his philosophy.

Deconstruction

The French philosopher Jacques Derrida (1930–2004) built a system of 'deconstruction' in the attempt to displace the sovereignty of the human self. He called for a radical uncertainty, an ongoing acceptance that our knowledge of anything is deeply provisional, a perpetual alertness to the power games of our thought and language. Like Sartre, Derrida was painfully aware of the sheer disturbance that the presence of the other can bring, and regarded the entire history of western philosophy as an exercise in averting one's eyes from the other.[8] In his later writings, he pondered at length about the coming of a Messiah, arguing that we must remain perpetually open, always looking for this great 'other' to break into our experience. But this expectation, this waiting, this theoretical openness to the other could never be allowed to become a reality. For Derrida, if the Messiah ever turned up, said John D. Caputo, 'that indiscretion would ruin the whole idea of the messianic'.[9] This is because, in the end, Derrida is profoundly prescriptive about the Messiah, who becomes a personification of otherness. Derrida knows exactly who this mysterious Messiah can and cannot be, and as such the Messiah's otherness becomes little more than a projection of his own desire. Unconsciously, Derrida domesticates the other, subjects the other to my own expectations – while keeping all the language and pretence of openness. In Derrida's thought, the sovereignty of the Self is never truly overturned, and as such, he is never truly postmodern.

- Derrida seeks to overcome modernity's 'sovereignty of the Self' by putting the human self 'under erasure', by denying the self. But his attempts at denying the self turn out to be an insidious, subconscious affirmation of the self.

- Fish seeks to relativize the self, by locating it within an interpretive community. But Fish's communities are places where the sovereignty of the self is amplified.
- Postmodernity does not get beyond modernity's sovereignty of the self. The human self has not been dethroned, denied, deconstructed or relativized in any meaningful way. For this reason it is often termed 'late-modern' or 'high-modern'.
- As Bauman had seen, modernity is ultimately a place where the other is silenced, demonized and, if necessary, terminated.

Conclusion

The human readiness to engage with otherness has been a concern of philosophers throughout history. And yet, it seems, this desire to engage openly with that which is fundamentally different from us is hampered by a base human tribalism that no amount of social evolution or technological progress can overcome. In primitive human communities, survival depended upon close affinity with others *within* your community, but an active hostility to those *beyond* your community. This is not only true of territorial disputes between proto-human tribal groups. It takes little insight to argue that, in the modern era, an unacknowledged but deeply rooted tribalism is still learned in the playground, practised on the sports field, demonstrated in the boardroom, expressed in the ballot box, manipulated by politicians, taught by religious leaders and preached by the media. No human advance has ever suppressed this primal instinct.

This chapter has tried to show that, throughout history, humanity has struggled to engage well with otherness, especially in times of crisis. That an alternative ethical framework is desirable for the contemporary world hardly needs stating. The twenty-first century opened with a stark reminder that mutually opposing cultures are well within the swing of one another's fists. Ecologically, the results of one nation's actions have tragic consequences upon another's daily life. The same can be said of the economic disasters that currently engulf the globe. The ethical here cannot be separated from the scientific; that is, our relationships with others cannot be considered in isolation from our relation to the otherness of the world. Scientific advance continues to confront humanity with new questions: digital technology, ease of international travel, the expanse of knowledge not only into other universes but into other dimensions, all highlight the need to be able to engage with otherness. Open-mindedness has become the unspoken cardinal virtue, and though we live in an age of encounter, our default cultural philosophy remains one of withdrawal.

4.

The Otherness of Scripture

If the history of philosophy has failed to provide a sure-fire guarantee of engaging well with otherness, is there a possibility that the Bible itself may offer a means of doing so? For many, the very nature of Scripture speaks of the exact opposite: it closes down all thought, openness and critical engagement with otherness, because it provides unquestionable answers offered by none other than God himself. Hence it is often referred to as the 'Word of God'. Ironically, there could not be a less biblical name for the book, and not only because nowhere in Scripture are the texts of Scripture referred to as the Word of God. More significantly, a crucial characteristic of Jewish and Christian texts is the critique of claims to power, claims that become idolatrous the moment divine sanction is assumed for human decisions. This is certainly the function of the leader cults of the ancient world in which human leaders were seen to represent God himself, and where religions served to legitimize human power claims. This religious worldview is critiqued throughout the scriptural narratives, as the present chapter will show. However, by turning the Bible itself into the 'Word of God', it thereby becomes a tool in the hand of anyone wanting to justify their opinions by quoting chapter and verse at their opponents. Treating the Bible as the 'Word of God' in this way thus undermines one of the core features that make it a 'holy' book. It is the attempt to reverse the incarnation, squeezing the Word-made-flesh back into the Word and away from real life – a Christendom endeavour to spiritualize Christ out of politics and confine him within the covers of a book.

The present chapter offers an overview of key points in the biblical narrative, showing how Scripture as a whole offers a particular way of engaging the other. The voices of Scripture, which have often evaporated into the atmosphere of Christendom, nevertheless address concerns that Christian and atheist alike have rarely acknowledged. With the passing of Christendom, the authors of Scripture are no longer compelled to speak through an 'authorized' interpretation, and their voices may pull the rug from beneath the feet of the faithful and the faithless.

A Divine Resource

The Scriptures themselves are comprised of various types of histories and biographies, stories and accounts, various kinds of liturgies and prayers, of letters and propaganda, of theology and philosophy. Some are the product of communities, gently fashioned over the course of time; some read as the hurried scribbles of individuals in crisis. Some of its texts are written from the perspective of the victor, some of the loser. But all of these varied literary landscapes have been flattened by a double-impact literary missile: the establishment of chapters and verses.

If the whole Bible is 'God-breathed', it has been widely assumed that every single part of it must be infallible, which in turn means that no verse can be of greater weight than any other. This leads to the conviction that isolated verses – removed from the context that validates them – can be read as self-contained nuggets of eternal truth. Read this way, the Bible's historical context and literary genres are disregarded, the beauty of its poetry is marginalized, and the function of narratives ignored. The result is an arid, featureless and two-dimensional resource of timeless (and therefore, pointless) truth. In ascribing divine status to these documents themselves (rather than that to which their authors seek to draw attention), their true voice is almost silenced.

This is certainly a convenient view of Scripture for powerbrokers of the Christendom era. While hierarchical structures filtered biblical truth into the minds of the populace, all was well. When, however, Scripture became more widely available after the Reformation period, what was to prevent revolution? If the subversive nature of these documents was rediscovered by the masses, how could political stability be retained? For those who sought to revere these scriptures, then, chapters and verses flattened the texture of their documents into a smooth plane in which readers would see little more than their own reflection. The Bible became a source of proof-texting what the reader already knows to be true – providing divine endorsement for human worldviews and thereby inverting the very dynamic that made Scripture holy. It is little wonder that atheists throughout the modern era have ridiculed scriptures. Christendom had transformed them into a single, ridicule-worthy document. On such a reading, the command to 'love thy neighbour' is of equal status to the injunction to put unbelievers to death. But isn't any other way of reading Scripture 'selective', where the reader picks convenient texts and ignores those which are inconvenient? This would be true only so long as it is assumed that the text contains a static essence called a 'meaning'. The act of interpretation would then be understood as wresting the correct meaning from the text, which may subsequently be applied in the reader's life.

There are alternative ways of engaging with Scripture, however, which take seriously both its claim to divine revelation and its all-too-human origins and stories. Karl Barth, for instance, described Scripture as a 'strange new world' that genuine readers enter at their peril. The human authors of various scriptures each had witnessed different dimensions of divine identity, to which their writings point. Readers are thus invited to situate themselves as closely as possible to the author, in order that his or her 'authority' can be taken seriously. The reader, far from seeking to extract the correct meaning or learn valuable lessons, seeks instead to witness what the author witnessed. In this light, Scripture is not an end in itself. To treat it as such is to idolize it, ignoring its primary referent. Scripture points beyond itself, and invites readers, therefore, to see beyond themselves. This is the view of Scripture adopted below, looking specifically at how the different authors of Scripture deal with 'otherness'. If, in the last chapter, I argued that philosophers have struggled to offer an account for engaging well with otherness, particularly in times of crisis, it may be noted that it is the crises encountered by the Jewish people groups that precipitated a unique way of engaging with otherness. My post-Christendom readings of the Old Testament texts focus upon the fallout from three major pinnacles of crisis in ancient Jewish history.

Exodus

Hebrew (and Christian) identity is rooted in a Bronze Age pact between a nomadic farmer and his deity. This pact (referred to by Christians as the Old Testament) was that Abraham and Sarah – a childless, elderly couple – would have offspring who would grow into a nation with innumerable inhabitants. Abraham was chosen, not because of his righteousness, his piety or his morals (he scored very badly on each count), but because of his faith. In the context of the narratives, this type of faith has little to do with the psychotic performance of mental exercises necessary to draw comfort from a ludicrous fairy tale. It was, rather, his ability to live with short-term dissatisfaction, frustration and un-fulfilment, on the basis of the promise his God had made to him. The history of his descendants, who were subjected to experiences that would have destroyed not only the faith but the national identity of most people groups, bears out how this virtue was bequeathed to an entire nation. On the other hand, it shows in stark form how the Jewish nation constantly struggled to embody this impossible virtue in the face of one national crisis after another.

The first crisis was the exodus. Scripture narrates the formation of a people in the context of slavery at the hands of the Egyptian superpower sometime in the second millennium BC. Eventually, the Hebrew people crack under the growing excesses of their oppressors and attempt to flee the country. When they hit a dead end (the Red Sea) with the Egyptian military in hard pursuit, their leader Moses prays to his deity for a way out – in Greek, *ex* (out of) *hodos* (way, road, route). The waters move, the Hebrews escape. Once on the safety of dry land, the waters close behind them and engulf the Egyptian forces. Regardless of the historicity of this account, it functions in the narrative as a societal creation story. This is not the 'order out of chaos' narrative usually attributed to the creation accounts of Genesis. If anything, it denotes chaos out of order, the unjust order maintained by the slave driver's whip and the chaos that genuine freedom must bring. This exodus is a national baptism. That is, this is a nation whose identity is established explicitly in relation to chaotic, disturbing, liberating divine otherness – a point emphasized by the fact that this event is cited over 150 times in subsequent passages of Scripture. There is little, at this stage, to distinguish the Hebrews from other ancient tribal groups who believed themselves dependent upon a deity. However, as the story unfolds, this nomadic tribe receives a series of laws that begins to articulate something of their distinct identity – most notably, the Ten Commandments, or 'decalogue', which lie at the heart of the law, as Lloyd Pietersen points out: 'The text begins . . . with "I am the Lord your God" and ends with "your neighbour" (Ex. 20:2–17). Thus Jesus' statement that the two greatest commandments are to love God and to love neighbour (Matt. 22:34–40) reflects the structure of the Decalogue, which expands on what it means to love both God and neighbour.'[1]

At the heart of Judeo-Christian self-understanding is an injunction to engage well both with the otherness of the world as it is (i.e. that constructed by their distant, invisible deity) and with the down-to-earth otherness of other people. Underpinning the specific do's and don'ts of the Ten Commandments is the fundamental recognition that to be human is to engage with otherness both on horizontal and vertical axes. This is a vision of the human self that runs throughout Scripture, but is at odds with the modern view of the self which is built around the individual human subject.

This is spelt out by a further injunction, another essential component in the genesis of the Hebrew people: the command to welcome the stranger. In the Ancient Near East, comprised largely of nomadic societies, hospitality was a treasured virtue and by no means exclusive to the Hebrews. Had Abraham himself not shown hospitality to three strangers, their nation would never have come into existence.[2] Furthermore, so the logic ran, since the Hebrews had experienced as a nation what it meant to be strangers while they lived in slavery in Egypt, they – of all people – should show hospitality to strangers. By the time of the New Testament (most notably, the letter to the Hebrews), the injunction to welcome the stranger is not only practical but ontological – since by welcoming strangers one may unwittingly be welcoming 'angels' (quite literally, messengers), just as Abraham had. By welcoming the stranger, we discover who we are. The stranger represents not simply an opportunity to be kind, nor only a horizontal engagement with otherness, but simultaneously engages the vertical axis of otherness. However, once the Hebrew people had escaped Egypt and received their law, the ontological foundations of that law would often slip from their consciousness with disastrous effects. Within a generation of receiving the Ten Commandments on Mount Sinai, they would set out to commit genocide. These innumerable folk who had wondered through the desert now wanted a home of their own. Yahweh had promised them a land flowing with milk and honey, but this land was already the home of others. Whatever otherness the Canaanites represented was about to be destroyed, seemingly by divine command. The god who ordered the massacres of the Canaanites is, as Richard Dawkins complains, 'a vindictive, bloodthirsty ethnic cleanser; a misogynistic, homophobic, racist, infanticidal, genocidal, filicidal, pestilential, megalomaniacal, sadomasochistic, capriciously malevolent bully.'[3]

To modern ears, this is – beyond doubt – the god portrayed by the narrative. If Scripture is a two-dimensional source book of unmediated divine revelation, then no feat of interpretive acrobatics will excuse Christians from facing the fact that the true object of their worship here is Mars, the god of war. If, on the other hand, to interpret Scripture is to situate oneself as closely as possible to the author, then readers are drawn into the terrifying experience of unresolved horror, and then challenged to identify for themselves the character of the god who requires humans to commit such atrocities. Such texts are penned by human authors who have witnessed extraordinary events and tried to discern God's hand in them, and their authority can be recognized in precisely the act of rejecting their interpretation of the events they report.

This is by no means to be selective with which parts of the text are worth accepting and which are not. This is rather to recognize the picture of divine and human otherness that has developed through the narrative, precisely so as to be capable of identifying interpretations that are inconsistent with the narrative substructure. (As stated above, those preoccupied with chapters and verses and sloganized versions of divine interpretation fail to recognize the divinely inspired narrative substructures of Scripture.) To listen well to the text is to learn the discernment necessary to see when the human portrayals of the divine are questionable. The biblical conquest accounts, though consistent with similar accounts offered by other cultures in the Ancient Near East, contravene both the character of Yahweh and the spirit of the law he had given. Even biblical authors are prone to that all-too-natural tendency to seek divine legitimization for acts of human barbarity. This, however, is not to dismiss the text as divinely inspired. *To believe that every word of the text is inspired is not the same as believing that every word of the text is an expression of the divine will.*

Again, if the domain of the text is a two-dimensional flatland where every verse from documents written over the course of a thousand years is to be read in precisely the same way as every other verse, then one must accept Dawkins' view of God. Alternatively, if Christians believe in a God who can create a universe of astounding complexity, maybe his literary capacities extend beyond the ability to produce a two-dimensional celestial instruction manual. Maybe such a God would expect readers to use the full range of their God-given interpretive abilities in getting to grips with biblical texts. To the alert reader, the conquest accounts offer a shocking portrayal of how, within a generation of suffering oppression in Egypt, the descendants of Abraham became perpetrators of oppression and claimed divine backing for doing so. This would not be the last time the foreign policy of the chosen nation resulted in such natural and such destructive disregard for human otherness.

The Philistines

According to the Scriptures, once the Hebrews had settled into the land, they dwelt as separate tribes, sometimes battling with their neighbours and at times even with one another. Occasionally a larger threat would loom, and the tribes formed a temporary alliance under the leadership of a 'judge', but once the threat had passed the confederation would disband. Then came the Iron Age. This new historical era visited itself upon the people of Israel in the form of a strong, technologically superior and well-organized military aggressor: the Philistines. The tribal alliances were no longer sufficient to meet this new terror, and Israel responded with a radical social restructuring.

Here lies the origin of the Israelite monarchy. Believing that Yahweh alone was their king, many Israelites were clearly uncomfortable with the idea of monarchy. And yet, as the royal courts developed, the role of the royal prophet emerged. Prophecy was by no means a supernatural prediction of the future, but radical attunement to the divine will, enabling the prophet to offer to the king an 'other' perspective on his policies. The presence of a prophet at the royal court was a reminder to all that an Israelite king's authority was not absolute. The most celebrated king from the early period was David, who came to power during the Philistines' invasions.

The story of David and the Philistine champion is well known. The Philistines and the Israelites have agreed to settle their battle in single combat between two champions. Goliath, the 6 foot 9 inch warrior, has come forward from the Philistine camp, and the only Israelite with the courage to meet him is the young shepherd boy. When Goliath unsheathes his cutting-edge Iron-Age technology, David produces a crude but highly effective weapon, declaring, 'God saves not with sword or spear.' He then shoots his opponent, cuts off his head, and puts the Philistine army to flight. As such, he stands as an ideal monarch who presided over what later generations regarded as a golden age for Israel. David is the unlikely warrior-king who throughout his life remains radically and consciously dependent upon God.

The books reporting his career, however, are brutal in their honesty. David betrays one of his loyal guardsmen to death in order to sleep with the man's wife – at which point his career takes a downturn. The texts become deliberately critical of David's behaviour and link his treatment of other people with his relationship with Yahweh, integrating again the two axes of otherness. As the stories unfold, David's kingship becomes one of tragedy and loss. The most appalling episode of David's leadership is to be found with the writing of the third psalm:

A psalm of David. When he fled from his son Absalom.

Yahweh! Look how many enemies I have, how many people rise up against me, how many are saying (behind my back),'For him, there will be no victory from God.'
But you, Yahweh, are a shield around me, my glory, the One who lifts my head up high.

I will call out loud to Yahweh, and he will answer me from his holy
mountain.
I lay down and fell asleep; I woke up again, because Yahweh sustains
me.
I will not fear the multitudes who have amassed on every side.
Arise, Yahweh! Give me victory, my God!
Smash all my enemies on the jaw; shatter the teeth of the wicked.
Victory does come from Yahweh.
May your blessing be on your people.

The words are frequently used in Christian worship, but the context
in which the psalm is to be understood raises serious questions
concerning David's fitness as king. Absalom was David's second
son, whose sister was raped by David's firstborn son, Amnon. On
learning of this, Absalom is furious and goes straight to David.
David does nothing. Absalom then takes the law into his own
hands, and kills Amnon. The people, knowing his cause to be just,
side with Absalom against David. Civil war ensues and David is
forced to quit Jerusalem. This, we are told, is when David wrote
the psalm. It contains no sign of remorse, no hint of self-doubt,
and no recognition that he is in the mess of his own making; only
the assumption that God is on his side. However, this text emphasizes yet again the importance of genre recognition. That David
was aware of his own guilt is highly likely, given the way that the
narratives report his general character. In this instance, the text
serves as a biblical equivalent to the pre-battle speeches of Shake-
speare's Henry V. In other words, this reads as a prayer to rally
David's beleaguered royal guard – who are no doubt included
in David's royal 'me'. If the text is akin to a pre-battle speech,
then any self-berating guilt on the king's part would be entirely
egotistic and counter-productive. Here the text itself functions as
an invitation to identify with someone whose situation is hopeless, who is the victim of his own misdeeds, and yet clings desperately to his belief in divine favour, because that favour is based not
upon his conduct but upon the divine promise. Bearing in mind
the interpretive scheme offered above, to read this psalm well is to
enter into the world of David's guilty darkness. Psalm 3 may then
be read as David's plea for what – a thousand years later – would
become known as the gospel.

David's life as a whole is presented, in the historical books of
the Old Testament, as brutal and flawed; he is a leader abusing
his power with blood on his hands. When this figure stands as
the ideal, hero king for Israel, it says little for his successors. As
the story unfolds, his son Solomon consolidates the kingdom
that he had built, but after Solomon's death the kingdom splits
in half: Israel in the north and Judah in the south. The prophetic
writings of the Hebrew Bible show numerous attempts to call the
kings to account. This after all (rather than supernatural predic-
tions of the future) is the function of the prophet. But the prophets
in royal palaces often became royal puppets, and prophets from
outside the court went unheard. Their writings attribute the
misfortunes of Israel largely to the unfaithfulness and failure of
kings. In the end, the northern kingdom of Israel was destroyed
when the Assyrian war machine rumbled across the Middle East
in the eighth century BC, and the southern kingdom of Judah only
narrowly escaped with a last-minute act of national repentance.
Soon enough, it would face a monumental crisis of its own.

Exile

In the sixth century BC, a new hostile superpower (the Babylonians) arose, annexed the little kingdom of Judah and, after a
rebellion, took its leaders into captivity. A thousand miles from
their homeland, it looked to these dejected believers as though
their tribal deity had been defeated by the more powerful gods of
the new empire. Here, the technology was vastly superior to their
own, and the temples dwarfed the quaint structure built by their
ancestor Solomon back in Jerusalem. Yahweh, it seemed, had been
crushed, the entire worldview of the Jews revealed as a fairy tale,
and Yahweh himself brought no relief.

It was in this context that some of the most beautiful Hebrew
poetry began to circulate among the exiles. This is the creation
account reported in the opening chapter of Hebrew and Christian
scriptures. Far from being a defeated tribal deity, the god of the
Jews was the god who had created the entire universe. However,
this was not simply a poem offering otherworldly solace to people
undergoing a communal sense of dejection. It offered a stark

alternative to other creation accounts, not least those treasured in Babylon itself. The creation accounts of other nations and religious groups were fundamentally violent accounts. This is hardly surprising, given the violent nature of the world as it was known. Primitive human societies had to function on the basis of mutual support for those within their own tribe, since this was essential to survival. Equally crucial was communal animosity towards other tribes, whose very existence threatened the wellbeing of one's own. The creation accounts of other cultures confirm this view, and the novel dynamic of the Hebrew account is the radical alternative it offered. Lloyd Pietersen makes the point well when he notes that the Genesis account 'deliberately counters' the Babylonian:

> The primary text, *Enuma Elish*, portrays creation as an act of violence, so that violence is structured into creation. The gods are intrinsically violent; the cosmos is formed from the murder and dismembering of the goddess Tiamat and humans are formed from the blood of an assassinated god to serve as slaves to the gods. So, according to the prevailing creation account of the day, killing is in the very blood of humans. In stark contrast, the Genesis creation account poetically portrays the creation of the cosmos by the speech of God and the text subsequently denounces violence in the strongest terms.[4]

Far from being a primitive Iron Age fairy story for those who favoured myths about the creation of the universe because they had no access to science, this was a sophisticated propagandist document, subverting the empire's (and its victims') assumption that the way to deal with otherness is to attack it. It was also in this context that one of the most infamous and seemingly violent psalms was penned. Psalm 137 begins with words that set the scene for the exiles: 'By the rivers of Babylon, we sat and wept when we remembered Zion.' What follows spells out hatred for their captors, and lament at the loss not only of their freedom but of their worldview. The psalm then ends with a repulsive beatitude:

> Happy shall be the one who pays you [Babylon] back with what you dished out to us:

happy shall be the one who grabs *your* children and smashes them
against the rocks.

Needless to say, the latter section of this psalm rarely features in a
modern hymnbook. Remembering that the genre of this psalm is
worship, the psalm is a textual dwelling the worshipper is invited
to enter. Given the disturbing nature of the psalm, it is much
easier to pass judgement from outside on its supposed meaning.
But those who do enter properly into this text are destined to feel
something of the agony of unaccomplished revenge: an immoral
but thoroughly natural human longing, especially taking into
account the historical context. Whoever wrote this, it seems, had
witnessed their own children smashed against the rocks. (This
practice was common in ancient warfare, since invaders wish to
minimize the risk of future as well as present rebellion.) Failure
to pause here and enter into the psalmist's agonized memory is
failure to read the text. The closing beatitude does not read as an
incitement to hatred, but a response to it. That is, an unresolved
and tragic submission to the bitter reality that seems so at odds
with the promise that God had once made to Abraham. The subtext
of this psalm speaks of a seemingly genetic ability for Abraham's
descendants to suspend final judgement, engaging with their god
from amid the worst forms of human agony. The modern desire
to secure a 'meaning' from the text runs into confusion with such
open-ended, unresolved frustration when it is expressed this way.
   This frustration is shared by the 'Weeping Prophet'. Jeremiah
had warned of the disaster that was set to engulf Judah, not
because of a supernatural ability to predict the future but because
of a human readiness to listen to the past. When the Babylonians
were still on the political horizon, Jeremiah issued a reminder to
his fellow Jews to engage not only with the vertical axis of divine
otherness (and assume divine protection because of divine promises), but to attend to the horizontal axis of otherness, caring for
the most vulnerable members of society:

> Hear the word of Yahweh, all you people of Judah, entering these gates
> to worship Yahweh. Here is what Yahweh, Commander of Armies, the
> God of Israel said: amend your ways and your actions and let me live
> with you in this place. Do not put your trust in these deceptive words:

'This is the temple of Yahweh, the temple of Yahweh, the temple of Yahweh.'

Now, if you seriously amend your ways and your actions, if you seriously deal justly – one with another – you will not oppress the alien, the orphan, or the widow, nor will you shed innocent blood in this place, and if you do not harm yourself by going after other gods, then I will stay with you in this place . . .

Jeremiah again makes the explicit link between human justice and divine righteousness, drawing together vertical and horizontal axes of otherness. His words, however, were not welcomed and Jeremiah was imprisoned in Jerusalem, only to be released when the Babylonians overran the city. But this was no happy ending for the prophet. After his release, he discovered that many of those taken into exile refused to accept their plight, and that false prophets were spreading rumours of an imminent return. In his celebrated letter to the exiles, Jeremiah exhorts his people to accept the divine judgement, and to pray for the welfare of their enemy's city, because from it they will draw their own welfare. Only seventy years later did a new power rise to eclipse the Babylonians. When the Persian Empire came to power, their policy of winning hearts and minds led to the release of the exiles who – according to the text – were positively encouraged to 'return' to Jerusalem and rebuild the temple. Around the year 538 BC, the exiles emerged from Babylon (in modern-day Iraq), degraded, humiliated, divided, disoriented and anxious, but alive.

On their return, the temple was indeed rebuilt under the leadership of Ezra and Nehemiah, and something of the Jewish national identity was restored. But the experience of exile had entered the Jewish psyche, colouring their collective memory with a humility that shaped their understanding of their place in the world. Unfortunately, humanity being what it is, the propensity for extinguishing otherness reasserted itself remarkably quickly. Perhaps the primary text by which this story is told is the parable of Jonah, a late 'post-exilic' text concerning events from several centuries earlier.

Jonah is a prophet, sent by God to warn the people of the pagan city Nineveh to repent. Jonah refuses his divine calling, and attempts to flee. Then comes the legend of the three days he spends inside a fish, where he is forced to repent and accept his prophetic calling. The prayer he makes from inside the fish is a prayer of exile, speaking of his despair and longing to return to the temple. Once he has learned his lesson, the fish vomits Jonah onto dry land and he obeys the divine command. So far so good: Jonah, as a representative of Israel, has returned from exile and is restored to fulfil his calling. However, when he goes to Nineveh and unburdens himself at the city's inhabitants, instead of jeering and stoning Jonah, they listen to him and repent. Jonah is furious at such a response, and complains that Yahweh has shown mercy to a pagan city. The story ends with Yahweh breaking the news that not only the people, but even the animals of this pagan city are precious to him. In short, any form of nationalism that is likely to hamper Israel's engagement with human otherness is severely critiqued by this late prophetic text.

Religious nationalism, after all, remained an issue for the Jewish people long after the exile. The Persian Empire was displaced by the Greek, and the Greek by the Seleucid kings, against whom the Jews staged a successful rebellion under Judas Maccabeus in 110 BC. For almost half a century the Jewish nation enjoyed relative independence, but in 63 BC the great Roman general Pompey marched into the land which Yahweh had promised to Abraham and his descendants. The Roman Empire was unlike anything that had come before, and its presence in Judea precipitated a series of bloody rebellions, mounting towards the growing national catastrophe that had almost reached breaking point by the time the earliest documents of the New Testament were penned.

The Gospels

At about 14 years of age, a peasant girl from the obscure town of Nazareth believes that God has spoken to her through an angel. She bursts into a spontaneous anthem of political revolution, expressing the hope that her son would be known as a wise leader who would govern well and establish peace:

My being amplifies Yahweh, and my spirit is thrilled by God, my liberator.

Because he has paid close attention to the troubled plight of his servant.

Look: From now on, every generation will be happy for me, because the mighty one has done great things for me – even though his name is holy.

His mercy reaches out to people who respect him, from one generation to another.

He has performed mighty feats with his arm:
He has scattered the high and mighty in their inmost thoughts.
He has dethroned the powers that be; but has lifted up downtrodden people.

He has satisfied those who hunger with good things; but has dismissed empty-handed those who have become wealthy.

He has helped his servant Israel, remembering to be merciful to Abraham (and his descendants) forever, which is just what he promised to our ancestors.

The poem, known as the *Magnificat*, voices well the hope of Israel, hinting towards the regime change which – it was widely assumed – must take place if Israel is to be free. If Yahweh is going to bless his people who are suffering at the hands of an occupying power (Rome), then surely – so the logic runs – it must mean that Yahweh will use force (mighty feats with his arm) to bring liberation. It means that Yahweh's anointed leader (his Messiah) will defeat both the Roman prefect (Pilate) and Rome's appointed puppet-kings (Herod and his dynasty), i.e. 'the powers that be'. This liberator will put an end to the hunger of his people, and stop the nation's resources being syphoned off to Rome ('he has sent the rich away empty'). Surely, if Yahweh is going to 'help his servant, Israel', a people who are living under brutal oppression, then this is the only way to make it happen. Unfortunately, even after his resurrection, Jesus had not dethroned any rulers; downtrodden people were still being crushed; the rich were not sent away empty and there were multitudes of hungry people.

The *Magnificat* closes, nevertheless, with the expectation that Yahweh is going to keep the ancient promise he made to Abraham. His offspring were to outnumber grains of sand and the stars in the sky, and the whole world would be improved by these descendants. But the Roman Empire was here to stay, and

Abraham's offspring were a downtrodden, powerless and voice-less nation. Even so, the Jewish people still believed that Yahweh would keep his promise. The problem, spelt out by the Magnif-icat and echoing through the stories about Jesus' life, was not that people believed God would keep this promise, but that – for the many who did – they were also sure about *how* God was going to keep that promise: the Messiah would take up the sword against the pagan oppressors.

Such were the seditious hopes of a people who had read and heard, time and again in their holy writings, that kings come to thrones by force of arms. Their scriptures pulsated with stories of heroes employing violent strategies to bring about the purpose of God. The major strand of Jesus' teaching is invested in offering an alternative way of being Israel, which was unexpectedly in tune with their divine calling to engage well with the other. While this is a logic that pervades the entire career of Jesus as reported in the gospels, here I focus simply upon two key parables.

The parables of Jesus are not general wise sayings that leave otherwise clueless people with timeless truths to help them cope with the rigours of life. The parables are revolutionary political bombshells. They don't simply illustrate what Jesus is trying to say, but they make it happen. Always, the parables are a retelling of Israel's history, and a call to a new covenant, a covenant with Yahweh in which love for the other displaces rejection of the other. The most obvious (and tragically misread) example is the so-called 'Parable of the Rich Man and Lazarus'. Lazarus is a Greek version of the earlier Hebrew name, Eliezer. In the parable, Eliezer is a poor man, lying outside the gatehouse of a wealthy man. When both men die, everyone knows that the wealth of the wealthy man guarantees his status as a descendant of Abraham, whereas Eliezer's poverty is proof that he has no share in the covenant blessings of Abraham. So, when Eliezer is transported to Abraham's embrace, and the wealthy man finds himself in Hades (the pagan hell) something is severely wrong. The wealthy man begs for Abraham to warn his five brothers, but is told that if his brothers cannot hear the Scriptures, neither will they listen to someone who returns to them from the dead.

From the time of Yahweh's first covenant with Abraham, Eliezer has been present. Those who first heard this parable would be very familiar with the story. When Abraham was a childless old man, he lamented that his entire inheritance would not pass to a child of his own, but instead would go to his servant, Eliezer of Damascus. God replies to Abraham with the opening words of the covenant: 'This man [Eliezer] will not be your heir.' It is hardly surprising, then, that in the parable Eliezer is pictured outside the great wealth of Abraham's true descendant, the wealthy man. Nor is it surprising that the wealthy man treats Eliezer as though he were a servant, Abraham's servant. By picturing Eliezer in Abraham's embrace, Jesus is making a specific point: that the ultimate 'other', i.e. the original, ancient covenant-outsider, is not excluded from Yahweh's covenant blessing.

What does it mean to be a child of Abraham, beyond sharing his DNA? Plenty of Jewish people would answer with something along the lines of how faithfully their lives reflect the Torah, the law which Moses gave to the people. This was summarized into a famous saying, which Jews call the *Shema*: 'Listen, Israel: Yahweh your god is one god. Love Yahweh your god with every bit of your heart, your strength, your soul and your mind.' Another was added to this: 'Love your neighbour as you would like to be loved.'

When questioned by a Jewish legal expert, Jesus affirms the convention, but when the lawyer pushes him to define 'neighbour,' Jesus responds with one of his best-known parables. In Jesus' day, there was no such thing as a good Samaritan. Several centuries earlier, when the people of Israel had been dragged into exile, the Babylonians also shipped foreign captives into the area known then as Samaria. This meant not only that Samaritan blood had mixed with foreign blood. It also meant that the punishment for sins that God had dished out to Israel (in the form of exile) had not been dished out to the Samaritans. They were not part of the story of Yahweh's own people.

The parable itself is well known: en route to Jericho, a traveller is mugged and left half-dead in a roadside ditch. A priest and a Levite pass him by without helping, no doubt to keep themselves pure according to the detailed laws of Moses. As the legal expert would have known, they could not risk impurity by touching a dead body. However, a disgusting Samaritan, the representative of an impure nation, takes pity on the mugging victim, and goes out of his way to take care of him. But, by the logic of the *Shema*, the legalist is forced to admit that this hated foreigner is more of a Jew than the priest and the Levite, figures epitomizing the very pinnacle of essential Jewishness. Their true Jewishness is eclipsed by the worst kind of anti-Jew. The parable is not a general moralizing call to care for people in distress – endorsing the benevolent but harmless 'big society' morality so conducive to Christendom. It is set up to answer the legal question, 'Who is my neighbour?' It is assumed, of course, that neighbours are other descendants of Abraham, people just like 'me', with Abrahamic blood pumping through their veins and the Jewish law thumping in their hearts.

By redefining 'neighbour' to include Samaritans from beyond the borders of acceptability, and excluding the very worthiest examples of Jewish Jews, Jesus is making radical claims about Jewishness. It is not your DNA, nor even your faithfulness to the letter of the law, but your actions towards the 'other' that makes you a descendant of Abraham. If legal observance makes a good Jew, then some untouchable semi-Jewish foreigners are proving themselves worthier than even the best of the best within Israel. By turning Samaritans into neighbours, Jesus redefines what it means to be Israel. This echoes what Jesus has been telling his supporters all along: 'If you only love the people who love you, what does that gain you?' To be Israel, in accordance with the *Shema*, will mean acting well towards the other. Ultimately, behaving differently towards a Samaritan requires a radical shift of worldview. Not a simple ethical transfer from being selfish to being ready to help others and 'hug a hoodie'. Instead, adopting a worldview in which people who once were thought to be repulsive become potential agents of Yahweh's justice in the world.

These parables express a strand that runs through the gospels. Mary, along with countless others in Israel, longed for a Messiah who called upon divine otherness to conquer human otherness: God's anointed Warrior King who would defeat God's pagan enemies. In so doing, the Jews believed justice would be done in the world, Roman oppression would cease, and the nations would be free to praise the God of Israel. The parables, like the rest of the Messiah's ministry, offered a radical alternative. Not an Israel rebuilt on military foundations, but reconstituted on the basis of radical exposure to divine and human otherness. This is the way of life that – according to Jesus – was most truly human, most truly life-affirming, and yet most radically subversive. Not by the power of the sword, but by self-giving love, would justice be established.

To those who believed that one must first seize power if one is subsequently to establish justice, Jesus said, 'Take up the execution stake to which you will be nailed, and come with me.' To those who thought military force could bring about divine justice, he said, 'If your enemy forces you to carry his pack for one mile, go with him two.' To those who revelled in the privilege of their tribal genetics, their Abrahamic bloodline, their ancestral heritage, he said, 'You must hate your father and mother.' His entire ministry had sought, in word and action, to be faithful to the Jewish heritage of engaging well with divine and human otherness.

The Jewish people were covenanted to offer the world a particular way of being human and as such were called to be a light to the nations. Unfortunately, their human nature all too often dragged this calling into the mire where countless descendants of Abraham simply wallowed in their ethnic privileges. In so doing, they would lose the very capacities of engaging otherness on which their covenant identity was grounded. Again and again Jesus offered stark, political alternatives. When faced with racism, he blessed foreigners. When faced with religious supremacy, he praised pagans. When faced with nationalism, he welcomed collaborators. He frequently confronted the popular custodians of the religious, social and political authority for dislocating the people from their true heritage. He insulted Pharisees for making Yahweh inaccessible, rebuked scribes for making Scripture inaccessible, and condemned the Sadducees for making the temple inaccessible. It was finally his prediction that violent resistance against Rome would lead to the destruction of their precious temple that would seal his own fate. The temple was the intersection of divine and human otherness, the crossing point of these two axes, a 'house of prayer for [the benefit of] all nations'. Jesus denounced it as serving precisely the opposite function, a hotbed of nationalist fundamentalism. It was a costly move.

The result was betrayal, arrest, condemnation and execution. Such, it seemed, was the end awaiting anyone naive enough to believe the world could be changed by relinquishing rather than exerting power; that justice could come by radical listening to others; that engaging well with the other would lead to anything but defeat. Those followers who had found this Messiah convincing were forced to accept that his call to engage with otherness was helpless against the dispassionate and insuperable realities of imperial, religious, judicious power. Cold, imperial justice had the final word. Humanity was forever enslaved by the primitive urge to conquer the otherness of other humans, a brutal enterprise sanctioned by the divine otherness of whichever god happened to be in power. With the crucifixion of Israel's Messiah, Yahweh is overpowered, the kingdom of god defeated, and the world of humans devoid of hope, of justice and of otherness. For those who had followed this messiah, darkness had engulfed not only Israel, but the plight of humanity.

Resurrection

In this light, claims that the Messiah had returned from the dead are not to be read as a mere miracle. Taken as a whole, the New Testament documents do not present the resurrection simply as an event within history, so much as the event that makes sense of history. This is not because the resurrection offers some kind of proof that God can do the impossible. (If this had been the case, the prescient resurrected Jesus could have solved two thousand years of scepticism by marching into the Antonia Fortress and saying, 'Nice try, Pilate!') Far from offering any kind of proof of the supernatural, the resurrection is the vindication of Jesus' way of being human. It suggests an ontological substructure for human existence, an endorsement of the way of being human that Jesus envisioned and embodied.

The way this vision is fleshed out in practice is the subject of other New Testament documents, most notable of which are the letters attributed to Saint Paul. If Jesus had proclaimed that the Jewish community were called to display the faith of their ancestor Abraham, Paul took this same call still further out into the non-Abrahamic world. Here, in light of the resurrection, he reinterprets how the ancient promise to Abraham is to be fulfilled. He claims that Abraham's descendants are identified no longer by their bloodline or their religious heritage, but by their faith – specifically their faith in the person of Jesus of Nazareth. (This is the true meaning of what Christians often call 'salvation by faith'.) The rapid expansion of believers across the Gentile world of the first century is seen as the beginning fulfilment of the ancient promise: innumerable Abrahamic descendants. However, the growing multitudes of believers also posed a threat to the Roman Empire.

As shown in chapter 1, the 'Son of God' was the emperor's title, the 'gospel' was a celebration of the emperor, so when these words are taken to apply to a failed resistance leader, it is hardly surprising that Roman suspicion should be aroused. The book of Acts reports both the growth of this new Abrahamic movement and the opposition it evoked both from conservative Jews and wary Romans. In fact, the book ends with Paul awaiting trial in Rome and the unresolved question of whether he is guilty of inciting rebellion. To exhort patriotic Roman citizens and conservative Jewish subjects to engage with otherness is to run the risk of undermining political and religious systems of control that have become totalitarian. However, it is not only conservative Jews who rejected the Christian message on religious grounds. By the final book of the Bible – Revelation – the Christian community at Laodicea has lost the core of its faith dynamic: Jesus is pictured standing outside, excluded from the church that claims to be worshipping him. Christian religion, according to the New Testament documents, has no privilege over Jewish or philosophical systems when it comes to engaging well with the otherness upon which its existence is founded.

Conclusion

The challenge to root our identity in that which is outside ourselves is a prominent strand of the biblical narrative from Genesis to Revelation. Throughout Scripture, we see a portrayal of the human self, confined within its own limits, its own boundaries, its own securities. This is not simply an individual trait, since there is such a thing as a communal self, a community spirit, a national identity. Support for those within one's group and revulsion at those who do not belong (love your friends, hate your enemies) is an evolutionary survival mechanism, a primal, instinctive impulse known as tribalism. Whether individually or corporately, Scripture regards this trait as both inescapable and as 'sin', which, as one theologian said, is 'man turned in on himself'.[5]

Whatever history has done to the concept of sin, and however it has been used as a means of controlling the masses, its root lies in a simple, inescapable, primal reality: the tendency to withdraw from engaging with otherness as Adam and Eve withdrew from one another (behind fig leaves) and from God (who had to go searching for them). It is the spirit of radical self-sufficiency, the self-preservation that manifests itself in rejection of otherness. And yet, through the varied writings of Scripture, God is holy (other) precisely because he identifies himself with the stranger, with the outcast, with the marginalized and rejected. The Christ of the Gospels calls his followers to do likewise.

Translated into contemporary culture, this form of radical encounter has settled into the treasured virtue known as 'open-mindedness'. As such, it can become a glib and shallow quality we might expect to gain with a bit of moral effort in order to become a more rounded individual, a charming trait we might learn to manifest in polite conversation. Of course, it is easy – and conventional – for secular modernists to regard themselves as open-minded in general and in theory, but rare and highly unconventional to change one's mind in the course of (or as a result of) an actual conversation with a real person.

In neither the traditions of Scripture nor of western philosophy is the capacity for open-mindedness taken so lightly. The ancient Greeks had understood well the traumatic nature of altering your view once your mind had already been made up. Knowing that to abandon a hard-won 'mindset' was a gargantuan feat, they describe such action using a compound of the word for 'after' (*meta*) and 'mind/knowledge' (from *nous*). This near-miraculous capacity to move beyond a deeply treasured and highly valued 'mindset' was called *metanoia*. Although the word appears frequently in the Greek New Testament, strained through the translation filters of Christendom it has devolved into a religious transaction designed to remove personal moral guilt: repentance. Properly understood, *metanoia* is neither just a rite of spiritual purification, nor a demonstration of open-mindedness, but a radical reorientation of the affections, the mind and the will. To abandon the convictions that have shaped our understanding and experience of the world entails a rupture in the human psyche, disruptive, disturbing and literally catastrophic. Such is the cost of genuine thought. As Montaigne famously declared, 'To philosophize is to learn how to die.'[6] This experience of death is where the Christian story begins.

Interlude

RESURRECTION

To be modern is to celebrate the sovereignty of the Self. So far, I have argued that atheism inevitably asserts itself as the default belief-system of modernity, a natural expression of its cultural egocentricity. Unfortunately, the spirit of modernity also manifests itself in a radical rejection of that which is genuinely other. The aggressive rejection of God is a necessary consequence of this almost militant rejection of otherness. Even so, modernity is not to be lamented as an exclusively destructive force. The present argument is simply that the modern mindset, though 'tuned in' to an infinity of wonder to which humanity might otherwise have remained oblivious, can *for that very reason* blind humanity to other sources of infinite wonder and hope. Resurrection, as the beating heart of Christian practical and political hope, is destined to remain incomprehensible to those captivated by the spirit of modernity.

The model of thought in which a thinking *subject* observes, examines and patiently reflects upon the nature of another *object* is very much a modern innovation. Apart from the helpful clarity of thought this distinction offers, it can sometimes have the effect of alienating us from the otherness of the objects we consider, be they people, events, texts or inanimate things. The position from which I (the subject) observe facts (the objects) is a point of cool, unpolluted detachment. I am a spectator. These things are fundamentally external to me, separate from me, and I can understand them perfectly well from my current, isolated viewing platform, 'outside' the things I observe. For some branches of scientific observation, this is perfectly sufficient. It is problematic, however, when grappling with questions like resurrection that involve my own personal being.

To restrict consideration of the resurrection to its historicity, its scientific possibility, its ethical or political implications, its social effects, even its personal transformative impact, is destined to remain a mechanical, two-dimensional exercise, conducted at a safe distance from the event reported in New Testament documents. Such considerations, though necessary, are not sufficiently attuned to the nature of the event. Resurrection is always, invariably and irreducibly resurrection-as-it-impacts-me. If it is true, resurrection is self-involving because it entails at least some form of personal experience of death in all its horror, and something happening within the experience of death. Throughout history, philosophers have issued the challenge to take death seriously, because doing so can deepen appreciation and understanding of existence. To consider resurrection, however, not only requires that we consider our own death. It is a doctrine most fully comprehended by those who already inhabit the experience of this-worldly manifestations of death.

Resurrection is an event in the darkest, bleakest and loneliest moment of human desolation: in the abysmal, stateless, agonizing silence – there, without consolation, without meaning, without love, there and precisely there, in the place of absolute loss, where anything and everything is cruelly engulfed by the darkest, coldest nothing. An emptiness unsympathetic and infinite, where there is nothing but nothing, reveals itself as the origin and the end, the alpha and the omega, of human existence. Millions throughout history have no doubt experienced something of this sheer absence, and though they have tasted it this side of the grave, the only language available, should they attempt to describe it, is language associated with death. Resurrection is not an antidote to such comfortless experiences, nor does it offer any short cut around them, nor even a happy ending to them. Resurrection, if it is to have any genuine force in relation to death, is something beginning inside death. Those who believe well in resurrection believe that, precisely in the midst of such inconsolable, impersonal and all-encompassing nothingness, there is something. Resurrection is the emergence of 'something' out of the dark, abysmal 'nothing'.

The modernist reaction to such claims is to extract this 'something' away from its context, and abstract it away from the experience of death. This 'something' may then be defined, categorized and analysed, until eventually an objective and rational assessment can be made from a safe distance. The explosive, disruptive charge that makes this unquenchable 'something' what it is, is thereby ignored. Resurrection thus evades modern attempts to classify it.

Alternative approaches to engaging with the Scriptures reporting the resurrection are available: to 'enter into' a text, to en-counter its impact in one's inner being, rather than observing it safely from outside. To hear the voice of a text is not simply to try to extract the correct meaning out of it, but to enter fully enough into the author's world to see what that author is pointing towards. To view resurrection from the perspective of the Scriptures is to enter a region undergoing an earthquake. The closer one comes to the authors, the nearer one comes to the epicentre. This earthquake destroys the myth of a detached, dispassionate observer. This is – at root – what makes Scripture 'holy': it is a place where the reader is exposed to radical otherness. Here is the distinct possibility that the reader's entire worldview will come crashing down.

However, to believe in the resurrection cannot be to live in a perpetual state of existential crisis. Nor can Christian believers presume that, having once experienced the traumatic destruction of their worldview, they are destined to remain in a permanent state of wounded openness. (The histories of Israel and of the church show this clearly enough.) Rather, the resurrection-shaped life is one in which believers do not 'get over' the dark experiences of nothingness, so much as 'get used to' them. In so doing, the character is formed and re-formed in relation to otherness. Some contemporary writers have claimed that the harrowing exposure to nothingness, though it leaves its wound, does not leave the believer in a state of despair.

At the personal level, for instance, the philosopher Gillian Rose (1947–95) paints a chilling picture of human hope in her reflections on death in *Love's Work: A Reckoning with Life*, a rigorous autobiographical engagement with death in light of her advanced state of ovarian cancer. 'Keep your mind in hell and despair not' is the book's epigraph, highlighting how love is found in facing head-on and holding the gaze of the horror that often surfaces in the course of life. The result is a readiness to become fully human by a profound but hard-won openness to that which is truly other: 'To grow in love-ability is to accept the boundaries of oneself and others, while remaining vulnerable, woundable, around the boundaries. Acknowledgement of conditionality is the only unconditionality of human love.'[1] This belief gave personal expression to Rose's philosophical research, in particular her controversial reinterpretation of Hegel. As argued in chapter 3 above, Hegelian 'dialectic' (thesis, antithesis, synthesis) has been extremely influential – especially when applied to history. Traditionally, Hegel is criticized for seeking to conquer otherness, bringing otherness into my world of comfortable familiarity by means of 'synthesis'. Rose, however, offers a different reading of Hegel. It is precisely the event of synthesis – the point of conflict between my world and that of otherness – that constitutes life in the midst of a broken world. The most natural reaction when faced with the threat of otherness is to retreat into a secure environment: hurrying towards the consolation of a satisfactory but premature synthesis, hiding from the disturbance of otherness, avoiding the pain of being broken and remade. On the other hand, 'love's work', for Rose, is to battle with the pain and suffering interwoven throughout lived experience. This, it seems, is precisely what Hegel meant with his call to 'tarry with the negative'.[2]

The Marxist literary critic Terry Eagleton offers a political interpretation of resurrection along precisely the same lines. The sinful, fallen world described by the New Testament is often grossly caricatured as the individual's spiritual status in heavenly eyes. Eagleton puts flesh onto the notion of fallenness as 'the lamentable state of humanity'. That is, 'the prevalence of greed, idolatry, pollution, the depth of our instinct to dominate and possess, the dull persistence of injustice and exploitation, the chronic anxiety which leads us to hate and maim, the sickness, suffering and despair which Jesus seems to associate with evil.'[3]

The human experience of nothingness often arises from our capacity to inflict horrors upon one another: the unacknowledged greed in which wealth is venerated and increasing power is conferred upon those who are already excessively wealthy; the necessity to keep the economic machine running smoothly by exploiting poverty-stricken workers, enforcing migrations, tolerating preventable child mortality; the political short-termism that keeps world leaders so obsessed with the next election that the major long-term issues set to engulf humanity in ecological terror can never be truly addressed; the militant nationalism and worship of Mars that transform the horrors of violence, war and military aggression into virtues; the cult of celebrity, in which hero status is achieved not by discipline, moral exertion or genuine self-sacrifice, but by luck-of-the-draw; the corporate erosion of education systems, the dehumanizing mechanics of the divorce industry, the reverse-Darwinism of an advertising environment in which humans devolve into consumers; the list could go on, but must climax with the corporate, political and media propaganda that shelters privileged westerners from seeing all this as the true state of the world, along with the cowardice, apathy and indifference that feed our contentment with these delusions. The insurmountable power of these faceless and soulless forces that grind the humanity out of the human condition are precisely the forces the church once meant when it spoke of original sin. These are what Saint Paul referred to as the 'spiritual forces of evil in the heavenly realms'. This is not to deny their spiritual reality (or their capacity to reach into the human spirit) but to draw attention to the sheer weight of the forces that shape human fate but cannot be overthrown by human force.

Regardless of how Christian believers may wish to justify seeking power in order to fight for a better world, the point of Christianity is precisely that such power games are incapable of winning justice. This is why, as Eagleton states:

> The only authentic image of this violently loving God is a tortured and executed political criminal, who dies in an act of solidarity with that the Bible calls the *anawim*, meaning the destitute and dispossessed. Crucifixion was reserved by the Romans for political offences alone. The *anawim*, in Pauline phrase, are the shit of the earth – the scum and refuse of society who constitute the cornerstone of the new form of human life known as the kingdom of God. Jesus himself is consistently presented as their representative. His death and descent into a hell is a voyage of madness, terror, absurdity, and self-dispossession, since only a revolution that cuts that deep can answer to our human condition.[4]

There is no vitriolic celebration here, as though Christians armed with fairy-tale beliefs about resurrection need no longer worry about death. Here is the unnerving reminder that the Christ who said, 'Follow me', was on his way to the cross. Christian belief is not the suicidal abandonment of the preciousness of life, but the knowledge that the insurmountable 'powers that be' will only be truly countered with self-sacrifice. The image of the church as the 'body of Christ' is worth reconsidering in this light: the body of Christ is the tortured, mutilated corpse epitomizing failure and shame. If this, according to Saint Paul, is the body in which Christ lives by his Spirit, then the church's experience of resurrection is to be found by following this Christ into the abyss. For Eagleton, Jesus' descent into hell was a descent into precisely this absurdity:

> Only by preserving a steadfast fidelity to failure . . . can any human power prove fertile and durable. It is by virtue of this impossible, stonily disenchanted realism, staring the Medusa's head of the monstrous, traumatic, obscene Real of human crucifixion full in the face, that some kind of resurrection may be possible. Only by accepting this as the very last word, seeing everything else as so much sentimentalist garbage, ideological illusion, fake utopia, false consolation, ludicrously upbeat idealism – only then might it prove not to be quite the last word after all.
>
> The New Testament is a brutal destroyer of human illusions. If you follow Jesus and don't end up dead, it appears you have some explaining to do.[5]

In both Eagleton and Rose, then, we see the determination to take death (in its personal and political manifestations) with utmost seriousness. In this light, Christianity is not primarily an attempt to make a better world. In the first instance, it is the readiness to engage with otherness in its most disturbing manifestations, and to engage with it in the most personally open manner. At root, belief in resurrection is radical openness to radical otherness. This brings us all the way back to the nature of faith that underlies the covenants of Scripture. Not faith in some divinity who promises happiness because he can perform miracles and offer life after death. In the case of Abraham, as we saw in the previous chapter, faith was the ability to endure the hardships, the difficulties and the tragedies of the present on the basis of the divine promise. It is little surprise that the original covenant forming the basis of Old and New Testaments comes to Abraham as he undergoes a 'deep and terrifying darkness'. Faith is the ability to 'tarry with the negative', to live with the intolerable.

All of this is to say that Christian faith has little to do with intellectual assent to the existence of a divine being. At its basis is the formation of communities of people struggling in the midst of fear, injustice and pain, seeking liberation not by use of physical force against the powers pressing in upon them, but rather, through the blood, sweat and tears of radical openness towards the other. This hard-won radical openness is called 'faith', and the otherness discovered is a source of loving transformation. In sum, Christians believe that resurrection is discovered most fully by those whose situation is most frightful. As Eagleton points out, 'The trouble with the Dawkinses of this world . . . is that they do not find themselves in a frightful situation at all . . . beyond the fact that there are a lot of semideranged people called believers all around the place.'[6]

In this respect the New Atheists and their followers come remarkably close to the position of the Sadducees of the first century. The Sadducees did not believe in resurrection, as is well known, but their non-belief had little to do with intellectual capacities or liberal sensitivities. The Sadducees were drawn from the wealthy and privileged elite of Judean society and benefited from the Roman imperial regime from which so many others suffered. They knew well enough that the Jewish beliefs in resurrection entailed the breaking up of the current order, and the establishment of a new order according to the revolutionary expectations of a feral underclass. Their refusal to believe in resurrection arose naturally from a desire to conserve their own privilege against any form of otherness that threatened it.

- Resurrection is always resurrection-as-it-affects-me.
- Modern attempts to 'understand' resurrection usually consider it only from a safe distance, a position of detachment.
- Resurrection begins in the experience of the nothingness of death. To enter into this nothingness is a disturbing experience.
- Gillian Rose showed how her own struggle to face the otherness of death as it really is, was to 'tarry with the negative'.

- Terry Eagleton implies that the injustices of the world constitute a form of death, and shows that radical Christianity faces the otherness of the world as it really is.
- Exposure to the monstrous nothingness of death is a necessary part of believing in resurrection.

The resurrection is only properly considered when the world is seen for what it is: when we face the horrors of injustice that modern history has learned to disguise; the stark reality of death as the ultimate hindrance to progress. The practice of openness to others and to the world is not simply another set of moral commands, a hermeneutic strategy for reading Scripture, or a set of ideal values to apply. Being open is not something that an individual can one day decide to start doing. To engage with otherness is not an ability that can be turned on and off at will. The capacity to engage well with otherness is, from the Christian perspective, a mere symptom. It is the manifestation of those who genuinely believe in the resurrection of Christ: of those who face the reality, the mortality, the fallibility and vulnerability of their own existence in the fullest sense; of those who see the injustices, the degradations, the dehumanizing political realities of the world as they really are; of those who – despite the horrific state of the world – cling to the belief that hope is every bit as real and is to be lived out in the form of radical, self-giving love as personified in Jesus of Nazareth.

Christian belief in resurrection is, of course, rooted in the historical resurrection of Jesus. This is not merely an event that could have happened to anyone, since Jesus is portrayed as the pre-existent *logos*, the reason why the universe behaves as it does, present from the beginning, an agent of creation, the source and the enlightenment of human life. So begins the Gospel of John, whose introduction climaxes with the claim that this pre-existent *logos* became a human being, the *Word became flesh*. So when this embodied universal *logos* takes human flesh, does he take charge of his people as would be expected, i.e. like a cosmic emperor? The Christian story is that Jesus was a peasant who showed that leadership need not be authoritarian, that power need not be coercive, that greatness need not be success. Instead he shows a counter-intuitive way of life, marked by brutal fragility, unmitigated political love in the face of constant frustration and ultimately

disastrous failure, but a way of life in which something monumental takes place on the far side of failure. Theologians have
sometimes referred to the day of resurrection as the eighth day of
creation, where a specific moment in time and space has an impact
upon every time and space. What kind of impact?

Resurrection Power

The nature of resurrection described above does not suggest itself as
a source of power useful for those seeking to run a successful empire.
Hardly surprising, then, that throughout the Christendom era, resurrection has been more popularly conceived simply as proof that an
omnipotent God can do the impossible, that he can forgive sins, and
that he can offer life after death. The personal trauma and the political revolution that belief in resurrection entails have rarely featured
in the Christian story told by the oppressive powers of Christendom.
Post-Christendom believers are not so much concerned with the
actual *abuses* of power that the church has committed throughout
history, but with seeking to resist the *trust in* the kind of power that
is open to abuse in the first place. The power dynamic arising from
belief in resurrection is drastically incompatible with models of
Christianity that seek to harness secular forms of power for the sake
of goodness. The Christian drive to establish justice by first gaining
political, cultural or social power is a dubious exercise because it
abandons all belief in resurrection. It rejects the perilous, life-threat-
ening, failure-prone lifestyle of Jesus of Nazareth through which God
– finally – reveals his true power at work. If God cannot be trusted
to save the world from a position of utter powerlessness, so the logic
runs, then we must give him a helping hand by first manoeuvring
ourselves into positions of power from which we can then seek his
blessing on our well-meaning action. Christendom is the name of any
version of Christianity that has no stomach for genuine resurrection.

Beyond Theism

In order to get to grips with what resurrection says about how
a divinity may exert alternative forms of power in the created

order, an alternative framework of imagination is required. For the most part, Christian and atheist alike assume that a god who is active and present in the universe must, of necessity, be the god of *theism*, i.e. the counterpart of the god of *deism*, both of whom were invented in the seventeenth century. Deism is the product of a world in which authority was being slowly withdrawn from the Pope in Rome to the princes of individual nations. This was the era of the 'religious war' at the end of which God had to be promoted to a realm where he could cause no more bloodshed on earth. The result was deism – with a God who wound the world up and left it to tick, a divinity with the good sense not to meddle in the world of politics and social order.

Theism was a Christian reaction to deism, defending the existence of a god who micro-manages the universe, who answers prayers, who communes with believers and is active in the life of the world and the church. Always and everywhere, however, the god of theism was rooted in the Christendom picture of an omnipotent, omnipresent, omni-benevolent, praise-hungry cosmic emperor. This was also a god filtered through the new view of the universe unveiled by the Scientific Revolution. The Newtonian worldview determined the character of this God: the laws of nature were absolute – and the theist god was compelled either to obey or to suspend them. This was a god whose action in the world could sometimes be viewed as 'interfering', flouting the very laws by which he expected all his creatures to live. Divine involvement in the created order, then, was 'supernatural' whenever it was inexplicable.

Being supernatural, his divine providence was a matter of invisibly and miraculously controlling every minute action and reaction across the universe – which of course leaves him responsible for every evil as well as every good. However, he was exonerated from committing the evils that beset humanity on all sides, by providing his worshippers with the trump card: 'God moves in a mysterious way, his wonders to perform.'[7] Though this phrase offers an important insight, many distort its logic along these lines: if we question why an all-powerful and all-loving God seems to act in ways that are inconsistent with any sane notion of good behaviour, it is only because our minds are too limited to understand. We must simply tolerate injustice, disaster and downright evil, because – although God causes all these things – his ways are 'mysterious' to our pathetically finite minds. Theism is thus a life-support system for the Christendom god whose hideous character is beyond reproach, enabling him to survive artificially throughout the modern era. Little wonder that atheists of every brand would like to see the machine switched off.

This is certainly not a conventional portrayal of theism. Most view theism simply as the belief that God is active in the world. More precisely, however, theism is a belief about God's relationship to the world. As such, theism is welded to a particular set of beliefs about what the world is – and it is those beliefs that are problematic. Theism is the name for belief in a god who created and is intimately involved in a world from which otherness is systematically excluded. As shown in chapter 3, the world of modernity is a world constructed around the ego of the free-thinking individual. Any god at home in such a world is clearly an object of human imagination – a god created in humanity's own image. Is such a god active in the world? Then he is able to act only in ways that humanity is able to imagine. Is this a powerful god? Then his power is simply human power multiplied into infinitely greater proportions, i.e. power limited to the confines of omnipotence.[8] Is this a god who speaks? Then what can we hope to hear but the echo of our own voice? The god of theism is a modern god for a modern world, best laid to rest in the graveyard of modernity.

If, in a postmodern, post-Christendom era, we feel compelled to use the word 'theism' to describe belief in an active god, it must be a theism drastically redefined. Otherwise, we run into the inescapable problems so effectively highlighted by modern atheisms: is God all-powerful, all-loving, and active in the world? If so, then this god not only allows but causes suffering and is a grotesque, malevolent supernatural demon masquerading as a benevolent do-gooder. There are alternatives.

An 'Ontological' Dimension

If – in accordance with the Newtonian worldview – the universe we inhabit is a three-dimensional entity, those things we cannot explain must automatically be supernatural. However, the contemporary physicists proposing 'string theory' currently subscribe to the belief that our universe has eleven dimensions. Actions in one dimension spill over to affect those in another. In which case, those who wish to believe in a Creator God might similarly imagine that he could create multiple dimensions through which he makes his presence felt. These would be dimensions that span every corner of time and space, a thoroughly natural, pre-planned, fundamental, ever-present strand of a complex created order. If we are to believe in a God of providence, a God who is active in the world and has universal, overriding power and authority, it is perfectly conceivable that he expresses his *universal* being through a *particular* channel of influence. That is, through a particular dimension. Such a dimension of the universe could, I propose, be described with a term borrowed from philosophers.

Ontology is the study (*logos*) of being (*ontos*) which underlies all existence. It asks the question of why anything at all simply 'is'. If the universe is a given, some branches of human enquiry explore *how* it came to exist, whereas ontology is concerned with the prior fact *that* it exists in the first place. What does it mean that there *is* anything at all? What is 'is'? Even if nothing exists, it still exists! Such concerns are so fundamental, so basic, so foundational to who we are that they are often seen as an irrelevance or abstraction. Ontology, then, highlights the relevance of the most obvious, deeply rooted, but ill-considered dimension of the universe: that it 'is'.

If there is an ontological dimension woven through the fabric of the universe, to be a human *being* in the fullest sense is to access this dimension. I am by no means suggesting that God's own being is exhausted by this dimension, or that this dimension is identified with God himself. Rather, I claim that such a dimension *may* exist, and will write below as though it *does* exist. If it does, then by entering this dimension at divine invitation, this God may be actively encountered. This, in fact, is close to the dynamic of Sabbath celebration in Hebrew scriptures: that to celebrate Sabbath is, in the first instance, to stop (*shavat*, in Hebrew). As one psalmist put it, '*Stop* faffing, and know that I am God.' In the struggle for existence, in the hyperactive carrot-and-stick busyness of living and surviving, to celebrate Sabbath is to stop and to be reoriented within the purposes of God. Rabbi Abraham Heschel described Sabbath as 'a palace in time',[9] into which we may dare to enter and face the depths of our own humanity. Ontology principally addresses not what we do or think or strive towards, but *who we become* in the process of doing and thinking and striving.

The way I use the term 'ontology' assumes the picture of human *being* I have advanced in chapter 3: that to be human is to be engaged most openly with that which is genuinely 'other'. To enter the ontological dimension is to enter a 'palace in time', a temple in which we stop to become attuned to sheer otherness. To abide with the intolerable otherness of other people, of the world we know, and of the universe beyond our knowing. I claim that whatever and whoever we encounter in this dimension may have the capacity to affect other dimensions of our life and world. This encounter is the true context for what Christians describe as worship.

Conclusion

If the resurrection offers a means of exerting force in the world, it need not be the coercive power generally associated with the politics of the Christendom order. A Creator God may leave the universe to run itself, though remaining present and active to it through an ontological dimension. Events that appear miraculous may simply have their natural cause in this ontological dimension. This dimension, though in a sense 'hidden' beyond the scope of modern (though not necessarily future) physics, is at the same time universally accessible to human beings. However, as I claimed in the first part of this interlude, resurrection power cannot be seized to serve some other end, because to believe in resurrection is a profoundly disruptive, traumatic, life-altering endeavour.

If to believe in the resurrection is to enter an ontological dimension, it is an activity beset with paradox. To engage with the otherness encountered in such a dimension is at once both attractive and repulsive, the most natural thing in the world and the most counter-intuitive, the most sensible and the most senseless, strange and yet familiar, captivating and yet liberating, terrifying and yet comforting. Christians believe that resurrection is rooted in a historical event that was hidden from the public eye and that took place on the Sabbath in the 'middle of time'.[10] All valid Christian belief revolves around this event located like a black hole at the centre of history.

5.

Science and Miracles

Christian theology is based upon engaging openly with that which is genuinely 'other'. In theory at least, this places theology and science in close harmony with one another, pursuing radical openness to radical otherness. However, since the collapse of Christendom and the Scientific Revolution of the seventeenth century, theology has been widely perceived as the drag queen of the sciences: making claims about truth and fact but trading in superstition and myth; accepting the supernatural while masquerading as a serious academic discipline. Scientists, on the other hand, are often assumed to have a monopoly on openness, and to build their own claims about the truth of the universe upon secure foundations. These scientific claims are usually thought to be at odds with the claims of theology. As such, until the late twentieth century, the relationship between religion and science was often portrayed as one of conflict. Naturally, a key theatre in this mythical war has been the question of miracles. This chapter will argue that, while scientists are compelled to accept the possibility of miracles, Bible-believing Christians are compelled to reject all belief in anything supernatural.

Sunset over the Scientific Empire

Creedal atheists subscribe universally to a dated but largely unquestioned historical narrative of the relationship between science and religion. The story runs something like this: in the dark mists of our unenlightened history, humans knew little about the world and so took refuge in mystery and myths. The dominant myth in the history of the West is, of course, Christianity. The leaders of Christendom, so the story goes, opposed the advance of science – and with good reason. The more science expanded its territory, the more God himself was forced into retreat. The church of Christendom, seeing the threat and desperate to defend the divine fairy tale against the rational onslaught, reacted violently. Science must be opposed. The great scientific traditions of ancient Greece and Rome were silenced by the church with its insistence upon blind faith and unthinking dogma. Only with Copernicus (1473–1543) did true science rear its head again, re-ignited as a force that would march forwards through time, evicting God from the public sphere to take up residence in ever-shrinking 'gaps' beyond either the reach or interest of science.

After the Scientific Revolution of the seventeenth century, during which Isaac Newton uncovered universal laws governing the behaviour and movement of all material, the prevailing picture of divine involvement in the universe was radically altered. This was no longer a hyperactive, plate-spinning divinity that interfered on a daily basis to keep the universe running like clockwork. Divine causality could now be viewed as a one-off act when a prime mover ignited a big bang (deism), rather than a god who answered prayers, performed miracles and flouted the laws of nature (theism.)

By the nineteenth century, the wonder of science was increasingly celebrated in the popular mindset. Its principal weapon in its expansive endeavour was something called 'scientific method', or more precisely, 'inductive method'. That is, the careful observation of an object, by a detached, dispassionate, free-thinking subject (the scientist), and from that observation, moving to a general understanding of how the world works. That such a view became and remained dominant for so long is hardly surprising. It worked. Fires burned, liquid heated, engines rumbled, aeroplanes flew. The technological progress of the Victorian era was undeniable, bringing assured results in the world of sanitation, medicine, agriculture, transport, housing. The list could go on, as the progress offered by science was so widely seen, felt and celebrated.

After three centuries in which the scientific empire enlarged its territory by accumulating knowledge, wresting truth out of the unknown, God himself had aged considerably and was forced to accept his weakened status. Having once been a powerful, malevolent dictator, he was now shuffled out of the world of public life, away into a celestial retirement home where he can still be visited by kind-hearted or curious souls. From here, any claims he makes are heard as the toothless, meaningless and pointless ramblings of a being who has lost all connection with reality.

Such is the story of the relationship between science and religion, a narrative to which modern atheism continues to cling. *It is, of course, mythological – in the sense that it tells a story for theological purposes but is devoid of historical authenticity.* Its credibility in the world of contemporary peer-reviewed historical scholarship is identical to that of a seven-day creation or a literal worldwide flood. It is a persistent myth, nevertheless, passionately defended by those who believe that science and religion are mutually incompatible. The myth is based upon a particular (but discredited) philosophy of science, termed 'scientific imperialism'. This view describes not only the belief that science is an ever-expanding empire of factual knowledge, but also the conviction that this factual knowledge applies to every important dimension of life. Anything that does not fall within the realm of science cannot, with any certainty, be described as 'true' or 'false'.

Unwitting Philosophies of Science

While few would assume that being a motorist thereby also qualifies you as a mechanic, nor that being a miner qualifies you as a geologist, many assume that professional scientists are automatically authorities on the philosophies underpinning what science is and how science works. Practitioners who apply and extend the techniques and insights of scientific research on a daily basis are by no means guaranteed to reflect on the nature of what they are doing. For instance, Peter Atkins, a respected Oxford chemist, ranks the validity of every academic discipline against the supremacy of his own, dismissing philosophy as 'a complete waste of time'.[1] Unfortunately, Atkins is delightfully unaware of the philosophical claims that validate his own popular and widely published arguments on science and religion. Even the brilliant Cambridge physicist Stephen Hawking pronounces philosophy dead before launching into a book that unwittingly relies upon and endorses a dated and dubious philosophical framework.[2] Practitioners of science are not necessarily the best qualified to see what science actually is, especially when it is assumed that all the important mysteries of the universe can (eventually) be accessed exclusively via the particular discipline in which they happen to be expert. As the old saying goes, 'To a man with a hammer everything looks like a nail.' The imperial spirit continues to manifest itself in the scientific community, even in the enlightened quadrangles of our senior universities.

Scientific imperialism is based largely upon the accumulation of evidence, technically known as 'empiricism'. The word itself is rooted in the concept of 'empire', that is, a domain – in this instance, of knowledge – that seeks to expand, enlarging its boundaries by conquering new territories. For those subscribing to the 'conflict myth', that new scientific territory is captured from none other than God himself and the accumulation of evidence is how empiricists fight the good fight. However, the empiricist can make no claim without hard evidence. While we may legitimately claim that we have no evidence for the existence of God, to conclude (in accordance with modern atheism) that there is, therefore, no God is profoundly anti-empiricist. After all, the principle that *the absence of evidence is not the evidence of absence* remains a stain on the lab coat of empiricists wishing to deny the existence of God. Philosopher Julian Baggini, for example, invites us to sidestep the logic of the very empiricism he claims to treasure:

> Consider the simple question of whether there is any butter in my fridge. If we don't open the door and have a look inside, there will be an absence of evidence for the butter being there, but this would not add up to evidence of its absence. If we look inside the fridge, thoroughly examine it, and don't find any butter, then we have an absence of evidence which really does add up to evidence of absence.[3]

Even in his own illustration, Baggini misses the simple point that the absence of butter is *not* the absence of evidence. The absence of butter *is* positive evidence, namely evidence that the butter is not there! But Baggini does not stop to notice his blunder, and merrily steamrolls across all rationality in the belief that his access to the great mysteries of the universe is as unlimited as his access to his own fridge. And all this, to make the philosopher's 'case for atheism'. Empiricism is, of course, a crucial dimension of scientific progress, but those who use it to deny the existence of God display a fundamentally closed-minded engagement with otherness.

Counter-Imperial Movements within Science

Scientific imperialism, as again the title suggests, is a form of empire – an expansive, aggressive means of accumulating power either by explicit or covert means of conquest. As with any empire, the Scientific Empire proved a mixed blessing. The success of the sciences had warranted great optimism and hope, and brought tremendous potential benefit to humanity. However, in the twentieth century, scientific progress also turned relatively anonymous parts of the world into the Somme, Auschwitz and Hiroshima. Not only did these events place an enormous question mark over the kind of progress science represented for humanity, but other moves were also at work to inject humility into the heart of Scientific Imperialism.

Alternative Philosophies of Science

Contemporary philosophers and many practitioners of science, in theory at least, encourage a more open attitude to otherness. As early as the nineteenth century, belief in the objective, detached and dispassionate scientific observer of evidence was recognized as profoundly naive. Firstly, scientific research is rarely conducted for its own sake. Research requires funding, and those who provide the funds require certain outcomes from the projects they finance. This is true not only of companies with their own research and development teams. At universities and research institutes, scientists invest significant energies in submitting applications for funding, usually requiring extensive detail about the projected findings of their work, showing how it will benefit the wellbeing of society. Science is bound by economic, ideological and political practicalities, which quietly shape the directions it takes.

Secondly, there is the principle championed by the neuroscientist Stuart Firestein. His provocative book, *Ignorance: How It Drives Science*, begins with the citation of an old proverb: 'It is very difficult to find a black cat in a dark room . . . Especially when there is no cat.'⁴ He continues:

> When most people think of science, I suspect they imagine the nearly 500-year-long systematic pursuit of knowledge that, over 14 or so generations, has uncovered more information about the universe and everything in it than all that was known in the first 5,000 years of recorded human history. They imagine a brotherhood tied together by its golden rule, the *Scientific Method*, an immutable set of precepts for devising experiments that churn out the cold, hard facts. And these solid facts form the edifice of science, an unbroken record of advances and insights embodied in our modern views and unprecedented standard of living.⁵

Firestein dismisses this belief as a media myth and a high-school caricature. Instead, he says, 'it's black cats in dark rooms',⁶ arguing that groping and grasping in the dark is precisely what makes science interesting and exhilarating. Real scientists are less interested in facts, he claims, than in mysteries, in hunting, searching, exploring.

In light of all this, Scientific Imperialism has been largely displaced by a more contemporary scientific philosophy which accepts that our observations are perspectival, cautious and loaded with our own interpretive assumptions. Further, it could be argued, science is simply one among many necessary and complementary ways of looking at the world. Science is, literally, a word for knowledge. Given that we experience the world in a variety of ways, that we accumulate, assess and absorb knowledge in a variety of ways, science is simply one means of understanding who we are. There are other equally important and no less valid means of experiencing the world. The parent–child relationship, for instance, proceeds, deepens and flourishes by means of a sophisticated exchange of knowledge. It is no less scientific than astrophysics. It is simply a different form of knowledge. The parent and the physicist are both doing science; the question is whether they are doing it well or badly. Clearly, to do science well requires a more radically open engagement with otherness than scientific imperialism allows.

Big Bangs and Black Holes

It is not only philosophers of science who have highlighted the unscientific nature of the imperialist. Those scientists now labouring to 'know the mind of God' by exploring atoms and galaxies have not so much solved mysteries as exposed humanity to a gaping expanse of mystery, beauty and sheer uncertainty that leaves the scientific imperialist floundering in a previous epoch.

Since Newton, sets of laws governing the behaviour of matter have proven useful in developing technological advancement in the everyday world. However, physicists now study the behaviour of the tiniest atoms that make up our everyday world. Quantum physicists look still further, at the 'subatomic' particles that make up the atom (the protons, neutrons and electrons). They then study the movement of the even tinier 'quarks' that combine to form those protons and neutrons (both of which are called 'hadrons', from the Greek word for sturdy/solid/thick). However, the energy that holds the quarks together as a hadron makes it virtually impossible to break the hadron into its component parts. The only way to achieve this is by manufacturing immensely high- energy, high-speed collisions. By using a 'hadron collider',[7] physicists crash particles into one another with such force that they are broken into individual quarks, whose movements may then be traced. The results are the business of quantum mechanics, which undermines any belief that the laws of nature with which we are familiar are, in fact, universal. The quantum world, it seems, behaves very differently from the everyday world.

This is not to say that there are not manifestations of the subatomic world within the everyday world. The mushroom cloud of a nuclear explosion is evidence enough: whereas it was once thought that there were such things as 'inanimate' objects, physicists revealed that anything with mass therefore has energy. In fact, in order for solid matter to exist, an enormous amount of energy is required to keep its component parts bonded together at the sub-microscopic level. In other words, even the most concrete object we observe bristles with high-energy particles moving around at immeasurably high speeds. Every object we see, touch or hold is alive with movement, undetectably pulsating with its own raw energy. Such is the wonder of the everyday world that modern physics has revealed. To 'split the atom', then, is to break particles down in order to release their energy into a form of power that is usable. However, the links between quantum theory and everyday life are still barely understood and have opened up vast fields of undiscovered, unexplored possibilities along with unanswered and perhaps unanswerable questions.

For 250 years, scientists were content with Newton's theories, and, though offering only partial explanations, they were widely held to be the only laws governing the behaviour of the universe. Then in the twentieth century, Einstein's theory of general relativity built upon, and in some ways, displaced Newton's theory of gravity, but again, served as a universal theory by which all movement in the universe could be understood. With the advent of quantum theory, however, an alternative set of laws emerged. Since both theories are, in a sense, universal, the challenge taken up by many contemporary scientists is to reconcile the two into a 'Unified Theory of Everything' (UTE).

The existence of the black hole highlights the issue. A black hole, thought to be triggered by the implosion of a star, generates such enormous gravitational pull that nothing, not even light, can escape it. Which theory should be used to understand black holes? General relativity, dealing with objects of enormous mass, should be the prime candidate, since the imploding star retains its massive weight despite its astonishing reduction in size. However, since that star has reduced to the size of a particle, it comes under the domain of quantum physics. Unfortunately, general relativity (a theory that works extremely well for stars and galaxies) and quantum physics (a theory that works extremely well for tiny particles) are not compatible. The quest for the Unified Theory of Everything is the attempt to reconcile these two incompatible theories.

Of the several different routes towards reconciliation, best known are the various forms of superstring (or more commonly, 'string') theory which then feed into M-theory (M standing for the membrane of which strings form a part). String theorists propose that, if we were able to observe the tiniest particles of the universe, we would discover that they are comprised of one-dimensional energy strands – strings. These strings vibrate, producing the equivalent of a musical note, which determines the type of particle they form. Since, it is claimed, everything in the universe from the tiniest particles to the largest stars is comprised ultimately of this same one-dimensional strand of energy, the theory is indeed a theory of everything. However, the nature of this 'everything' is drastically counter-intuitive. Three dimensions (plus time) are no longer adequate to account for the universe as we know it. M-theory requires an additional eight dimensions, all of them running throughout the great expanse of our universe but curled up so tightly as to be unobservable. This has led many scientists (including theoretical physicist Stephen Hawking and the cosmologist Martin Rees) to explore the possibility that we do not live in a universe at all, but in a 'multiverse' – where an infinite number of other universes run in parallel to our own.

Where once such speculation might have been regarded as the groundless imaginings of philosophers, theologians and novelists, the existence of multiple universes is a hypothesis based upon mathematical modelling and cosmological observation. However, its only drawback is that it is – and might well be destined to remain – an untestable hypothesis. It is speculation only, and as such is viewed by many as philosophy rather than science. While M-theory is notoriously tentative and, as mentioned above, only one of several paths striving towards a Unified Theory of Everything, we may nevertheless draw one firm conclusion: Newtonian certainty concerning the laws that govern the behaviour of the universe has now been comprehensively undermined by radical uncertainty.

How does quantum physics, then, relate to scientific imperialism? In the first instance, as already noted, the belief in universal laws of nature is radically undermined. At the subatomic level, everything – including time, space, movement and communication – behaves in ways that are fundamentally at odds with the traditional Newtonian physics upon which Scientific Imperialism is founded. Secondly, this means that laws have long been regarded as absolute are in fact only relative. Even the understanding we thought we had amassed, and will continue to amass, is destined to be partial at best. Thirdly, this destabilizes the knowledge and scientific belief we once thought secure. We are increasingly aware not only about how wondrously little we know, but how tentatively we know it.

Summary

Scientific imperialism, then, has long since been defunct in the world of science and scientific philosophy. Its method for dealing with otherness is no different from that of any other empire in history: otherness is there to be conquered. That mystery yields itself to research is to be celebrated, but when I assume that the otherness of the material world can be explained solely (or at least predominantly) according to my particular scientific expertise, when I belittle other sciences and disciplines in the process, and when – as a result – I conceive of the whole breadth and infinite complexity of human existence solely on my own terms, the crude imperial power dynamic is at work. Otherness must yield to my desire. This is scientific imperialism, and its pulse beats live and strong in the hearts of creedal atheists, including those generating (and consuming) the floods of best-selling atheist literature. As a prominent champion of scientific imperialism, the late Christopher Hitchens declared that he and his fellow non-believers have no belief structure, and 'distrust anything that contradicts science or outrages reason'.[8] For Hitchens, 'science' and 'reason' are simply ideological castles from which he dare not venture out, demonstrating his favour for a philosophy of science as closed as Julian Baggini's fridge. As Terry Eagleton has pointed out, it would be plausible to claim that 'science contradicts itself all the time, and that this is known as scientific progress.'[9]

In sum:

- The supposed clash between science and religion is technically known as the 'conflict myth', and though this myth no longer has any currency in scholarly circles, it remains an article of faith for countless modern atheists.
- The conflict myth rests upon a philosophy known as 'scientific imperialism': the belief that 'science' is an ever-expanding field of knowledge that has forced the god of Christendom into a permanent state of retreat.

- Scientific imperialism itself, however, is a dated and discredited philosophy that has been superseded by more open ways of engaging with otherness.
- New breakthroughs in cosmology and quantum physics invoke humility in order to proceed and evoke humility as they uncover ever greater and more puzzling mysteries concerning the universe.
- The modernist attempt to invalidate Christianity by using the insights of something called 'science' has now become a futile endeavour.

The frequently heard claim, 'As a scientist, I could never believe in miracles', is thus more accurately phrased, 'As a scientist, I cannot believe my present understanding of nature ever needs revising.' Which in turn means, 'I am not a real scientist.' This by no means provides creedal Christians with licence to adopt undisciplined beliefs. Since science is simply a way of knowing, Christians in post-Christendom seek to engage as openly as possible with the texts they hold as authoritative. In taking Scripture seriously, they will discover that belief in the supernatural is at odds with core Christian convictions, as I will now show.

Monotheism vs Supernaturalism

Although later chapters of this study will show that belief in miracles is treasured as much by contemporary sceptics as by the most creedal Christians, it is widely assumed that to be religious is to believe in God on the basis of miracles.[10] And yet Scripture itself contains no miracles and nothing remotely supernatural. This, in the first instance, is because both Jews and Christians are monotheists. You cannot *both* be a monotheist *and* believe in miracles. Jewish monotheism is not simply the mathematical doctrine that there is only one God. It is rather that, *since* there is one God, and since this one God is also the Creator God, he does not arrive late in the day, into a cosmos with a pre-existent set of laws which he must either obey or – if he wills to interfere with human affairs – suspend. Monotheism entails the conviction that the causal laws of the universe – those governing personal relationships or foreign policy, or the death of a loved one, or the thunderclap from above – are learned by experiencing the world which God made.

The distinction between the natural world (which we experience on a daily, matter-of-fact basis) and the supernatural world (where divinities from other planes of existence live) is in itself a dichotomy derived from Greek polytheism, not Hebrew Scripture. The boundary between the world we know, and the reality of a God in heaven, is not a frontier between the natural and the supernatural, but between the created world and its Creator. The supernatural God is one who may intervene in the world, flouting the laws of nature at will, favouring or punishing those individuals lucky or unlucky enough to warrant his attention. In sharp contrast, the God of Scripture works creatively, and the human (and scientific) response from the Jews was to construct a worldview around what they had experienced *within* the natural world, in the belief that Yahweh was Lord *of* the natural world. There was no aspect of life that did not come under the authority of this one God. This is monotheism. Like Baggini, the Hebrew people would not have sought anything outside their experience of naturalism.

How, then, could they believe in miracles? The language of the gospels contains no reference to 'miracles' (derived from a Latin word), describing the actions of Jesus as astonishing, as 'powerful action' (*dynamis*) or as signs (*semeia*). These were not performed as demonstrations that he could suspend the laws of nature at will, nor were they interpreted as such. For those who witnessed what we have come to call 'miracles', it was their empirical experience (with all its fallible interpretive apparatus) that required a change in their understanding of both the natural and the social order. This, after all, was the point of the miracles as they appear in the gospels. They were, in short, enacted parables – designed to subvert the social order.

The Politics of Miracles

Given that the social order of the day (including its brutalities and injustices) was almost indistinguishable from the natural, eternal, divine ordering of human life, society and universe, to subvert that order would require a so-called 'mighty act' or 'sign'. For instance, those who were crippled by poverty were often considered divinely cursed, whereas those who were wealthy were widely considered blessed. Those marginalized by religious and political hierarchies felt, and were made to feel, like outsiders. One's social position was bound up with the divine will and the unchangeable reality of the natural, created order of things. The parables, miracles and exorcisms performed by Jesus were ideological explosive devices, shattering these dehumanizing myths and offering an alternative worldview based upon universal human dignity. The belief that Jesus performed miracles simply to convince gullible peasants to believe his fairy tales is as ridiculous as it is widespread. These events were designed to subvert his hearers' view of their plight, their world and their God. They were revolutionary acts, dislodging the certainties of the natural order with explosive political consequences.

If we postpone the question of whether these miracles are scientifically viable, and first ask how – if they did occur – they would fit into the structures of Christendom, the objections concerning their viability appear in a different light. Christendom, as we have seen, is what the Roman Empire became when it learned to recite Christian creeds. As shown in chapter 1, the Jesus endorsed by the empire was no longer a political revolutionary, and the kingdom of God was no longer a beleaguered cry for regime change. If Christendom was going to run smoothly, it could only do so by maintaining a strict hierarchy and social order. Such an empire has no room for the kind of revolutionaries who gave birth to the Christian faith. Throughout the Christendom era, nevertheless, groups like the Waldensians, the Lollards and the Anabaptists sought to rekindle the radical beliefs of which they read in biblical documents. Not surprisingly, when their beliefs brought their lives into conflict with the authorities, they found themselves facing persecution, sometimes even execution. The hierarchies of this Christian empire needed citizens to remain peaceful, content with their lot, convinced that the status quo was divinely ordained.

In Christian artwork, for instance, the Messiah and his revolutionary band of peasant followers were gradually transformed into their exact opposite. Jesus was no longer the friend of sinners, but the emperor of Rome. Peter was no longer a fisherman, but a bishop. The disciples were no longer depicted as peasants, but as Roman senators. As the empire became more Christian, Christianity became more imperial, and Christian beliefs served to endorse the authority of Rome. The most convenient faith for an empire is, as chapter 3 showed, an otherworldly faith: a set of beliefs passionately held, but politically harmless, socially sterile, incapable of threatening the smooth running of the imperial machine. The preaching, the miracles, and the subversive behaviour of Jesus which the gospel records show, are thus absent from every creed recited throughout the realms of Christendom. This is not to say that the miracles are to be disbelieved. The creeds themselves require assent to the resurrection and the virgin birth. However, selective as the articles of the Apostles' and Nicene creeds may be, of more significance is the nature of belief they engender.

In scriptural language, to believe something is to act upon the strength of it – to embody in one's life the conviction to which you subscribe. The political, social, ethical lifestyle of Christians was simply the manifestation of their convictions – demonstrated *by life* – the origin of the English word *belief*. In Christendom, in order to keep Christians from disrupting the social order, a new manner of believing was required. Where previously one's convictions and one's life harmonized to become belief, Christendom severed the harmony. Convictions became otherworldly, imaginary, mental assent to ideas that had no impact on real life. The articles of the creed were non-material, spiritual doctrine – whose application in real life was determined by those authorized with spiritual and political authority. You could recite the Creed your whole life, you could believe in the truth of resurrection and virgin birth, and not worry about the social, down-to-earth practicalities of those doctrines. Belief had become an otherworldly affair.

This brand of belief, developed to serve the Christendom hierarchies, is the very same model taken up by modern atheists. Relating this back to the question of miracles, the atheist can be humble enough to grant the remote possibility of the miraculous components of Christian belief. However, since those miraculous components of belief have no bearing on the real world, the atheist is perfectly justified in trivializing those beliefs, comparing them to belief in fairies (Richard Dawkins), cosmic teapots (Bertrand Russell) or 'truly everlasting gobstoppers' (Julian Baggini).

However, I have argued that the so-called miracles of Jesus are not otherworldly affairs, but events that brought genuine hope for the most marginalized members of ancient societies, because they disrupted the seemingly immutable laws of nature and society. This was the kind of harmony between spiritual conviction and socio-political life that inspired the Donatists, the Waldensians, the Lollards and the Anabaptists. If we reject the Christendom pattern of belief as a sterile acceptance of otherworldly doctrines, and view belief instead in the more biblical sense of embodying one's convictions with practical political consequences in the real world, then we are compelled to ask modern atheists a basic question: who, in the history of the world, has ever claimed to believe in (to live on the strength of) fairies, cosmic teapots or everlasting gobstoppers? The authorized beliefs of Christendom are no more likely than the tooth fairy to inspire a student to defy a column of tanks in Tiananmen Square, a black woman to refuse to relinquish her seat to a white passenger on a segregated bus, a young Indian leader to defy an oppressive empire by peaceful means. Russell, Baggini and Dawkins have succeeded in highlighting the remote possibility but pointless beliefs of Christendom.[11]

In sum, the power brokers of Christendom thus transformed the nature of belief in miracles. In Christendom, miracles are genetically modified to relieve them of their explosive, subversive, revolutionary impact. All that is left is a supernatural act taken as a demonstration of the authority of Jesus, and therefore of the priesthood that represents him. On the other hand, those who genuinely believe in miracles may well find themselves defying natural and social laws that were once thought absolute.

Is it possible to defy Newton's laws? Rejecting the possibility of miracles on the basis of some supposedly superior worldview offered by 'science' is itself a product of the Christendom heritage. In chapter 3 we saw how, through the influence of Aquinas, the pronouncements of Aristotle gained infallible status within Christendom. It is from Aristotle that we have learned there are five senses, a doctrine that prevailed for centuries and that still holds sway over those who reject the possibility of miracles. But was Aristotle right?[12] Science has traditionally restricted itself to contemplating only five, but a genuinely post-Christendom (post-Aristotelian) scientific mindset recognizes that human beings have a limited range of measurable perception. For sure, the microscope, the telescope and the particle accelerator have extended that range into a realm that previous generations may well have regarded as miraculous. As a result, many creedal atheists now place their faith in an unlimited expansion of human science and technology in the future. But might it be possible that such scientific perception is itself destined to remain severely limited, because there are other ways of knowing and experiencing the world that are currently viewed as 'unscientific' because they do not fit Aristotle's model? Is it possible that there are major facets of the universe that simply do not register on the radar of human perception? To insist that everything in the universe gains its existence from revealing itself to the five senses identified by an ancient Mediterranean philosopher hardly sounds scientific. The 'Unified Theory of Everything' is more precisely a 'Unified Theory of Everything We Are Currently Aware Of'. The infallibility Christendom bestowed upon Aristotle continues to assert itself through the secular arguments of science – proving that, even in the sterilized sanctity of the lab, 'history just burps, and we taste again that raw-onion sandwich it swallowed centuries ago.'[13]

To recap:

- Monotheism is the belief that one God has set up the entire universe (or multiverse). There are no alternative deities managing different regions of space and time. *Monotheism is the religious basis for a 'Unified Theory of Everything'.*
- Christian Scripture contains nothing supernatural, because monotheists build their understanding of 'natural' around their experience of the world. The idea of the supernatural comes from Greek polytheism, where gods intervene in the lives of mortals.
- In Christian Scripture, miracles are concerned with challenging people's experience of the world, redefining what is 'natural' – not so much in scientific terms as in social and political terms.
- Belief in miracles is not belief in fairy tales. During Christendom, what people *believed* was distinct from how people *lived*. In Scripture, *to believe in miracles is to challenge the social, political and natural laws of the day.*
- The challenge of miracles is thus to live not on the basis of what you are able to do, but upon what you decide to do.

In post-Christendom, then, Christians may agree with anyone else that there is a natural explanation for anything and everything. The challenge, however, is for an alternative vision of nature – a challenge that today is issued by scientists no less than Christians. This also requires an alternative vision of the God both Christians and modern atheists have inherited from Christendom.

Beyond Deism, Theism and Scientific Imperialism

In the previous chapter I claimed that modernity has restricted our pictures of God to one of two alternatives: deism and theism. After the religious wars of the sixteenth and seventeenth centuries, God was seen as a divine troublemaker and had to be promoted above the down-to-earth running of countries and business of daily life. While still pictured as the omnipotent Creator, this was a god who – having lit the fuse of the big bang – withdrew to a safe distance where he can enjoy the fireworks. This *deist* god remains aloof from the realities of the world, little more than a 'prime mover' who set the stage of the universe as we know it but has little ongoing, intimate involvement. The *theist* god, on the other hand, interferes with the creation on a daily basis, micro-managing every conceivable sequence of every physical action: every flap of every insect wing, every flight path of every pollen grain, every course of every bacterial cell. This is the god who carries bullets from gun barrels into victims, who supplies water for tsunamis and who nurtures cancerous tumours in those we love. Thankfully, in his kind-hearted moments he also guides believers to parking spaces, grants visions of Mary and inspires great works of art. This omnipotent and schizophrenic deity is the image projected by those seeking to defend the Christendom version of God for the modern era.

To the modernist, if there is a God then he is either a *deist* or a *theist*. Strictly speaking, these are not pictures of God as such, but function as laws that determine how God is permitted to exert influence within the created order. Neither picture is consistent with Scripture, and they are certainly not the only possible ways of conceiving of how an almighty and benevolent God might be active in a world where pain and suffering are common to all.

An Ontological Dimension

As I suggested in the previous chapter, suppose that a divine Creator has woven a (currently undetectable) strand throughout the fabric of the universe, and suppose we call this strand the *ontological dimension*. Ontology is concerned with the root of human *being*, with the question of how human identity is radically shaped in relation to otherness. Suppose that within this dimension humanity may find space to encounter the active presence of the divine Creator, and that what happens in this dimension spills out into the more traditionally observable world.

It remains entirely conceivable that a Creator can build into even the most closed, predetermined, naturalistic and non-miraculous system of existence an entire dimension of being. That is, a dimension that may yield itself to those who engage with the universe in particular ways, a dimension whose effects manifest themselves through the actions of those who have adopted particular ways of being. This would be a universally accessible dimension, however, whose mechanisms have yet to reveal themselves to the apparatus developed by life-forms who have not adopted a particular way of being.

This is not a long way from some of the reflections offered by the great twentieth-century philosopher of ontology, who also happened to be atheist, namely Martin Heidegger. For Heidegger human beings are thrown into a 'fallen world', but not in the sense that we are surrounded by sin. The idea is rather that we are afflicted by a deep-seated cultural amnesia, in which most human beings have forgotten what it means simply to be. Everything in our world is geared up, he says, to divert our attention from the ultimate questions that really matter. In his later writings, he focused upon how the technological mindset blinded and deafened us to questions of being. In the technological era, we tend to interpret the world, other people, and even ourselves, as little other than resources to be used. Their otherness is thereby ignored. If there is such a thing as an ontological dimension, then Heidegger believed that modern humans are almost incapable of gaining access to it.

With these claims about 'ontology' we are drawn back to a pre-modern argument for the existence of God – one that is unlikely to sound remotely convincing to modern ears. Namely, that if so many people believe in God, he must therefore exist. Of course the modern mindset cannot begin to entertain the validity of such an argument. But this may not simply be because modern people know better than their unenlightened ancestors. In many ways, they know far less well. Though technology has advanced (to our great benefit), it has also distanced us from the natural world. Double-glazing, central heating and air conditioning minimize our exposure to the seasons; supermarkets and freight transport distance us from the land that feeds us. Plastic wrapping and ready meals protect us from the reality of the plants and animals that nourish us. While the widespread and all-year-long availability of food is to be celebrated, there is something here to be lamented. For Heidegger, that would be our incapacity to access the ontological dimension of our world. The modern world has bestowed upon us a worldview in which we no longer see ourselves as part of an eco-system.

For instance, the geographer Steve Trudgill traces our modern relationship with the soil which once was cultivated with respect but now is plundered without thought. An increasingly mechanized world closes our minds and emotions to the 'voice' of the soil that sustains us. As we lose our relationship with it, the earth loses its otherness. In the end, the soil becomes nothing other than a resource (and one that is disturbingly finite). Trudgill's case reaches its climax with a citation from John Steinbeck's *Grapes of Wrath*, as the farmer climbs onto his tractor, losing all contact with the earth he works:

> He could not see the land as it was, he could not smell the land as it smelled; his feet did not stamp the clods or feel the warmth and power of the earth. He sat in an iron seat and stepped on iron pedals . . . He did not know or own or trust or beseech the land . . . He loved the land no more than the bank loved the land . . . Behind the tractor rolled the shining disks, cutting the earth with blades – not ploughing but surgery, pushing the cut earth to the right . . . Behind the harrows, the long seeders – twelve curbed iron penes erected in the foundry, orgasms set by gears, raping methodically, raping without passion . . . And when that crop grew, and was harvested, no man had crumbled a hot clod in his fingers and let the earth sift past his fingertips . . . The

land bore under iron, and under iron gradually died; for it was not loved or hated, it had no prayers or curses.[14]

In other words, even modern farmers have a different way of knowing, that is, a different 'science' from their predecessors, one that has a different relation to the natural world. Might it be that those with a deeper exposure to the natural world are likely to experience, feel and think about life, the universe and everything in a different way? Might it be that such folk – though moderns may dismiss them as culturally and scientifically inferior – have access to valid ways of knowing that are no longer available to modern people? If this is the case, then only with humility can the inhabitants of the modern, technological era dismiss the kind of assumed experience of the divine which their predecessors seemed to acknowledge. Here Trudgill has offered just one example of humanity cutting itself adrift from the ontological dimension of the universe.

To summarize again:

- The relationship between science and religion tends to be stuck with the split personality of a seventeenth-century god: that of deism or theism.
- An alternative would be a god who (like the deist) creates the universe and allows it to run itself, but who (like the theist) reveals core features of his identity through a dimension that is both hidden and accessible.
- This 'ontological' dimension, might currently be beyond the reach of traditional scientific methods, but accessible via certain ways of being – of relating to otherness.
- The 'fallenness' of the world refers to the human capacity to divert itself from engaging with the ontological dimension of life.
- Events traditionally regarded as miracles might simply be the manifestation of actions within an unknown (but natural) dimension, into the midst of dimensions with which we are familiar.

Feeding the Five Thousand: An Atheist Miracle

We are now in a position to recognize that the miracles reported in
the New Testament documents are fundamentally atheist events.
The most widely reported and perhaps well known of the miracle
stories is the feeding of the five thousand. Crowds have gathered
on the hillside to hear Jesus speak, but evening approaches, there
is little food, and his disciples suggest he dismiss everyone. Jesus
replies, 'You give them something to eat.'

Throughout history, providing bread has been a crucial function for any political leader. Moses is the most frequently quoted
and relevant link in this regard, 'miraculously' providing his
people with daily bread as they wandered through the desert.
But providing bread to hungry people is almost the universal
function of a lord in any society. An Anglo-Saxon 'lord' was
literally a 'loaf-giver'. In ancient Greece, the cult of the bread
goddess eventually became the state religion of Athens. And,
most importantly, in Roman society, a good emperor was
expected to provide his citizens with bread. Bakers were given
special privileges by the emperor, as 'people important to the
welfare of a nation'. That bread would be brought in from every
corner of the empire, including Israel, whose own people were
going hungry.

So Jesus, as the *Messiah* (i.e. the political leader anointed to lead
his people to freedom), has amassed a crowd of five thousand and
does what the emperor of Rome spent his life struggling to do: he
gives bread to his people. More significantly, he provides bread
for those whose own bread has been taken by the empire. Jesus,
whatever he intended, is effectively usurping the authority of
Rome. And yet, he had issued no direct threat, and to prevent the
crowds seeing him as any kind of military rebel leader (the texts
tell us there were five thousand men, without reference to the
women and children) he immediately disperses them. Given that
there were no more than six thousand Roman soldiers in the entire
province of Judea, Jesus might well have marched on Jerusalem –
especially if his troops had no worries about rationing. Instead, he
subverts many expectations by dismissing his potential army *after*
he fed them. No violence, no attempt to seize power, no stirring
revolutionary speeches. Just the provision of bread for hungry

people: not for Roman citizens, nor for privileged Jews, but for Jewish peasants in a political backwater.

Are we to regard this as a supernatural event? The first point to mention is that this miracle destabilizes the social order of the empire, and in so doing, destabilizes what many perceived to be the natural order. The second point is that Jesus did not perform this so-called 'miracle'. He told his disciples to do it. '*You* give them something to eat!' If we are to read this within the context of Luke's gospel, Jesus is suggesting an alternative power dynamic to what was popularly expected of a Messiah. This is an exercise in giving oneself to the other.

If we entertain the notion that this is a historical incident that actually happened, then – as shown above – it must have been a natural rather than a supernatural event. As such, could it be that Jesus accessed something akin to an ontological dimension that manifested itself in the form of matter? Might it be manifest in accordance with laws of nature, with laws of cause and effect, related nevertheless to the being and the way of being of those present? The power dynamic of the gospel rejects the attempts to conquer, extinguish or exterminate the other (as many expected the Messiah to do to the Romans). Instead, the power dynamic embodied and encouraged by the Messiah is one of radical self-giving love for the sake of the other ('You give them something to eat'). Are the causes of this event to be found in an, as yet, undiscovered dimension of the natural world?

The logic of Christianity is that such a possibility cannot be assessed without experiment. The Messiah's invitation to conduct this experiment is found in the practice described above as *metanoia*, generally translated into the Christianized English word 'repentance'.[15] This call to 'repent' has less to do with negating sin or guilt than with a positive and radical reorientation of the mind, the affections and the will. *Metanoia* is – at root – a challenge to encounter ourselves, other people and the world differently, a call – in other words – to an ontological reawakening. This, it seems, is the point of the miracle in question. Jesus is by no means attempting to display his super-powers. Instead, he is calling his followers to an alternative way of being. This is a way of being that defies both Mars and Venus, the prevailing gods of his age. Lloyd Pietersen's post-Christendom reading of the miracle runs in close harmony with this claim:

The miraculous provision of food for the hungry . . . suggests a profound anti-imperial emphasis. Rome famously had the bread dole to feed its hungry citizens from the bread baskets of the empire. Jesus' role in feeding the masses out of compassion is implicitly contrasted with Rome's ability to do the same by means of military conquest (as Rome itself could not provide the grain to meet the needs of its population).[16]

As Pietersen points out, one gospel account explicitly states that the crowds experienced this miracle as an imperial claim, and attempted to make Jesus king. By refusing to use his power for military ends, by refusing to lead his crowd to expel the Romans from his homeland, Jesus explicitly rejects the military way of the god Mars. He also rejects the economic allure of the goddess Venus, as Pietersen implies: 'The combination of themes from Psalm 23 (the "green grass" of Mark 6:39 echoes Ps. 23:2) and the Eucharist suggest the imagery of a table prepared in the midst of occupied territory (Ps. 23:5). Eucharistic feasting is to be a profound means of economic sharing which subverts the economy of the empire.'[17]

However this miracle is understood, it constitutes an act of sedition against the gods of the age, against the warmongering of Mars and the economic unfairness of Venus. It is thus an atheist miracle and speaks of the nature of power that miracles display. This is not the three-dimensional coercive power useful to a Roman emperor. Instead, it offers an entirely different framework for understanding the power that makes the world work.

Conclusion

We are now in a position to view the astonishing events reported in Christian Scripture, not as miracles, but as perfectly plausible, historical, natural phenomena. Miracles do not 'break' the perceived laws of nature, but challenge those who witness them to rethink and redraw the laws of nature. Those familiar with the Asgardian characters of Marvel Comics will know of the fictional characters of Thor, Odin and Loki – popularized most recently in Hollywood blockbusters such as *Thor* and *Avengers Assemble*. In the comics, while these characters are portrayed as gods with divine powers, those powers are entirely natural but simply beyond the reach of human science. As such, their powers are conceived in the way that the miracles of Jesus have been portrayed in this chapter. But there is a fundamental difference: the power exerted by Jesus is not a coercive, observable power feeding the religions of Mars and Venus. The power of Jesus' miracles, though manifesting itself practically, is – from start to finish – based upon giving oneself to the other.

The miracles are acted parables, which deliberately subvert oppressive power structures, particularly those of the Roman Empire and the Jewish religious hierarchies. The gospels themselves bear this out. When the disciples witnessed miracles, they were often 'astonished' (at the calming of a storm, the miraculous catch of fish, the exorcism of a demon etc.), but on one occasion, they were not merely astonished, but '*exceedingly astonished*': when Jesus declared it almost impossible for a wealthy man to 'inherit the kingdom of God' his followers were exceedingly astonished. More shocking, it seems, than Jesus' readiness to defy the laws of nature was his readiness to subvert social and religious convention.

By suggesting that divine action might be rooted in a dimension with real effects in the real world, but which scientists cannot currently access, is this chapter portraying a God-of-the-gaps? The answer is an enthusiastic 'yes'. This is precisely my intention, and for several reasons. Firstly, as this chapter has emphasized, 'gaps' are all there is. Modern science has taught us that there is no way to know just how much or how little we know. Do we know 1 per cent of what there is in the universe? Or 1 per cent of how life on our planet functions? Or 1 per cent about my next-door neighbour? How can we possibly speak in such terms until we grasp what 100 per cent is? We live inside a Russian doll, and while we may marvel at our ability to see beyond our own layer, we have no idea how many larger dolls contain us, nor how many smaller dolls sit in our hand. There is simply no way of knowing how much there is to know, and how much of it we know. In light of extra dimensions and an infinite range of new possibilities, supposed 'gaps' are in the habit of expanding. Secondly, science has yielded factual knowledge about how the world works, about how galaxies and molecules and atoms and brains behave. But always and without exception, the knowledge we have wrested out of the gaps is still based upon what remains in them. Our knowledge simply offers a glimpse into the abysmal infinity of the gap. Scientific methods can identify causal links between one point in a sequence and another, and can predict outcomes with great accuracy and confidence, but a genuinely open scientist accepts that all we know could be undermined in a moment by an unexpected piece of new evidence. Thirdly, if God is to be found in the gaps, then this is not where he hides, but where he invites us to encounter otherness.

6.

Sources of Ethics

Ethical debates raging between atheists and Christians usually follow predictable patterns of argument: Christians claim that, without God, there can be no ethics. Without some belief in a transcendent deity, there is no objective standard against which to measure human behaviour, nothing big enough to give meaning to words like 'good' and 'evil'. Instead, so many Christians fear, there can be only competing moral claims, all of them hopelessly adrift on the bottomless ocean of moral relativism. No universal standards of right and wrong, no timeless moral truth, and therefore, no ethics. Atheists respond with the undeniable catalogue of Christian hypocrisy that fills the pages of history, with each Christian generation boasting more than its fair share of individuals and institutions behaving poorly by any standards, and inflicting terrible evil on others and upon the world. This is hardly surprising, says the atheist, because the character of the fictitious God that Christians worship is a jealous, interfering bully, abusing his divine power by inflicting suffering upon his creatures.

This chapter argues that every human being is ethical because every human has an *ethos*, a character that will manifest itself in various kinds of behaviour. For many, ethics is a set of morals, virtues or values we must recognize and apply in order to be good. Alternatively (and the line followed here) ethics concerns the prior formation of the human *ethos*, which predetermines whatever ethical principles we may later come to learn, choose or treasure. Christians believe that their ethos is formed in relationship with their God, but what kind of a God forms such an ethos? A God who is both all-powerful and all-loving?

Rejecting Omnipotence

The evolution of omnipotence within Christian belief is a complex narrative usually told without reference to political power. If it were simply a word meaning that God's power is infinite in its scope, then it would remain consistent with the teaching of Scripture and the doctrine of resurrection outlined in the interlude above. Unfortunately, omnipotence also smuggles into Christianity a whole army of concepts radically hostile to the teaching of Scripture. Before Christ, *Omni* (all) *Potens* (power) was a title already enjoyed by certain Roman emperors, not to mention Roman gods. It speaks explicitly of the *extent* of a ruler's power, but also speaks implicitly about the *nature* of that power. As one philosopher notes, 'Without telling themselves so, the founders of the theological tradition were accepting and applying to deity the *tyrant* ideal of power.'[1] This, after all, is how we assume God must govern an otherwise inanimate universe, a divine puppet-master pulling the strings of an otherwise lifeless creation.

Is there an alternative? Is it possible that there are alternative forms of power, more effective than coercion? The doctrine of the incarnation suggests that, in Jesus of Nazareth, the Almighty God became human, and it is surely to this Jesus that Christians must look in order to see how God himself governs the created order. However, the doctrine of the incarnation makes God so intolerably fragile that Christians often recoil at its radical implications.

The majority assume that God is not so much *revealed* as *concealed* in the person of Christ: the omnipotent God, we are told, does not *show* himself, but *disguises* himself as a weak and vulnerable peasant; the monarch of heaven does not *express* his power, but *suppresses* it in order to become human; Jesus is not the 'Word become flesh', he is only 'veiled in flesh'. None of this warrants the title 'incarnation'. Instead, it presents the life of Jesus as an act of divine espionage, in which God becomes something other than he really is in order to infiltrate the ranks of humanity. The only honest route of incarnation available for this omnipotent God is for him to be born an emperor.

The Christ of Scripture is a vulnerable outsider, subject to all the dominant social, economic, religious and political powers of his day. And yet it is under the shadow of such forces that he displays his divinity. Never does he attempt to overcome these forces with redemptive violence, military force or any form of coercion. God's very nature is manifest most clearly in the body of a naked, mutilated and humiliated political criminal, in the kind of power that gives itself to failure, to defeat, to utter and abject powerlessness. A power expressed in the capacity to allow one's enemy to have the final word, to gloat over his victory, to display his triumph – but to remain present, nevertheless, to that enemy. This Christ reveals the nature of God through radical self-giving, world-saving love for the other. By inviting his followers to do likewise, one might assume, he invites them to a way of life destined to futility and failure, in which the machinations of human power brokers destroy the gentle beauty of the humble Christ. This, of course, is what we witness at the crucifixion. Jesus, his way of life, and the kingdom he proclaims come to a violent end at the cold hard justice of the cross.

Christian belief, however, revolves around his resurrection. Before anything else, the resurrection is a vindication of the kind of power wielded by the Son of God. And if this is how God works through his Son on earth, we might reasonably assume that this is how God works throughout the infinite regions of time and space. Not a God who clicks his fingers to bring lifeless objects into conformity with his imperial will, but a God whose drastically alternative power dynamic is known as 'the kingdom of God'. The possibility of an ontological dimension through which divine power is genuinely exerted and experienced is entirely consistent with resurrection as described above. Scripture points to a God whose power is of an entirely different order from the crude, mechanical, cause-and-effect power structures of omnipotence.

Rejecting Theism

Theism refers explicitly to the conviction *that* God's power is active in the world, but also brings with it an implicit set of beliefs about *how* God is active. As such, it is entirely plausible to believe in God's active presence, without believing in modernity's theistic deity.

An almighty God whose way of being present in the world is exclusively channelled through an ontological dimension might have a particular way of exerting force upon our world. The kind of force that can be exerted through this dimension is not coercive. It is the force that is based upon and thrives upon engaging well with otherness, but a force that has real effects in the real world. It is quite conceivable that human actions and patterns of behaviour can spill over from this dimension into others in such a way as to affect individuals, histories, and nature itself. The God of providence, who communes with those who worship him, who answers prayers, and is active and present in the world, may well channel his presence through this ontological dimension. Does this mean that God is fully present in the world? In terms of the universal possibility of access to an ontological dimension we may answer 'yes'; In terms of God being present, with every humanly conceivable type of divine power (including imperial power) at his disposal, we may answer 'no'. God's universal presence and infinite power come to humanity in *particular* ways.

The particular ways in which the god of theism is present are different from the ways in which a post-Christendom God is present. Here modernity is best understood as what happened when God the Father lost a custody battle for the world he loves. Content with being separated from his children, the deist god remains an absent father. Theism, on the other hand, refers to a father who visits at weekends to take his children on a cinema trip and a visit to McDonald's, but who nevertheless must act in accordance with the terms laid out in the contact order drawn up in the seventeenth century by René Descartes and Isaac Newton. (So much for his divine omnipotence!) This is a god pushed outside the closed universe so that he is compelled to be not natural but supernatural, who must now 'intervene' in human affairs and, by so doing, break the immutable 'laws of nature'. Theism is the belief that God is present within a closed universe – a universe in which God is bound to act in certain ways.

A more open view of the universe leads to different possibilities concerning the presence of God. In such a world, human awareness of the mechanics of nature is both impressive beyond measure *and* partial, tentative and minuscule. Scientific progress has brought humanity far enough to outgrow the certainties of modernity, far enough to be humbled by the vastness and the intricacy of the universe, far enough to treasure openness towards the otherness of the physical world. With such a view of the world, the questions of God's presence and the manner in which God exerts force remain open. With an open world, the existence of a divine being whose character is consistent with the deity of Christian Scripture also remains open. Modernist versions of theism, which strictly speaking are the *only* versions of theism, have accepted God's eviction from the universe and thereby restricted his involvement within the universe. Those restrictions impose upon this alienated God a set of behavioural patterns at odds with both ancient scriptures and modern logic.

Seen in this light, an ontological dimension offers a possible account of how the kind of power witnessed in the New Testament is not a magic wand that will fix the world's problems straight away. The kind of power exhibited here is not one that will dethrone the world's malevolent tyrants, eradicate poverty and hunger, end all injustice. The oppressive powers that be, along with other cruel forces of nature such as drought and famine, earthquake and volcano, will continue in accordance with the mechanics of the universe as it is. The violence, the terrors, the cruelty of the world will continue despite the presence of an ontological dimension. What this dimension gives, however, is a way of living within a cruel world that offers realism and hope, that does not allow the last word to the powers of nature – be they political or social, cosmic or geological powers.

But couldn't this claim be conceived as a psychological con trick, a pointless kind of power that enables people to live with *the way things are* but not to change *the way things are*? Is this nothing more than the reassurance from a God who will console victims without confronting bullies, an emotional crutch offered by a God who is happy to leave intact the oppressive powers that be? This, after all, is why many of Jesus' followers abandoned him (he would not overthrow the evil dictators) in favour of Barabbas (who at least had tried).[2] The ontological dimension from which divine energy might be drawn is not a means of solving the world's problems, but of defying them. To enable victims to live amid the suffering of the world is by no means simply to tolerate injustice and unfairness. It is precisely the kind of power that subverts the apparently omnipotent forces of nature, so to answer this question properly requires that two aspects of nature be considered, firstly nature itself and secondly its subcategory, human nature.

Nature

This chapter argues for the possibility of a God who creates a world on the one hand, leaving it to its own devices with all the cruel and violent forces necessary to its evolution and the development of life. On the other hand, running through this natural and evolutionary process is an ontological dimension in which there are forms of divinely provided power which, though accessible to human beings, are not the kind of powers that will end the cruel and violent forces of nature. The first question to ask, then, is why a loving God would create a world in which cruelty and violence are universal and necessary. The entire context for human life, the environment in which we flourish, is a violent explosion that began 13.7 billion years ago. The swirls of the galaxies, the movement of the planets, the beauty of the seasons, the days and nights, all are part of a massive explosion still underway. The universe is, first and foremost, a violent explosion, and human life is part of that explosion. Violence, in other words, is not simply a regrettable aspect of the world; it is the stuff of life. This is true both of the biological and the cosmological aspects of evolution. Violence is what we see when we gaze at the stars of the Milky Way, and when we marvel at the intricacy of a spider's web.

The biological world was inherently violent long before the evolution of tooth and claw. Violence is how plants colonize ground that can accommodate them, conquering new territory with no less aggression than Europeans colonized the Americas. Anyone responsible for a garden has seen as much. But it is not only weeds or carnivorous plant species that are violent. Plants' tenacious adaptability to new environments, their capacity to develop defence mechanisms against animals and insects, and their ability to clone themselves if necessary show their desire to cling to the life they have – and anything with a desire to survive has the capacity for violence. All living organisms develop strategies in their battles with environments and competitors. For plants, those strategies include their sheer plasticity, their regenerative power and their ability to produce a multitude of chemical compounds. Mammals, on the other hand, have developed the capacity to hunt and to flee. Obviously, the violence endemic to mammal life is much more closely akin to the violence more easily recognized by humans.

How, then, could a loving God justify creating a world in which violence is the norm? Why did he not create a world of bliss only, something closer to the kind of afterlife imagined by so many Christians? Is this not the sadist God caricatured so frequently by creedal atheists, and followed so faithfully by creedal Christians? As Christian apologists often point out, what alternative could there be? Is it possible that a deity *could* create a serene, luxurious, couch-potato existence, devoid of all suffering, pain and death, and yet an existence that would still be precious, worthwhile and have supreme value? Should the Creator God have invented a non-violent universe? While this question cannot be answered with any certainty, those who believe it unjust for God to create a violent universe like ours must answer that God *could* have created meaningful life without violence. This, after all, is what an omnipotent God can do: he can create ecosystems in which different species are not interdependent, where the life of one does not depend upon the death of another. To do so, of course, is tantamount to creating a rock so big even he couldn't move it.

Life, however short and apparently meaningless, however painful it might be, is still immeasurably valued by those that have it. Why does a mammal run from a predator? When caught, why does it fight until its dying breath? Life itself is a mind-bogglingly limited resource, but if it were not, would it still be precious? Life on earth is life in the midst of a violent explosion – but this is the only conceivable context in which God-given life can flourish. While such an observation does not necessarily bring a final answer, it does show that a God who created a violent universe is not necessarily a malevolent, sadistic tyrant of cosmic proportions. Only when we have stepped outside the context of our own violent universe is there even the remotest possibility of considering an alternative pattern of valuable life. To claim that God *could* have created a non-violent world in which life is precious is thus to assume supernatural powers of imagination, and to assume that a Creator God is also automatically an omnipotent God. The real question arising from universal violence is the question of how to live with it, which brings us to the question of human nature.

Human Nature

The view of God offered in this chapter is very close to that of the deist. That is, consistent with belief in a 'prime mover' who sets the world up and allows evolutionary processes to unfold. In this sense, the evolution of human life requires no supernatural intervention. The struggle of biological organisms, of different species to compete, to adapt, to survive, culminates in the unfathomable beauty of human life. To see the development of human life as the product of a helping hand from a well-meaning Creator destroys the very notion of human life as a gift. In the light of the entire evolutionary sweep that has gone before human life, the first 99.999… per cent of the life of the universe would all be rendered pointless, futile and dishonest if, at the end of it all, the Creator cheats by plonking artificial, ready-made human beings onto planet earth.

A far more satisfactory point of view, from a Christian perspective, is to accept the universe in which the spark of life is even possible, as a divine gift. The creation's response to its Creator is then precisely the evolutionary struggle into existence, the tenacious, dogged, drive to value the life that it has – honouring that life by battling to treasure, maintain, extend and expand it. In this sense, the human species is the culmination of billions of years of struggle and as such can value itself, have a legitimate pride and a hard-earned dignity. Human life is not a cheap trick, conjured up at the whim of a cosmic emperor who could choose to throw such supernatural novelties at the created order any day he chooses. This omnipotent God who might click his fingers and prepare a ready-made creation at any moment might well be perceived as a shallow, lazy, impatient and boring individual with no need to value the life he creates. If, on the other hand, the Creator has spent 13.6999… billion years waiting for his big bang to bear human fruit, then he has patiently invested himself in his craftwork and is part of the story.

This belief, as discussed below, runs in deep continuity with the creation poetry of the book of Genesis. Far from parachuting into the Garden of Eden from a different region of the multi-verse, Adam was drawn from the living earth – a natural part of the world as it came into being. The point at which human self-consciousness emerges is the point at which humanity becomes consciously attuned to the ontological dimension, receiving from the Creator both divine and self-awareness. What then may be said of human nature when human life emerges from the natural processes of evolution?

Perhaps the primal human instinct is expressed well in the moral injunction to love your friends and hate your enemies. Support within the tribe and hostility to other tribes is an evolutionary survival mechanism recognized long before Richard Dawkins published *The Selfish Gene*. Despite Dawkins' belief that humanity can overcome nature to become altruistic, Scripture's account of human fallenness suggests that no amount of evolution or civilization is able to suppress the human instinct for violence towards the other when that other is from beyond my own group or tribe.

An Atheist Ethos

Not all contemporary scientists and philosophers agree that we are prisoners of our violent genetic nature. Steven Pinker draws together the work of Peter Singer[3] and James Flynn,[4] to argue that human beings are becoming more civilized, pacified and morally intelligent.[5] Thus, Pinker contends, human beings are showing, in increasing measure, their natural capacity to engage with the otherness of those beyond our parochial domains of self-interest, to consider the wellbeing of all people. This conviction forms part of his argument that human societies are slowly becoming less prone to violence. Gathering vast arrays of data from across centuries, he traces the declining rates of violent deaths and acts of physical violence as evidence that we are outgrowing our morally inferior ancestors.

Pinker's book is a fascinating tour through the history of violence, buttressed by hundreds of pages of evidence to show a gradual climb out of a past in which violence was commonplace, towards a future where it may one day be eradicated. Pinker makes some outrageously counter-intuitive claims, such as his conviction that the twentieth century was less violent than many other centuries. However, his evidence for claims of this nature does appear sound. More questionable are his attempts to interpret his facts. In the first instance, despite several hundred pages of text, Pinker fails to discuss what actually constitutes violence. His data is restricted to the kind of violence that can be measured by mutilated corpses or criminal records. No reference is made to anything other than the crudest, most identifiable and calculable forms of violence. It would be entirely plausible to take all of the raw data he provides and interpret it along entirely different lines.

If I were to claim that since the Enlightenment humanity has been learning to disguise its own acts of violence from itself, I could cite Pinker's evidence (and his logic) in support of my belief in a growing lack of cultural self-awareness. For instance, Pinker presents a convincing list of motives for violence: exploiting others as tools for one's own ends; the desire for dominance or supremacy; the moralistic hunger for revenge; and most importantly, ideology (militant religions, nationalism, fascism, Nazism, communism). Never does Pinker consider the causes underlying these motives. Only that 'the better angels of our nature' can overcome them: self-control; empathy, fairness, and above all, reason. What has changed historically for our better angels to overpower our motives for violence? The establishment of nation-states – with their monopoly of legitimate violence – and, as stated above, increased and scientifically enabled capacity to identify with others beyond the bounds of our familiar world.

Pinker's analysis, however, is astonishingly partial. Nowhere in this book is there any acknowledgement that those who already face the ravages of man-made global warming are the victims of violence; nowhere does he consider that those who suffer extreme poverty because of international economic and trade laws are the victims of violence. After all, Pinker believes that capitalism and international trade are a good reason for increased peace levels around the world. Hence the conclusion that a 'country that is open to the global economy is less likely to find itself in a militarised dispute.'[6] Pinker fails to see the late modern shift in how one country can invade and dominate another.

Take the IMF's dictates for Madagascar, which resulted in loss of funding for a crucial project – a mosquito eradication programme – and, in turn, in the deaths of 10–15,000 people, at least 5,000 of them children. This kind of man-made disaster does not register with Pinker, even though it resulted in widespread death. Features of the aggressive forms of capitalism in the late twentieth century do not constitute violence. The children who died in Madagascar do not feature in Pinker's statistics because the agents of violence were mosquitos instead of soldiers.

Since there is no easy, direct, identifiable link between those who suffer and those who benefit, then – by Pinker's reckoning – no violence has been committed. If I, the perpetrator, am protected by the complex systems of modern economics and technology from the victim who suffers as a result of my actions, I can wash my hands and presume no violence is done. If I choose to buy low-priced chocolate or climb on an aeroplane for an unnecessary journey, never will I be regarded as committing violent acts – even though such actions have consequences that inflict suffering upon others. The further I can distance myself from direct dependence upon human and natural ecosystems, the less I will care about the other. Although these are complex questions, his book celebrating the primacy of human reason does not demand that I address them. Instead, Pinker's book exonerates me, furnishing me with the smug satisfaction that I have outgrown my morally retarded ancestors[7] because with my increased capacity to reason I am blissfully ignorant of the violence my very way of life inflicts upon others.

As a moral defence of modernity and reason, the ethical structure of Pinker's work leaves the individual, thinking subject at the centre of the universe. The expanding circle of reason that eventually (and theoretically) allows me to consider the otherness of those from beyond the boundaries of my own world is still a circle centred upon me. As such, it is, finally, an inadequate attempt to engage seriously with the otherness of the distant other, effectively silencing today's victims of economic and ecological violence in the name of enlightenment. Although Pinker is convinced that his work undermines the legitimacy of any religious text (texts written by ancestors who condoned and encouraged violent behaviour), a serious engagement with those texts suggests otherwise.

The Roots of a Christian Ethos

Here, the Christian ethos has something genuinely distinctive to offer. At its roots is the question of what it means to be human at all. Since the advent of modernity, it is assumed that a human self is – first and foremost – a self-contained entity. I learn, first of all, how to be an 'I' since I am at the centre of my universe. Only later do I learn how to relate to a 'you', and later still, a 'they'. The world, in other words, is the construct of my imagination. Although other people may be important to me, they are somewhere out beyond myself, external to me. Modern ethics is built largely around belief in the freedoms of this kind of individual: 'My freedom to swing my fist ends where your nose begins.' An ethics of restricting the freedoms of individuals is necessary to living together with others in community. This kind of ethics is problematic precisely because it affirms the primal state of a human individual as free to do as he or she likes, and an ethics based upon restricting a person's freedoms is ultimately an ethics of conflict and hostility towards the other.

Christian beliefs about human identity take an entirely different route, in which the individual is not an isolated being, but is grounded upon relation to that which is not itself. Some Christian ethicists have described this view as the external constitution of the self. Here, for instance, we may draw together the work of Augustine on the one hand, and Martin Heidegger on the other. For Augustine, the self is not a free-floating, isolated unity. The self is grounded in the reality of God, shaped in the first instance by divine otherness. Equally, Heidegger's notion of 'thrownness' highlights the human experience of being thrown into a world, discovering oneself in relation to the things and people around. I discover that I am an 'I' only secondarily as I receive myself back from the 'you' on whom I am dependent. For Augustine it is relation to divine otherness that grounds the human self; for Heidegger, it is the complex relation of human otherness. In short, the human self is given, by its relation to divine and human otherness, a view running in deep continuity with the creation poetry of Genesis. Adam is created consciously in relation to Yahweh and to nature, and it is not good for him to be alone. Hence the creation of Eve, who is drawn from the rib of Adam not to show his authority over her (he cannot be human without her), but to show that their mutual selves are fundamentally related to one another – their identity rooted in the other. The mutual *ethos* (of divine and human interrelatedness) is the natural basis for their ethics – the way they live. There is no need of moral commands or codes of conduct. However, disaster strikes the Garden of Eden the moment Adam and Eve begin the game of ethics, taking fruit from the tree of the knowledge of good and evil. Here, the desire for ethics (knowledge of good and evil) is sought without reference to the hard work of engaging well with otherness. Hence their withdrawal from one another (behind fig leaves) and from God (who had to go looking for them.) The subsequent history of the Hebrew people, as Scripture recounts it, is a catalogue of escalating ethical violence towards the other.

For Augustine, ethics is grounded in active communion with God. Hence, his famous ethical phrase, 'Love, and do as you like.' In other words, love God, love others, and ethics will look after itself. Ethics is secondary to the *ethos*, and, from a Christian perspective, that ethos is shaped in relation to divine and human otherness – just as Jesus of Nazareth followed the convention of his day, summarizing the law and prophets with the dual command, 'Love the Lord your God with all your heart, soul, mind and strength', and 'Love your neighbour as yourself.' Such a command is not simply a moral code demanding that the individual should 'do as you would be done to' *and* sing hymns of adoration to a psychologically needy divinity. It is rather the rooting of one's identity into the wellbeing of others and, in so doing, discovering that this is where Christ might be encountered. Christ himself claims that 'whatever you do for the least of these [the lowest, most marginalized, voiceless and powerless], you do for me'. Thus he identifies himself with the powerless, not just sharing their company, but rooting his divine being in theirs. This draws us back to the doctrine of incarnation, in which the life of Jesus points to who God is and how he behaves. This is not a god who needs to move into a position of influence before he can exert influence. Nor is this a god who needs to become rich before he can help the poor. This is not a Jesus who performs miracles (Greek, *dunamis/semeia*) because he is supernatural, but whose astonishing actions (*dunamis*) are signs (*semeia*) drawing attention to the true nature of the power that underpins what the universe is and how it works. This Jesus is not superhuman, but so radically, thoroughly, fully human that he is attuned to natural, hidden dimensions that shape the created order. This is the Christ around whom any Christian way of life is structured.

- If God is omnipotent and loving, there should be no suffering in the world.
- Omnipotence is useful to the Christendom power dynamic but at odds with Jewish and Christian scriptures.
- The God of Scripture may not be able to create a world in which life is precious but suffering is absent. This does not rob the world of its beauty or God of his goodness.
- The entire structure of the created order is an order of violence. We are, after all, in the middle of a big bang.
- In order to survive in a violent world, human beings have evolved to learn co-operation with their friends and hostility towards their enemies.
- Most forms of ethics are concerned with co-operation between humans.
- Christian ethics are distinctive, because they teach love for one's enemies as well as one's friends; love does not halt at the boundaries of one's own tribe.

Epicurus had declared that if God is willing to prevent evil, but not able, he is impotent. The problem with this view, adopted by countless adherents to the Christendom ideal and the Enlightenment worldview, is the assumed understanding of what power really is. As discussed in the interlude on resurrection, the Sadducees did not believe in resurrection because it meant revolution, the last thing you want if you are benefiting from the status quo. When they attempted to ridicule belief in resurrection, Jesus accuses them of not understanding the power of God. Traditionally, this is taken to mean they did not understand the *extent* of God's power, but it is more likely that their privileged position had blinded them rather to the *nature* of God's power and the manner in which it is exerted. Epicurus follows the same flat-footed logic, seeing power only on a sliding scale between omnipotence and impotence, rather than realizing the different forms of power.

When Saint Paul claimed that God's strength is made perfect in human weakness, he was not planning to wield that power to surround Rome and defeat the emperor. This is not a power that will end violence and injustice, any more than this divine power will stop the violence of the big bang in which all human life is inescapably caught up. The evils of nature and human nature will run their course unhindered by divine intervention. However, we may encounter, within an ontological dimension, something akin to what C.S. Lewis called 'a deeper magic from before the dawn of time.'[8] This deeper magic may be conceived as an ontological substructure that determines that, when certain courses of action are adopted, certain consequences will be inevitable. Such a dimension would be entirely consistent with the entire narrative sweep of the Christian Scriptures – even if a thousand years of Christendom have numbed our ability to consider it possible.

The kind of God outlined above is one who has created a universe and is ontologically present to it – not offering the same old coercive power as those who claim it, but offering a different form of power exemplified and enabled by the death and resurrection of Jesus of Nazareth. The post-Christendom form of mission is not an invitation to consider, in objective, cool detachment, the possibility of a loving and omnipotent God. No belief in God was ever conceived that way. Instead, it constitutes immersion into the world in all its ugliness and beauty, loving those with whom Christ identified himself, having the courage to 'tarry with the negative', and seeing what experience of God emerges.

Ethics as an Expression of Worship

Ethics, in the post-Christendom world, takes its lead from Kant's attempt to find an account of moral obligation that is universally acceptable because it is based solely upon pure, undiluted, apolitical, reason. 'Act only according to that maxim by which you can at the same time will that it should become a universal law.' Those who seek to make pronouncements about ethics tend then to proceed by seeking some general belief in the 'good life', some value, some commendable overriding principle, around which moral reasoning may be structured. Thus the question of how to be good in the world can be based upon abstract principles and beliefs that are kept at a safe distance from who I really am as a person. That is, they require no personal engagement with the ontological dimension of life.

What, then, is to prevent a central claim of this book (that humans engage well with divine and human otherness) from being the heart of just another modern attempt at conventional ethics? Another attempt to propose an objective, detached set of moral obligations – even if those obligations are to be fundamentally open to engage well with otherness?

Christian ethics is not, at root, a desire for openness towards the other so much as a readiness to welcome the stranger. That is, Christianity does not encourage an abstract openness to the other, an openness that need never come to any tangible fruition. This is theoretical openness propounded by Derrida, who applauds the perpetual open-endedness of waiting for the Messiah, but who absolutely cannot abide the idea that the Messiah would have the ineptitude to arrive. Christianity has nothing to do with an unachievable abstract state of openness, but is fleshed out in relation to the content-full presence of Christ. Hence, it is the church's engagement *with* Christ in worship, *as part of* the body of Christ at worship, which constitutes the particular form of engaging with otherness offered in this book.

As stated in chapter 1, this worship is no imaginary encounter with a supernatural realm. There is no politics and no ethics and no belief in a better world that is not based, consciously or otherwise, upon worship. Worship is simply the name of our relation to the things that we value. The lives that we live, the worlds that we construct, the beliefs that we hold are always, and in every conceivable sense, based upon that which we treasure. Politics and ethics are unavoidable expressions of our prior commitments to the things that we value, namely, our worship.

New Atheist Worship

What then is the liturgy of the New Atheist? Is the worship of the atheist likely to invite opposition from the powers that be, opposition that has been faced throughout the history of atheism? As argued in chapter 1, atheism is a rejection of the gods of one's own age. One of the major arguments of this book is that, since the demise of Christendom, the gods of our own age have new identities, and the New Atheists are submissive to them. In fact, if there is anything 'new' about the New Atheism, it lies in the subservience to (rather than subversion of) the contemporary powers that be. What are those powers? I have argued that they are the dehumanizing forces that have tangible, damaging, effects in the real world – but cannot be easily identified. Walter Wink (1935–2012) has offered a persuasive assessment of the contemporary powers of society in his trilogy, *Naming the Powers* (1984), *Unmasking the Powers* (1986), *Engaging the Powers* (1992).

In this series, Wink contends that 'the powers that be' are the *domination systems* under which we live. These are ideological, structural realities that shape the way we think, feel and believe, that restrict our freedoms and diminish our humanity. But the powers are not in the hands of humans who enjoy individual power, nor is this some religiously conceived conspiracy theory. Wink offers a way of explaining the powers that shape human destiny but seem beyond the reach of human influence. Hence Wink famously deconstructs what he calls 'the myth of redemptive violence'. Nevertheless, it is only by violence that the domination systems in politics and law, economy and commerce, trade, media and religion can maintain themselves. As stated above, for instance, at the simplest level, the luxuries I – as a wealthy member of a privileged society – enjoy will often come to me at the expense of some powerless person who suffers as a result. The link is not person to person, nor is it direct, because the entire technology masking cause and effect shields me from witnessing the violence required to keep me in the life to which I have become accustomed. In other words, the gods of our age are those that require (and celebrate) violence as the means of protecting my interests.

Of course, this goes against the claims of Pinker, who believes that humans are slowly eradicating violence. In support of Pinker we might turn to recent movies for both children and adults, in particular the modern and postmodern versions of *Star Wars* and James Bond. The 1970s *Star Wars* movies saw Luke Skywalker merrily killing storm troopers, albeit with his 'elegant weapon

from a more civilized age'. A generation later it is no longer acceptable to inflict violence upon the all-too-human storm troopers, so
the movie's intergalactic cannon fodder becomes robots. Robots,
that is, with highly sophisticated weapons systems, precise and
intelligent motor movement, independent reasoning capacities,
but monotone voice-boxes based upon electronic spelling games
developed on planet earth in the 1980s, just to remind us that they
are robots, so to slaughter them *en masse* is not cruel. The victims
of violence are literally dehumanized. The same development in
our apparent distaste for violence may be identified in the difference between the modern and postmodern James Bond. The old
Bond kills his victims, graces their corpses with a quip about
the manner of their death, brushes himself down and orders
his Martini. The new Bond is scarred by his acts of violence and
grasps his Martini as a refuge from his wounded memory. Despite
the realism, however, and the implication that audiences have, in
the last generation, a slightly more evolved moral sensibility, both
sets of movies are entertaining precisely because they are violent.
They still reinforce the story that violence is a regrettable necessity
in order for good to prevail – endorsing what Wink has called 'the
myth of redemptive violence'.

A principal god of our age, then, may be identified as Mars, the
Roman god of war. The identity of Mars, however, is to be sharply
distinguished from that of Ares, his Greek counterpart. Ares represents a glory in violence in itself, for its own ends, a sentiment with
which few moderns (or ancients) would be comfortable. Mars, on
the other hand, is a guardian, the god whose violence is exerted
for the sake of defending the interests of Rome. Not surprisingly,
it was under Caesar Augustus that reverence for Mars flourished.
By Wink's logic, this is the god still revered as the guardian of the
Domination Systems we value today.

The relationship, then, between the New Atheists and the
warlike deity of Mars is tragically straightforward. In fact, it is
reverence for Mars that spawned the entire New Atheist movement into existence. As is widely perceived, there are no new
intellectual components in the arguments they offer but there is a
more aggressive hostility to anything religious. The movement is
– at one level – simply a publishing decision. Publishers, however,
will publish only what sells, and in the wake of the 9/11 events,

religious fundamentalism became a popular concern. Not surprisingly, for the New Atheists, all religion is fundamentalist – and non-fundamentalist believers are simply not being faithful to their religion. On 11 September 2001, Mars failed to prevent not only an atrocious loss of life, but a powerful blow against the principal ideological symbols of the modern West. The worshippers of Mars soon went to work.

This is not to say that the New Atheist thinkers adopted their ideologies in response to 9/11. Dawkins, for instance, has long been fiercely atheistic. It was rather the publishing world that opened up debates previously circulated only by minor, specialist publishing houses to well-financed, heavily marketed mainstream publishers. After 9/11, publishers set the stage and the New Atheists gave the crowds what (the publishers believe) they wanted. As stated in chapter 2, the New Atheists are almost unanimous in their support for the war on terror.[9] Dennett critiqued the manner in which the war was fought, but not the necessity of fighting it. Hitchens was an outspoken supporter. Least cautious among the New Atheists, however, is the gun-toting rhetor Sam Harris, whose Islamaphobia has been widely published:

> What will we do if an Islamist regime, which goes dewy-eyed at the mere mention of paradise, ever acquires long-range nuclear weaponry? If history is any guide, we will not be sure about where the offending warheads are or what their state of readiness is, and so will be unable to rely on targeted, conventional weapons to destroy them. In such a situation, the only thing likely to ensure our survival may be a nuclear first strike of our own. Needless to say, this would be an unthinkable crime – as it would kill tens of millions of innocent civilians in a single day – but it may be the only course of action available to us, given what Islamists believe. How would such an unconscionable act of self-defence be perceived by the rest of the Muslim world?[10]

Such comments render Harris a high priest to the god of Mars. (One wonders, for instance, what would happen to a Muslim believer living in the US who disseminated this kind of rhetoric.) This unconfessed endorsement of the gods of the age is certainly alien to genuine atheists, even those of recent history. Anyone familiar with the writing of a Bertrand Russell will be acutely aware of how far the latter's atheism led him in the opposite ethical direction from a Harris. Russell himself had faced considerable opposition for his beliefs, to the point of being arrested at an anti-nuclear campaign in his ninetieth year. Harris, who has devoted an entire book to the belief that 'science can determine moral values', frequently displays the *ethos* that drives his violent suggestions: 'Where ethics are concerned,' he says, 'intentions are everything.'[11] Harris' intention is to nuke otherness out of existence.

Conclusion

Since the atheist critique of the Christian God is precisely the critique of Christendom's, the first part of this chapter was given over to offering a different picture of God but one that is consistent with the God of the Judeo-Christian Scriptures. This is the God whose power is effective but not coercive, who created a violent universe but does not abandon human beings to that violence, the God whose creatures become most fully human as they engage well with otherness. The ethos of such a God is a long way from the ethos of violent or omnipotent deities. However, atheists themselves, like all other human beings, are worshippers of something. The default gods of our contemporary culture are, I have argued, headed up by the Roman god of war, Mars. This is the deity pulling the strings of the New Atheist movement, a god accurately described as 'jealous and proud of it; a petty, unjust unforgiving control-freak; a vindictive, bloodthirsty ethnic-cleanser; a misogynistic homophobic racist, infanticidal, geno-cidal, filicidal, pestilential, megalomaniacal, sado-masochistic, capricious, malevolent bully.'[12]

Dawkins' description of the Old Testament god is no less true of the deity whom the New Atheists unwittingly serve. The latter part of this chapter has sought to make that point:

- Post-Christendom followers of Christ, seek – in the first instance – not to be ethical, but to expose their *ethos* to the transforming power of Christ.
- That power, though effective in the world, is not the violent, coercive power of Christendom that can be asserted *over* others.

- Human beings structure their political, social, ethical lives around that which they value. All humans 'ascribe worth to', i.e. worship, something.
- Atheists have always rebelled against the gods of our age.
- New Atheists serve the gods of our age, especially the Roman god of war: Mars.

The belief that without the God of Christianity there can be no absolute, objective moral standard for ethics is of little concern in the post-Christendom world. Ethics, as presented in this chapter, does not refer to a set of rules, of rights or wrongs, goods or evils. These are values that remain external to who I am, and do not necessitate the disturbing, transforming engagement with divine otherness that Christians call worship. Ethics can all too easily become a substitute for the painful but ultimately liberating transformation of the human ethos. *Christians need only demand an eternal and authoritative standard of ethics when they cease worshipping an eternal and authoritative God. Adherence to the former is a substitute for worship of the latter.*

I have argued that all ethical systems are built upon and perpetuated by that which we worship. This is no less true of atheists, New Atheists in particular, many of whom are unwitting devotees of the god Mars. This god is leading our world to destruction, and any who engage in Christian forms of ethical action will find themselves, consciously or otherwise, in defiance of this warmongering deity. In other words, an ethical Christian is a practical atheist.

7.

Economics, Venus and the Whore

The previous chapter argued that the Roman deity Mars is one of the principal gods of our age, but he does not work alone. Venus, in Roman mythology, is frequently pictured as the companion of Mars, a relationship rooted in the older Greek relationship between Ares (the god of war) and Aphrodite (the goddess of seduction and wealth). Roman tradition holds *Venus Genetrix* as the ancestress of all Roman citizens, the goddess of motherhood and domesticity, with both Julius and Augustus Caesar claiming direct descent from her. In 46 BC Julius built a temple to her in a prominent position of the newly established Forum in Rome. There, like her counterpart had in Athens, she also embodied the virtues of seduction and wealth necessary for the sustenance of the empire of which she was mother.

Worship of deities like Venus is not simply a superstitious activity for those longing to be wealthy or successful. Located in Rome's Forum, the focal point of the empire's trade, wealth and universal appeal, the temple of Venus churns out one of the central ideologies necessary to maintain the empire. The temple and its cult pronounce to every citizen, soldier, slave and pilgrim that the gods who rule over all are gods who favour the empire and its emperor. Those gods are themselves not merely superstitious projections of a people unable to explain lightning and scared of thunder. For instance, the individual's ability to acquire wealth depends largely upon forces beyond the control of the individual, i.e. wider economic forces. Although Venus represents this kind of 'supernatural' force over humans, not even she is able to confer wealth upon her worshippers unaided, because she is not omnipotent. Other forces (such as an act of individual or national violence) can sweep away whatever wealth Venus may have ordained with her invisible influence. What Thomas Friedman declares of the contemporary global economy is equally applicable to the exertions of Venus: 'The hidden hand of the market will never work without a hidden fist.'[1] Venus needs Mars.

As this chapter will show, *the predominant pattern of economics in the present world demands universal worship*[2] *of all that Venus embodies.* Regardless of their disavowal of the supernatural, the New Atheists are among the worshippers of Venus. Modernity may have provided twenty-first-century individuals with an increased capacity for mental abstraction – in this case, to consider wealth as an abstract reality rather than a supernatural god – but the effects in daily life are different in only one respect: abstract or divine, timeless quality or playful divinity, wealth is a powerful force worshipped by humans, shaping the lives of humans. The ancients who worshipped wealth as a deity who could exert force over them often acted with more self-consciousness and world-awareness than the moderns, who (with their naive conceptions of freedom) believe themselves immune to the immortal power of forces like wealth. Ancients who worshipped Venus knew what they were doing; modernists who unwittingly worship her are locked into smug self-denial and blissful, disastrous ignorance. This chapter will focus upon how gods like Mars and Venus are free to behave once humans deny their existence.

Economics may not seem like the most natural subject to address in a book about atheism, but it is the burden of this chapter to unmask how economic realities arise from and generate religious convictions. The world's dominant economic systems today are not abstract ideas with no impact on real life, but reach deep into the soul of every human alive in the twenty-first century. What is more, beneath the surface of economic method and theory there is a theology, a set of religious beliefs and commitments, an unacknowledged devotion to what once were called gods. Only after Christendom did such an economics evolve, and only after Christendom are gods like Mars and Venus freed from the restraining effects of Christian principles and the pretence of Christian morality. In order to get to grips with the sheer extent of their power, this chapter will focus explicitly on contemporary, everyday examples of the influence they exert, and is likely to have a more journalistic style. As John Maynard Keynes wrote in 1936, 'The ideas of economists and political philosophers, both when they are right and when they are wrong, are more powerful than is commonly understood. Indeed, the world is ruled by little else. Practical men, who believe themselves to be quite exempt from any intellectual influences, are usually slaves of some defunct economist.'[3] How does that unwittingly slavish subservience to the gods manifest itself today?

Economics and the Evolution of Capitalism

'Economics' and 'ecology' are both words with Greek roots. Both refer to the word for 'house' or 'household' (*oikos*). Ecology refers to the logic (*logos*) of the household. Economics refers to the law (*nomos*) that governs a household. Since the law must be based upon the logic, economic laws *should* arise naturally from ecological reality. Ecology, in other words, refers to the resources available to a household, and economics refers to the ways in which those resources are managed. So, above all else, economists are 'eco-lawyers' whose role is to ensure that the resources at our disposal are governed well. Obviously, the current economic and ecological crises that engulf the globe suggest that those responsible for our 'household' have not governed well. However, that depends upon whom we choose to include within our household. So long as those with power and wealth are concerned only with their peers, then Mars and Venus continue to deliver what they promise. Those outside the household, however, may experience Mars and Venus as Beast and Whore.

The most pressing eco-ethical issue facing the world today, then, is the question of who is in and who is out of the household. Logically (i.e. according to ecology), everyone on the planet shares the fate of our planet. Legally (i.e. according to economics), there is a crude and brutal hierarchy of inclusion. At its centre is a highly privileged minority; somewhere within its compass are the average middle-class westerners; and banished to the unmetaphysical outside are the countless disposable humans whose well-being can be sacrificed for the sake of those within the household. The umbrella term for the eco-laws that created and maintain this current state of affairs is 'capitalism'. Only when Christendom disintegrated as a single entity could capitalism take root in western society. In essence, capitalism refers to a post-Christendom structure of economic practice in which:

- *Private owners* use their resources (land, factories, transport systems) to make profit and accumulate further resources.
- The aim to *make profit* (rather than aiming to meet human needs) is perceived as the best way to meet human needs.
- *Wage labour* operates: workers sell their time and energy to any private profit-hunters willing to buy it.
- *Market economy* is required; the larger the market, the more effective the system.

My intention here is not to offer yet another denunciation of capitalism, as though it were an option we could reject. I take the term to refer to an economic era rather than a vice. Capitalism is not only an economic theory but a social structure that shapes human life, thought and relationships. In the absence of an eco-crisis forcing the breakdown of society beyond conceivable repair, those who wish to escape capitalism are compelled to evolve their way out of it.

During Christendom, a market was a meeting place between those who bought and those who sold, an entity with a human face in which causes and effects were straightforward and where individuals could be held accountable for their actions. With the passing of Christendom and the establishment of nation states, the Market grew to develop an identity of its own. The Market became a force of nature, an entity that followed natural laws. Any who suffered as a result of the Market's behaviour could no longer be viewed as victims of injustice or unfairness. The Market is merely part of nature, and those who do not flourish under the Market economy are simply unlucky, underdeveloped or lazy. An economist may study its patterns and movements as a meteorologist studies the weather, so that its forces may be harnessed to good effect. But can this formidable power of nature, able to wreak both human benefit and sheer devastation, ever be harnessed? Traditionally the two major strands of capitalism are split over this question.

- *Free-rein capitalism* is the belief that the Market must be free of all interference and regulation; to benefit from the Market, humanity must submit to it. This has been variously described as 'free-market capitalism', 'laissez-faire capitalism', 'savage capitalism', 'disaster capitalism', etc.
- *Managed capitalism* is a system whose advocates do not trust the Market to be fair, and who seek to impose financial, trade and industrial laws to ensure human beings are treated fairly.

In the years following the Second World War, various brands of managed capitalism were favoured in the West: nations' natural resources were owned by the nation rather than powerful corporations, trade unions protected workers from exploitation, public money was spent on national health services and welfare benefits, and strong regulations prevented banks and businesses from gaining excessive power. The last generation, however, has witnessed a widespread shift towards free-rein capitalism, marked in particular by:

- Deregulation (ceasing to regulate how banks and businesses conduct their affairs)
- Privatization (selling publicly owned enterprises to private companies)
- Cuts (in government spending on benefits, health care and education)

In 2008 the world was shaken by the greatest economic catastrophe for almost a century, seen by many as the result of rampant, unrestrained capitalism. The specific cause was a mortgage value crisis in the US, a result of the inability of millions of citizens to keep up repayments on mortgages they should never have been sold, for houses that plummeted in value. A loss of confidence by US investors quickly led to a liquidity crisis that soon went global. In the non-real world of finance, it forced multi-trillion-dollar bailouts for banks, nosedives in stock market values, and threatened the collapse of major institutions. In the real lives of real people, job losses, benefit cuts and forced evictions made their unwelcome intrusions. Free-rein capitalism had failed. Or so it seemed.

After 2008

Despite the fact that the 2008 crisis is widely held as a consequence of deregulation,[4] far from abandoning this strategy, governments appear to be pushing it ever more fiercely.[5] Although the free-rein capitalists contend that wealth will spread to all, it is worth noting that before the crisis of 2008 the wealthiest and most powerful '1 per cent' of the US population (which includes those who had caused the crisis) enjoyed 34.6 per cent of the nation's wealth; after the crisis that figure had risen to 37.1 per cent in 2009.

How did the voting public respond to the corporate plunder of their resources? The most notorious reaction has been the Tea Party, a fake grass-roots movement which pointed the finger at those outside the household. Matt Taibbi's electrifying narrative shows how Tea Party champion Sarah Palin famously used the language of *we* (the white, working, traditional small-town Americans) against *they* who caused the financial disaster *we* now face. But this *they* are not the 'corporate titans' who rigged the economy against the honest hard-working Americans, but the lazy, needy recipients of welfare who cannot afford to keep the homes they were encouraged to buy. The Tea Party have always remained silent about the US government's bailing out of the banks that had caused the crisis. But when President Obama planned to spend a mere $75 billion (less than 1 per cent of the bank bailout) to help families facing eviction to stay in their homes,[6] there emerged the massive public outcry from which the Tea Party movement was born. Here, Palin parades as a priestess of Venus. Not merely by her widely celebrated sex appeal to middle-aged men, nor simply by her appeal to the maternal lifeblood of her nation's economy (the 'soccer moms'), but by her contempt for those towards the margins of her nation's household, and her veneration of those towards the centre.

Owen Jones' explosive survey, *Chavs*, traces the identical dynamic in British politics, unmasking the workings of the British propaganda machine, in unselfconsciously theological language, as '*the Demonization of the Working Class*'. For Jones, the demonization of the other is designed to promote the cultural supremacy of those towards the centre of power, to foster scorn for those towards the periphery and to protect the hierarchical structures of free-rein capitalism. In the wake of the financial crisis of 2008, Jones argues, 'What the media and the politicians have been able to do is redirect people's growing anger from the people that caused the crisis to the neighbour down the street.' The worst kind of neighbour is the 'chav', the under-educated lazy member of a 'feral underclass', widely portrayed as parasitic upon the hard-working middle class. Jones paints the alternative picture of a parasitic middle and upper class, feeding off the poorest and most voiceless members of British society. 'As a government of million-aires led by an Old Etonian prepares to further demolish the living standards of millions of working class people,' he concludes, 'the time has rarely been so ripe for a new wave of class politics.'[7]

Remembering that economics is the question of how we manage the resources at our disposal for the benefit of the household, it is worth revisiting the question of whom a radically free-rein capitalism includes within its household:

- The third world 'they' are comprised of disposable human resources who are definitely way outside the household.
- On the periphery, or begging at the gate, are the lazy citizens who receive undeserved assistance from the state, 'chavs' who contribute nothing, drain our resources, raise our taxes.
- Within the compass are the small-town Americans and members of the British middle class, the 'soccer moms', who believe their struggle towards affluence is hampered only by those further from the centre than themselves.
- At the centre stand the '1 per cent', those whose financial power games are too complex to be detected by the majority, and whose control of the popular press guarantees popular igno-rance of this fact.

Venus, Neoliberal Economics and the Financial Meltdown

Neoliberal capitalism is an umbrella term describing a recent form of economics in which governments are expected to interfere in the lives of citizens in order to keep them subservient to the domi-nance of the Market. By 'neoliberal', I refer to a new (neo) convic-tion that the market should be free (liberal) from democratic restraints. Neoliberalism itself has emerged precisely in tandem with the era of post-Christendom, the economic dimension of a world newly liberated from Christendom ideals and values.[8] But in this light, modern atheism is in reality a long way from being genuinely atheist. The Market itself has become a deity, not in the vague metaphorical sense that modern people idolize money, nor even because the Market displays the omnipotence, omnipresence and omniscience we traditionally associate with the god of Christendom.[9] Venus herself is the true deity behind the Market, not because she is the goddess of financial transactions, but because her seductive but hidden influence is deeply rooted, highly effective and virtually impossible to challenge. To get to grips with market dominance of Venus I turn to a reading of the current state of economics offered by Philip Mirowski, professor of economics and the history and philosophy of science at the University of Notre Dame.[10]

In the neoliberal economics that now dominates western culture, Mirowski identifies a capitalism that is neither restrained by governments, nor given free rein by governments. Instead, says Mirowski, the power of the Market is such that governments are not only powerless to resist the Market, but are among the very mechanisms that uphold its dominance. When the financial crisis of 2008 proved to all that the Market had failed, how and why was this not universally recognized and addressed by economists? Governments sank trillions of dollars into economies on the brink of collapse. Surely, this cold, hard, empirical fact shows that unregulated capitalism does not work. And yet, claims Mirowski, 'in the throes of the red-misted nightmare, it looks as if the crisis, otherwise so virulent and corrosive, didn't manage to kill even one spurious economic notion.'[11] Despite various pledges to tighten regulations here and there, no major changes have been proposed by any leading economist. Surely, if the Market ever was a god, it has been kept artificially alive only with the aid of public money – revealing that the Market is a long way from divine.

However, if we see Venus as the force that keeps the Market running smoothly, drawing wealth from the impoverished nobodies outside the household into the arms of those towards the privileged centre, then the 2008 crisis has not been a crisis at all. As noted above, the wealthiest '1 per cent' of the US population came out of the 'crisis' considerably wealthier, at the expense of their underlings. Venus proved herself a worthy goddess. For the '1 per cent' whom the Market is configured to serve, there was no market failure and no crash. The only crisis was the momentary fall of the curtain, as the rest of the world – if they were looking – caught a glimpse of Mars and Venus as Beast and Whore. Governments did not intervene to revive markets, because they were already mere mechanisms of the Market itself. The crisis of 2008 did not bring Venus to her knees; she was controlling the game all along, negotiating the paths of human progress with ruthless efficiency. She continues unflinchingly to fulfil her function, serving those with power and exploiting those without.

The masses are powerless to respond because Venus has instilled within them the deeply rooted inability to see the world as it really is. What *would* we expect to see if Venus were quietly commanding the worship and pulling the strings of western society? How does the world look when otherness is banished, and alternative possible worlds are concealed behind the illusory limits that hedge in our freedom?

Governments

Notions like government by consent, democracy, and the rule of law – all great triumphs of the Enlightenment – cannot be crudely set aside without mass public disturbance. Instead, under neoliberal capitalism, these pillars are cleverly reconfigured to serve the Market. No longer would we be 'citizens' but 'customers' of government services; democratic elections would be won no longer by ideals and policies, but by brands and advertising strategies;[12] those advertising strategies would be financed by corporations who thereby purchase the government (and the politicians) they require; fairness in law would be bought rather than assumed. Slowly but surely, *Homo sapiens* would devolve into *Homo economicus*, and – though remaining intelligent, sophisticated, effective servants of the Market – they would lose the insight, the language and the appetite required to make any kind of stand against the steady expansion of the reign of Venus.

Economics

Economics as an academic discipline is gradually severed from its ecological roots. It will diminish the otherness of other people and of nature, compressing both into resources to be exploited. If Venus ruled the world, her worshippers would barely notice their own gradual regress from human beings into human resources, and no amount of empirical scientific evidence would be sufficient to prevent the powerful from emptying nature of its finite resources. Economists would be incapable of imagining any genuine alternative to neoliberal capitalism, because the way that capitalism is taught would itself be determined by those with an interest in maintaining the status quo.[13] This has already been achieved in the university by the removal of the history and philosophy of economics, first from graduate and then from undergraduate courses, and the corporate takeover of academic economics journals. The result is a profession with a narrowly defined view of economics, and a genuine inability to consider alternatives to prevailing norms.[14] Academic economists who do not conform to the neoliberal model slowly lose their public voice, their professional reputation, and ultimately, their jobs.

Protest

In a society that treasures freedom and democracy, any hint of totalitarian regime is intolerable to the customer. Political philosopher Sheldon Wolin contends that under neoliberal capitalism citizens are victims of an inverted totalitarianism, in which they are not so much subjugated and oppressed as distracted from serious political engagement, diverted into obsession with the trivial. When corporations dominate a government, this is accepted as natural rather than criminal. The populace is kept in a state of apathetic indifference rather than brutal subjugation, and despite all this, people uphold the unshakeable delusion that theirs is a model for civilized democracy worldwide. For how long totalitarianism will remain inverted remains to be seen.

The human incapacity to offer any resistance to Venus is brought about by gradual, comprehensive and diverse means. This is by no means to suggest a conspiracy theory, in the form of a deliberate policy on the part of world's secret leaders. It is, rather, to observe that those in power know what is good for them. Key aspects of popular belief in Venus would nevertheless include infinite tell-tale signs, for instance:

- Media would present as heroic those people and values that grease the wheels of neoliberalism, and would ridicule any who question it.
- Education would devolve into assessing people's ability to pass tests, thereby conditioning them into subconscious compliance with the way things are and silently robbing them of the opportunity to think differently.
- Demands for moral goodness are deflected away from anything that would question the piety of the Market, and demonize those who (like benefits recipients) hamper the neoliberal system.
- Regardless of how they acquire their fortunes, the wealthy (including corporate gamblers who caused the crisis and were rewarded with public money) become people to celebrate and admire.
- Police and armies are used no longer to protect the public, but to protect the wealthy. Any who do protest economic abuses of those in power can be criminalized under anti-terrorism laws.
- Governments are compelled to subsidise enterprises that plunder finite resources and accelerate economic catastrophe, and are empowered to silence any protest.

Under the reign of Venus, human beings are compelled to worship the goddess who destroys them, oblivious to their own liturgical commitments, unable to see what is really happening in the world. Throughout history, various wings of resistance have helped to curb the excesses of those in power, but after Christendom's hold weakened, even these movements have been incorporated. The ideology of Venus gushes through every conceivable channel, through art[15] and music, literature and fiction, cinema and TV, through social media and advertising. An arbitrary glance across potential sources of resistance highlights the deep and widespread influence of Venus.

Speaking Truth to Power

Religions

While religions have long been a means of drawing people whose collective voice commands a hearing, a host of neoliberal virtues have imperceptibly sunk themselves more deeply into the modern psyche than religions have been able to reach. Take the virtue, 'freedom of expression'. Where once the philosopher would enjoin us to 'know thyself', the Muslim would entreat us to 'submit thyself', and the Christian encourage us to 'deny thyself', neoliberalism repeatedly commands us to 'express thyself'.

For example, religious adherents who demand their right to wear the cross in the workplace are by no means acting in courageous accordance with the central tenets of the faith they proclaim. (As though Christian faith is better expressed through the jewellery you wear rather than the life you live.) Generating their concern is no core Christian conviction, but a more deeply rooted, underlying obedience to the neoliberal commandment: 'Express thyself.' For such believers, the true object of their worship is not Christ but Venus. Churches may then view the defence of Christian rights (like self-expression) as a bold form of political action, rather than, say, engaging with the raft of horrific social and political injustices that Venus leaves in her wake.

The only religions Venus leaves intact are westernised forms of non-violent, peace-loving faiths imported from the East. While such faiths may allow modern westerners to express their lofty spirituality and gentle morality, any examination of these westernized faiths reveals that their very passivity leaves them ill-equipped to offer any effective resistance to the injustices that plague our world. Like all in a democracy (including even peace-loving Buddhists and Jainists) who remain ignorant or silent about the violent action of their own governments, they become default perpetrators of corporate violence.

Just as the religions in the Roman Empire were frogmarched into the Pantheon where they were subjugated to the gods of Rome, so in the neoliberal economy, even Christianity has complied with the religious dictates of the empire.

Journalism

Journalism is a major means by which governments might be kept in check by keeping an active voting public informed. In order to maintain the illusion that this remains the case, news reports are usually presented as being 'objective', meaning that an argument is presumed to have two sides and both must have an equal hearing. However, as the former war correspondent Chris Hedges points out, as a journalist, 'when you are "objective," it means that, in your reasonableness, you ultimately embrace and defend the status quo . . . It is safe and painless to produce "balanced" news. It is very unsafe, as the best journalists will tell you, to produce truth.'[16] The sentiment is echoed in the UK by George Monbiot of the *Guardian*, who advises would-be journalists:

> What the corporate or institutional world wants [is] a reliable tool, someone who can think, but not for herself: who can think instead for the institution. You can do what you believe only if that belief happens to coincide with the aims of the corporation, not just once, but consistently, across the years (it is a source of wonder . . . how many people's beliefs just happen to match the demands of institutional power, however those demands may twist and turn, after they've been in the company for a year or two).[17]

Far from supporting any notion of democratic accountability, if Venus ruled the world, then beneath the veneer of objectivity, journalism would quietly uphold the belief system of the powerful. As Hedges continues:

> These journalists and editors are besotted with their access to the powerful. They look at themselves as players, part of the inside elite. They went to the same elite colleges. They eat at the same restaurants. They go to the same parties and dinners. They live in the same exclusive neighbourhoods. Their children go to the same schools. They are, if one concedes that propaganda is a vital tool for the power elite, important to the system.[18]

If journalists and other news media outlets are designed to inform the public and challenge those in power, under Venus they would misrepresent the world to the public, and defend the interests of power.

Science

Surely, cold, hard, scientific facts should be sufficient to motivate reasonable members of a democracy to prevent their governments from accelerating climate change and pursuing models of economics that have clearly failed. Surely, science is an objective pursuit that can be trusted to correct faulty or dangerous courses of political action. How could Venus possibly assert any authority over the untouchable supremacy of scientific fact?

Consider the technology of fracking, the method of fracturing rock in order to extract increasingly scarce carbon-based fuels. The scientific genius required to perfect this method can blinker us from the reality that it constitutes a mad scramble to scrape fossil fuel from wherever it can be found. The staggering technological ingenuity of fracking draws attention away from the fact that, on any objective view, it is the frantic behaviour of the alcoholic, desperately seeking in any corner the substance that will accelerate his demise. At a time when the human race should be attempting to withdraw from dependence on nonrenewable energy, science is all too easily pressed into the service of Venus. Science, funded by the Market, accepts its place in the neoliberal hierarchy, and forfeits its status as objective guardian of truth.

For instance, the Chief Scientific Advisor to the UK Department of Environment concludes his advice that, in the current climate, scientists should be 'avoiding suggesting that policies are either right or wrong; and being willing to make the voice of science heard by engaging with the mechanisms already available through science advisory committees, by working with embedded advisers (such as myself), and by being the voice of reason, rather than dissent, in the public arena.'[19] Monbiot paraphrases the sentiment: 'Shut up, speak through me, don't dissent, or your behaviour will ensure that science becomes irrelevant.'[20]

Class

If social classes once provided a communal sense of identity and a source of resistance against those who would exploit them, Venus has now made class identity impossible. In a culture dominated by the Market, the working class are encouraged to better themselves by becoming middle class, and those who do not make the grade find themselves in a more deplorable state than before. Membership of a working class is no longer a source of pride. No longer is it possible to be poor but proud, since economics has hijacked pride, taking it out of the hands of the working class. As Owen Jones has pointed out, the archetypal working-class figure is no longer the hard-working blue-collar male factory worker, but the low-paid part-time female shelf-stacker.[21] Mirowski agrees, noting the key neoliberal doctrine that *'there is no such thing as a social class, and most decidedly, "economic" classes (working class, upper class, proletariat) do not exist.'*[22] The consequences barely need spelling out. If there is no working class, those with the lowest incomes in a modern society may be regarded no longer as full citizens, but as individuals who have failed to achieve middle class. Any potential political action on the basis of class is thwarted by the denial of a class system. Now that 'we' are all middle class, 'we' does not include certain people. Theologically, as I have pointed out, the incarnate Christ resides among those expelled from full citizenship in the modern West. In other words, Venus has quietly airbrushed Christ out of existence.

Atheism

Throughout this book, I have claimed that atheism is by definition a source of resistance to those in power – in particular, when the powerful rely upon gods to uphold their regime. Asking *whether* these gods exist is less important than asking *how* they exist. They are both idols (made, if not by human hands, then by human imagination) and demons (dehumanizing their own worshippers). These divinities are not mere metaphors of natural principles, since their power extends too deeply through too many dimensions and remains largely imperceptible, inescapable and unstoppable. Mars and Venus have proven themselves capable of overpowering human rationality, and exist to the extent that we see their effects in the real world. The task of the atheist, then, is not primarily to deny the objective, theoretical, ontological existence of these gods, but rather to prove they are not gods by threatening them, warring with them, making them bleed, remortalizing them.

Again, the genius of Venus has been to weaken atheism with diversionary tactics: namely, to keep self-perceived heroic atheists preoccupied with the war against the decrepit god of Christendom, a god whose real power in the world has long since faded. This frees the gods who are actually devastating our world to continue unimpeded by the very forces who valiantly claim to oppose them. The atheists who respond, 'But Mars and Venus do not exist', have failed to understand what gods are and how their existence is manifest. If Christendom was the era in which Mars and Venus disguised themselves in Christian fancy dress, in post-Christendom all pretence of Christian conviction is dropped. Instead, concealing themselves in the garb of a carefully crafted secular liberalism, Mars and Venus now operate with minimal restraints. As the poet Baudelaire famously declared, 'The most beautiful ruse of the devil is to persuade you that he does not exist.'[23] This is the essence of neoliberalism, and its overwhelming victory in blinkering the scope of human awareness. Beneath the radar of our perception, the gods are free to do as they please.

Conclusion

In sum, once Christendom's god fell from public favour, the Market became an independent, uncontrollable force in its own right. Such an entity, though wrought by human creativity, has all the characteristics of the Roman gods that shape human destiny, are widely revered, and (in the modern world) rarely understood. This chapter has argued that Venus and Mars conspire to shape human destiny, and that neoliberal capitalism is the means by which they would exert their influence most fully. As such, the 2008 crisis was a theological rather than an economic crisis: this was the global, ethical, economic and ecological consequence of the widespread worship of Mars and Venus.

These old Roman gods, nevertheless, do face pockets of resist-ance, voices which draw attention to the distinction between the wealthiest '1 per cent' and the masses, between 'the rich and the rest of us'.[24] *If economics constitutes the laws that govern a household, then the full extent of that household must be opened up to include or to benefit those who are currently outside it.* This is the economic dimen-sion of engaging well with otherness, of opening one's world to those who are excluded from it. It is an approach fundamentally at odds with the ideology of an empire, in which wealth is brought from the periphery to the centre, and laws are passed out from the centre (where people may flout them) to the periphery (where people must obey them). To interrupt the smooth running of this imperial machine is to defy the manipulative rule of Venus and to invite the vengeful wrath of Mars. *Such sedition against the gods of our age is genuine, perceptive, intelligent, courageous atheism in its most radical form. It is an atheism wholly lacking among those who seek to promote modern atheism in the twenty-first century.*

The greatest ethical question facing us today is whether humanity can muster its collective strength to overcome the dominance of Mars and Venus, or whether those gods will drive us headlong into oblivion. Capitalism, in its most savage form, is doomed. There are only so many times benefits can be cut, only a finite number of public companies to privatize, only a limited number of safety regu-lations to remove. The only question is whether its displacement will be a result of a deliberate remodelling of society or a result of a yet greater economic or ecological catastrophe. The tragedy of the twenty-first century is that the ecological catastrophe looks more likely. In light of the mass destructive behaviour of today's gods, despite the fact that Mars and Venus have dragged humanity into hopelessness and servitude, the New Atheists fail even to identify our most lethal and immediate divine enemies. Of course, they are not consciously colluding with Mars and Venus. Much more likely is that the New Atheists are the unwitting servants of the gods, embodying the servile ignorance they so deplore in the mindless medieval adherents of Christendom's belief structure. After Chris-tendom, I claim, a new and unacknowledged servitude becomes the default belief of the day.

Such servitude is by no means exclusive to the New Atheists. Neoliberalism has reduced the entire study of economics to the study of one dominant method. Economics, we have seen, no longer focuses upon history or philosophy, closing down alternative patterns of economic thought and concerning itself instead with refining one economic *method*. That is, maximizing the efficiency of a system around hallowed and unquestionable convictions. In the neoliberal sense, the divine supremacy of the Market is the dominant conviction, and its method is ever more thoroughly extended and applied throughout every conceivable aspect of the post-Christendom world. Neoliberalism thus favours further method as the response to the 2008 crisis. Interestingly, the word's Greek root combines *meta* (after) and *hodos* (way), the driving metaphor being the ruthless pursuit of a course of action. However, it is important to note, as one Plato scholar does, that the technical meaning of 'method' is rooted in the notion of 'pilgrimage to the presence of a goddess'.[25] The prime candidate for the goddess demanding such veneration in the world of neoliberal economics barely needs stating. The biblical alternative to servitude arises from similar Greek origins, *ex* (out of) and *hodos* (way), giving the concept of *exodus*, a way out. For a new exodus to be effective it must offer an escape not from capitalism, but from Venus.

This exodus does not begin by outlining a political manifesto for a new world order or a detailed plan for revolution, because to do so would simply be to keep us enslaved inside the projected futures dictated by method.[26] A genuine exodus comes only with the quest to reject our dominant theisms, to encounter the other, and in so doing, to enter an otherwise unimaginably alternative world. In a post-Christendom, neoliberal economy, this exodus is as politically dangerous as that of the Hebrews in the Old Testament, and as impossible as the new exodus that is resurrection in the New Testament.

8.

The Age of Encounter

This book has suggested an alternative to the either/or choice between the distant and disinterested god of *deism*, and the interfering micro-manager god of *theism*. Deism portrays God as the absent father, who plants his generative seed and hurries off-radar when his offspring need his support. Theism portrays an omnipotent do-gooder so busy answering prayers concerning lost keys, exam results and the distant relatives of churchgoers that he cannot save the lives of the ten million children who die needlessly every year. An eternity spent in the company of either of these deities would hardly be described as 'paradise'. But neither of these deities can be found in the writings of Jewish or Christian Scripture. Throughout this book I have tried to portray the alternative view of a God whose attributes of power and love are consistent with one another, with Scripture and with the world as we experience it.

This is a God powerful enough to create a universe whose complexities extend beyond each new scientific grasp at finality. It is also a God whose executive power is deeply embedded within an ontological dimension, a dimension concerned with 'being'. That 'being' is found in engaging well with other people within one's household/community, and other people beyond that community. The capacity to encounter otherness beyond the world of the familiar is inseparable from the ability to listen well to history, to wonder genuinely at the natural world, to think seriously and openly about global justice.

However, as Saint Paul observed in his own day, the God he worshipped is not the only god exerting force in the world. 'The God of this age,' he told the Christians of Corinth, 'has blinded the minds of non-believers.' The result is an inability to encounter the genuine, world-changing, life-affirming hope offered by the outsider-Christ. In the last chapter, I argued that the figure of Venus plays precisely such a role in shaping the ideology of citizens and subjects, be it throughout the ancient Roman Empire or the contemporary world of neoliberalism, destroying their capacity to engage with the other. This need not be regarded as a mystical, supernatural spell cast upon weak-minded peasants, but an ideology so deeply rooted in the psyche as to remain largely beyond question.

At the crudest level, we see this in modern advertising. Vance Packard's 1957 classic, *The Hidden Persuaders*, uncovered the psychological and subliminal techniques employed by advertisers to create needs out of nothing in order to keep the economy running smoothly. Fifty years later, and the modern consumer is more media-savvy, world-aware and harder to con – requiring an updated version of the approach Packard had identified. Today, we must be manipulated into believing that we are too smart for the manipulator, an approach known as 'murketing'.[1] Behind this dynamic, Packard's insight remains true to life. The average consumer must be made to feel inadequate: too fat, too thin, too ugly, too out-dated, etc. The inadequacy thus conjured up compels its victims to purchase the item on offer in order to redeem themselves. Once our needs have been met, new needs must be created so that we will never feel adequate, but must continue to buy our way out of personal inadequacy and social unworthiness.

This has more than a hint of the Christendom practice of priests selling forgiveness to guilt-ridden peasants. Both in this medieval form of selling indulgences, and in the updated version where divine remedies for human depravity are sold by the crudest contemporary evangelists, the Christendom power dynamic remains in force. Christopher Hitchens takes great delight in stealing Fulke Greville's famous insight that human beings are 'created sick – commanded to be well'.[2] (Presumably, Hitchens repeatedly fails to acknowledge its origin since it comes from a deeply thoughtful and committed Protestant Christian.) While this may be a valid critique of some Christendom missionary strategies, it is infinitely more applicable in today's world to the advertising strategies required by Venus. Advertisers pedal the belief that all humans are unworthy until they have bought the latest product – and the moment they have complied, they no longer have the latest product because it has been updated. The capitalist-shaped human, distracted away from 'being' and towards consuming, is a human created (and kept) sick, and perpetually commanded to be well. Hitchens and co, as priests of Mars and Venus, remain silent about the hidden indulgences their own gods require.

This is not simply a critique of advertising, as though mass advertisers were free to employ alternative tactics. Advertising is merely one manifestation of the entire culture of neoliberal capitalism, as advertisers manipulate individuals to open their souls like countries opening their economies to foreign investors. Once inside, the alien power dominates its host, instilling within them ways of being that, nevertheless, sometimes leave victims with the 'unhomely' feeling that they are living someone else's life. The diminished capacity to engage with actual human otherness, ironically, leaves modern individuals forever alienated even from themselves and compressed into the dominant social blueprint for what a human being should be. Heidegger calls this phenomenon the 'they-self'. The further we retreat from encountering otherness, the harder it is to imagine an alternative world, a world beyond the cycle of personal, economic and ecological despair to which Venus and Mars consign the masses and the planet.

The anthropologist David Graeber paints a bleak but realistic picture of how the capitalist belief system (both the military might of Mars and the 'propaganda engines' of Venus) evolved to prevent alternative worldviews from flourishing:

[I]t could well be said that the last thirty years have seen the construction of a vast bureaucratic apparatus for the creation and maintenance of hopelessness, a giant machine designed, first and foremost, to destroy any sense of possible alternative futures. At its root is a veritable obsession on the part of the rulers of the world . . . with ensuring that social movements cannot be seen to grow, flourish, or propose alternatives; that those who challenge existing power arrangements can never, under any circumstances, be perceived to win . . . To do so requires creating a vast apparatus of armies, prisons, police, various forms of private security firms and police and military intelligence apparatus, and propaganda engines of every conceivable variety, most of which do not attack alternatives directly so much as create a pervasive climate of fear, jingoistic conformity, and simple despair that renders any thought of changing the world seem an idle fantasy.[3]

Graeber is one of several key activists who realize the quest for global justice is theoretically possible, practical and achievable and yet, somehow, condemned never to arrive. If, morally, to reorder the world's economic systems requires little meaningful sacrifice, in reality tiny changes to economic structure are opposed with disproportionate force. The anger and frustration of activists like Graeber arises from precisely what Jesus of Nazareth commended as a 'hunger and thirst for righteousness', a compulsion to steal fairness from an empire whose being depends on the physical, political, military, ideological and, above all, subconscious oppression of its subjects.

In this light, a genuinely subversive atheism (which, I have argued, includes Christianity) faces a near impossible task in seeking to encounter the other. To encounter otherness is an act of self-sacrifice, an event that calls one's worldview into question. To 'en-counter' is to experience in one's own-most being, a reality *counter* to one's own. If that counter-position is in any way valid, then it calls into question all that we assume of our own worldview, all that we have achieved and treasure, all that we hope and aim for. This kind of genuine encounter is a painful, harrowing enterprise. Though it is commonplace to make a great virtue of encountering otherness with an open mind, all too easily such encounter becomes a self-delusional sham, crystallized into a set of unwritten secular commandments.

The Call to Artificial Encounter

The critiques offered below are not simply criticisms of the virtues treasured by secular humanism. Instead, I try to highlight the sheer contradiction between our treasured strategies for openness to the other, and the underlying compulsion to withdraw from the other. Secular calls to encounter the other, I argue, are based ultimately on compliance to the gods of the age: an inability to imagine alternatives, an aversion from the gaze of the other, a withdrawal from the demands of the other, a refusal to see that this is the case, and an unselfconscious submission to the gods whose existence we deny. My claim is not that we are all as individuals morally guilty, but that the default setting for an unreflective human being is to be a living, breathing, passionate expression of the spirit of our age with an inbuilt revulsion for genuine encounter.

Freedom of Choice

Whether the options are breakfast cereals or governments, choice is widely treasured as a right for the modern secular individual. The notion of choice is itself a complex phenomenon, but in a liberal democracy populated with literate individuals any form of dictatorship over thought, religion, politics or shopping is intolerable. Yet our age – like any other – has its gods, gods with appetites that need satisfying, who set rules the masses must obey. How then can such gods exist in a world that treasures freedom of choice?

The gods of our age do not wear nametags. Modern gods, I have proposed, assert their power most effectively by remaining incognito, and are worshipped most faithfully by those who remain most ignorant of their own acts of worship. Such gods function by instilling within their subjects the deep-seated belief that their blind captivity is a hard-won freedom. Neil Postman famously made a similar point by comparing the worldviews of George Orwell's *1984* (in which Big Brother explicitly and violently forces citizens into compliance) and Aldous Huxley's *Brave New World* (in which the masses are subconsciously conditioned by subtle programmes of mind-conditioning):

> What Orwell feared were those who would ban books. What Huxley feared was that there would be no reason to ban a book, for there would be no one who wanted to read one. Orwell feared those who would deprive us of information. Huxley feared those who would give us so much that we would be reduced to passivity and egotism. Orwell feared that the truth would be concealed from us. Huxley feared the truth would be drowned in a sea of irrelevance. Orwell

feared we would become a captive culture. Huxley feared we would become a trivial culture . . . As Huxley remarked in *Brave New World Revisited*, the civil libertarians and rationalists who are ever on the alert to oppose tyranny 'failed to take into account man's almost infinite appetite for distractions.' In *1984*, Orwell added, people are controlled by inflicting pain. In *Brave New World*, they are controlled by inflicting pleasure. In short, Orwell feared that what we fear will ruin us. Huxley feared that our desire will ruin us.[4]

In this light, Orwell and Huxley represent the works of Mars and Venus respectively. The implication is that Huxley's narrative is more fitting for modern western society (although with the rapid depletion of nature's resources, and the growing oppression of the lower classes, the vision of Orwell and the brutality of Mars may well return to prominence). From advertising fast food to mobilizing an election PR machine, the logic remains the same: while manufacturing the illusion that citizens are rational, free-thinking, informed members of a civilized society, advertisers manipulate citizens to make irrational choices founded upon ignorance.

How then has belief in freedom of choice become so widespread? Any consumer seeking to purchase any product, it seems, is faced with an infinite number of options. Infinity, however, can exist within *given limits*: between the numbers one and two stretches an infinity of possible other numbers. If our freedom of choice really were a universal 360-degree freedom, we could still find an infinite number of options between the given limits of, say, 180 and 181 alone. Mass corporations and governments may force-feed citizens the belief that freedom of choice is a good thing, but they rely upon citizens remaining hopelessly blinkered to the world of possibility that exists outside the given limits. I suspect it is for this reason that the choice between Choco-pops and Cocoa-pops seems like a real freedom, as treasured as the choice between electoral candidates Tweedle Dum and Tweedle Dee. Both candidates may exhibit the same subservient compliance to the gods of the Market; the only political difference between the candidates (be they Labour or Tory, Democrat or Republican) is the difference allowed to stretch between given limits.[5] How might the world beyond the given limits appear? It cannot be allowed to appear, since as Graeber pointed out above, any community, any enterprise, any religion that enables citizens to imagine a genuinely alternative world will find itself closed down by the propaganda or the muscle of the very empire that manufactures belief in freedom of choice.

Anti-Imperialism

Our enlightened sensibilities have taught us that empires are immoral. Anyone familiar with the original *Star Wars* trilogy knows why: the 'empire' is run by intergalactic bullies with English accents; heroes are the members of the 'Rebel Alliance'. The USA is a nation founded upon rebellion against [the British] Empire; that America could itself be an empire is a truth intolerable to countless contemporary citizens. Empires expand, invade and conquer – practices no longer acceptable to the enlightened inhabitants of an advanced civilization. Any civilized modern individual finds the practice of conquest repulsive.

Whether predators mark their territories with urine or coffee shops, conquest is the expansion of territory allowing one group access to resources already controlled by another. Modernity has failed to suppress the primal human instinct for conquest, which is rooted in the genetic drive for survival. Once the local resources available to a group are no longer sufficient to satisfy the growing demands of that group, new territory must be captured. This, it seems, was not only the case for the most primitive of human people-groups, since by the height of the Roman Empire the desire for perpetual expansion could not be deactivated. As Petroneus points out, 'The conquering Roman now held the whole world, sea and land and the course of sun and moon. But he was not satisfied . . . If there were . . . any land that promised a yield of yellow gold, that place was Rome's enemy, fate stood ready for the sorrows of war, and the quest for wealth went on.'[6]

It is difficult not to identify a link here between the power centres of the modern western military machine and the corner of the planet sitting on 80 per cent of the planet's 'black gold'. While Romans prided themselves on military conquest, the recent Gulf Wars required public construal of military action as a regrettable necessity rather than a glorious opportunity. Regardless of the motives, justifications and outcomes of these military adventures, modern people do not consciously support such crude and brutal conquest. James Cameron's blockbuster movie *Avatar* demonstrates such evolved sensibilities.

Avatar tells the story of a distant planet plundered for its resources by earthly (US) military forces, and an 'undeveloped' primitive people who successfully repel the colonists. The narrative immerses the audience in the world of the 'other', until that other world feels natural and precious, and the invaders (deliberately portrayed in US military terms) are revealed as the bad guys. The movie is largely concerned with establishing this shift in perception – as Adam Cohen of the *New York Times* rightly saw. The invading troops, unlike the story's main characters, have not experienced the 'humanity' of the natives – which enables them to treat the natives as mere obstacles. 'All of this draws on a well-known principle of totalitarianism and genocide – that it is easiest to oppress those we cannot see. This is one reason the Nazis pushed Jews into ghettos, and one reason that the worst Soviet abuses occurred in far-off gulags.'

Cohen celebrates the shift in perception achieved by the movie, but this is in effect a minimal and, as such, a delusional shift. To limit the applications to Nazi and Soviet abuses is to limit the notion of conquest to dated forms of military, violent, coercive force.[7] Conquest, however, is a role not only for Mars but for Venus also. This was the point cited in chapter 7, where it was shown that Stephen Pinker fails to see that capitalism rests upon forms of expansion and conflict which enable control of resources to change hands, just as though there had been a military conquest. For the victims the consequences of such peaceful expansion are no less brutal or tragic.[8]

Is the experience of watching a movie like *Avatar* likely to invite those who watch to inhabit a radically different worldview? Social commentator Slovaj Zizek thinks not. The helpless, exploited natives of the movie, he notes, are a pure fantasy (barely resembling today's victims of exploitation) designed to make viewers feel good as they identify themselves with the compassionate white colonialist. This fantasy helps the viewer to ignore the actual plight of people today suffering precisely the imperialist exploitation the film seems to lament. Zizek cites the example of the Maoist (Naxalite) people of Orissa who, suffering as a result of the sale of mining rights and forced into near starvation, responded with armed resistance:

> So where is Cameron's film here? Nowhere: in Orissa, there are no noble princesses waiting for white heroes to seduce them and help their people, just the Maoists organising the starving farmers. The film enables us to practise a typical ideological division: sympathising with the idealised aborigines while rejecting their actual struggle. The same people who enjoy the film and admire its aboriginal rebels would in all probability turn away in horror from the Naxalites, dismissing them as murderous terrorists.[9]

Zizek, though characteristically prone to overstating his case, at the very least highlights the possibility that modernity's most commendable attempts to extinguish the conquest mentality are destined to fail. Leaving intact the whole modern notion that the world is conceptually structured around the self-sufficient, autonomous individual, there is no escape from an ethics of conquest. Those modernists who do suppose themselves liberated from this imperial virtue are for that very reason more hopelessly imprisoned in their ideology than they already were.

Generosity

Perhaps a more positive approach would prove more effective. Peter Singer's *The Life You Can Save* offers a valiant call for wealthy westerners to contribute from their excesses to the plight of poor people. Pointing out that ten million children die each year from preventable disease, and that 1.4 billion people are living below the poverty line, Singer urges wealthy westerners to give money to aid agencies. As an atheist, Singer's ethical demand is refreshingly strong, based solely upon appeal to logic and reason:

> First premise: Suffering and death from lack of food, shelter and medical care are bad.

> Second premise: If it is in your power to prevent something bad from happening, without sacrificing anything nearly as important, it is wrong not to do so.

Third premise: By donating to aid agencies, you can prevent suffering and death from lack of food, shelter and medical care, without sacrificing anything nearly as important.

Conclusion: Therefore, if you do not donate to aid agencies, you are doing something wrong.[10]

Singer claims that we can reject his argument only by finding a flaw in his reasoning. The gaping flaw lies in his third premise, namely, the implicit assumption that aid agencies are the *only* means 'to prevent something bad from happening'. Working to change the economic rules and trade laws that perpetuate the very suffering Singer laments is the primary challenge – but Singer leaves the structures of savage capitalism untouched. In effect, he issues a commendable appeal *within* capitalism, more specifically an appeal for 'trickle-down' economics. That is, the now indefensible belief that wealth will inevitably radiate from the wealthy centre to the impoverished folk at the periphery and beyond. Leaving intact the structures of power that enable western societies to draw wealth from developing countries, Singer believes we should be altruistic.

This leads to a second and more important weak point. Singer's appeal is not to fundamental altruism, but to the secondary altruism that is based upon primary self-interest. Here, a seemingly commendable ethics (giving) is the sugar coating of a widely deplored form of ethics (accumulation), the selflessness arising from self-centredness. It is akin to drawing money from someone else's bank account, and exercising kindness by allowing them some of your loose change.

For Zizek, Singer's claim that altruism is good for humanity would be a dangerous delusion. It is, after all, the altruism of a consumer. Once we have bought a fairly traded item or committed to paying a portion of our income to charity, we can feel good about ourselves and thereby discharge all responsibility to work for a fairer world. The altruism of Singer is a commodity, a 'feeling' consumers may purchase without the inconvenience of climbing off the consumerist bandwagon. Ethically – as far as Zizek is concerned – this altruism requires no change of *ethos*, no genuine engagement with the other. Those others (the disposable humans outside the household) thus become the equivalent of moral toilet paper, to wipe away the culpability with which Venus stains the modern conscience.

If such capitalist-charity is all the consumer knows, then Zizek's critique stands. If, however, an individual living inside a capitalist economy does everything possible to establish a different social order, then that is likely to include supporting a charity – especially since many mainline charities are concerned with establishing different economic cultures. In this light, we may say that Singer's call for charity is necessary but not sufficient. Zizek – as a neo Marxist – is likely to respond, however, that Singer's type of charity is so overburdened with congratulatory self-deception as to feed the greater and growing violence that capitalism inflicts upon its victims. Rather like *Avatar*, the helpless underdeveloped natives remain entirely dependent upon the actions – good or bad (in Singer's case, genuinely good) – of the white colonialist. The minor acts of charity enable privileged members of the household to feel happy as they continue to benefit from the major acts of injustice that ensure their ongoing economic superiority. Zizek's and Singer's approaches, then, may both be identified in the famous words of Dom Carrera: 'When I gave food to the poor [Singer's approach], they called me a saint. When I asked why the poor were hungry [Zizek's approach], they called me a communist.'

No doubt, if everyone in the West – governments as much as individuals – adopted Singer's approach, all the extreme suffering of our world would be wiped out and the planet would be a much better place. It is for this reason Singer's approach is forceful and compelling. While it may not bring about an ideal world, it would bring about a better world in the short term. In fact, if more people follow Singer, a cultural mood swing may well occur that begins to deconstruct the savage capitalism Zizek so strongly opposes. However, it is the size of this 'if' that presents the problem. Here we return to the logical and ethical flaws of Singer's argument: the logical course of action for modern individuals in a world of diminishing resources is to prioritize their own security – a priority deeply instilled by primal human instinct and preciously guarded by the advertising industry and other ideological mechanisms. Appealing for altruism while endorsing a deeper self-centredness could well be an enterprise doomed from the outset.

Regardless of what conclusions we draw, Zizek helps to show a crucial dynamic of generosity. Many of the celebrated philanthropists of history are only such because they already benefited from (and defended) being in positions of great power, positions usually gained at the expense of others. This is precisely the power dynamic of Christendom, with all its good intentions and flawed realities: first capture power; then use that power for good. (And of course the process of seizing power redefines one's conception of 'good'.) Singer, as an atheist, endorses the very same power dynamic. Though he is deeply concerned about how we spend our money, he is not remotely interested in how we get it. As far as Singer is concerned, the goddess Venus is benevolent, and if her servants are not, then they jolly well should be. Why oppose a benevolent god? Singer enjoins us to serve her faithfully.

'Travel Yourself Interesting'

Travel is a principal means by which modern folk claim to experience otherness. Surely, to visit another country and experience another culture is likely to enlarge one's perspective, broaden one's horizons and deepen one's appreciation for other cultures. By so doing, the story goes, we become more open as individuals, growing in our respect of otherness. The essential postmodern, enlightened liberal will make a virtue of being 'well-travelled'.

In the first instance, there is the obvious problem that air travel inflicts environmental damage that hits first, and hits hardest, some of the planet's poorest communities. Any virtue in travelling for the sake of experiencing the otherness of other cultures is obliterated by the vice that air travel has recently become. The knowledge that air travel has destructive effects confronts us with an inconvenient case of otherness: an alternative ethic that threatens our previously conscience-free enjoyment of travel. However, leaving aside the fact that our rush to visit the vanishing corals of northern Australia accelerates the rate at which they vanish, the virtues of travel are questionable on quite other grounds.

Discussions concerning the benefits of tourism, of enjoying the otherness of alien cultures, universally lack a basic ethical question. Namely, the question of what happens to the visitor's *ethos* when the travel bug lands them in an encounter with members of an alien culture. Does being an observer of that culture guarantee any genuine encounter with their otherness? How do we allow persons of other cultures actually, practically, personally or politically to have any genuine, life-changing impact upon the traveller? Enjoying intelligent, thoughtful tourism is different only in quality from visiting Disneyland, where in one swoop the visitor may 'sample the culture and cuisine of fifty different countries'.

As modernists, are we prone to divert our own attention away from those unwelcome aspects of otherness that might actually threaten our worldview in any substantive sense? Zizek answers this kind of question with some force. Commenting on Michael Palin's BBC travel programmes, Zizek insists:

> Their underlying attitude of adopting a benevolent ironic distance towards different customs, taking pleasure in observing local peculiarities while filtering out the really traumatic data, amounts to postmodern racism at its most essential . . . Rousseau already understood perfectly the falsity of multicultural admirers of foreign cultures when, in *Emile*, he warned of the 'philosopher who loves Tartars in order to be dispensed from loving his neighbours.'[11]

At the very least, Zizek shows that experiencing other cultures in no way guarantees any form of radical encounter. Far more likely is that the experience of travel simply turns other cultures into commodities for consumption, a form of abuse that convention allows us to experience as virtue. One cannot, at the same time, extol the virtues of travel as necessary for human openness *and* be genuinely open to others. Venus laughs at those who consider themselves free of her influence.

Tolerance

In a divided and fragmented world, certain rhetorical devices enjoy wide circulation:

> I hear where you're coming from.
> Everyone's entitled to their opinion.

I disapprove of what you say, but I defend to the death your right to say it.[12]

The brand of tolerance embodied in such sentiments is the readiness to put up with people, situations or facts of life even when those things seem distasteful. We cannot change those people, so we must agree to disagree. Tolerance, in effect, assumes the total impregnability of one's own superior position over against that of the other. As such, it is the radical refusal to be confronted by the actual otherness of another person. It requires no engagement with otherness, no confrontation with a world that questions who I really am.

Tolerance, in this sense, becomes yet another self-congratulatory myth. Zizek cites the example of the construction of the Centre for Human Dignity – the Museum of Tolerance, a complex planned for a disputed patch of land in Jerusalem. The museum will promote harmony between different groups within Judaism, and between people of different faith groups. The only drawback is that the site – prior to 1948 – happened to be the main Muslim cemetery. (Claiming the site contained the remains of the victims of medieval Crusades, the Muslim community has appealed to the Supreme Court.) For Zizek, 'this dark spot wonderfully enacts the hidden truth of this multi-confessional project: it is a place celebrating tolerance, open to all but protected by the Israeli cupola which ignores the subterranean victims of intolerance – as if a little bit of intolerance is necessary in order to create a space for true tolerance.'[13]

Tolerance, in this sense, is only for those with power over others, and to promote it as a virtue is to celebrate that power. Indifference (to the plight of those outside the household) is disguised as benevolence (to allow them their strange ways). However, like all else in the neoliberal economy, tolerance is a finite resource. The more those outside the household come to threaten those within it, the more tolerance is tested. For Sam Harris – as we have seen – the point at which tolerance reaches its end is the point at which Iran develops nuclear capability. At that moment we can tolerate their difference no longer, and must nuke the region out of their intolerable state. Mars must allow Venus no competitors.

Free Speech

Harris, like most secular liberals, also believes in free speech. Take the wave of violence that followed *The Innocence of Muslims*, a western video designed to offend as many Muslims as possible. Harris is among those expressing a popular sentiment, condemning the Muslim violence the video was designed to spawn. Here he subscribes to the view that 'sticks and stones may break my bones but names will never hurt me'. That is, the belief that violence is physical only, that words alone cannot wound, and that symbolic acts should have no consequences. 'Here is where the line must be drawn and defended without apology: We are free to burn the Qur'an or any other book, and to criticize Muhammad or any other human being. *Let no one forget it.*'[14]

Apart from the fact that Harris' privileged 'we' hardly sounds like an enlightened household, such a view assumes that symbolic acts are not acts at all, and that words in themselves are sterile, serving only to express the speaker's mind but never to evoke a response. In reality, as speech-act theory has shown, the spoken word is a communicative act, and speech is an event with real effects in the real world. The context in which such communicative acts take place has an enormous bearing upon the type of act it becomes.

Neoliberalism, as described in the last chapter, speaks of a world with the powerful at the centre, the privileged within the household and, beyond the boundaries of our privilege, disposable humans. When speech is directed from the centre outwards it is an entirely different social exercise from speech directed from the outside inwards. Harris and those who share his view fail to distinguish between oppressive and subversive speech, between speech designed to belittle the other, and the beleaguered cry for justice. The result is to put Nelson Mandela's costly and outspoken demand for fairness in South Africa in the same category as hate-speech designed to inflame anger against Muslims. Free speech, when claimed by the powerful against the marginalized, is an abuse.

Those on the 'outside' who take offence at the free speech of the privileged do not thereby oppose a genuine freedom available to all humans. The freedom of speech enjoyed by the privileged members of the household is a freedom that rests upon certain societal and ideological structures of thought, belief and politics.

Here, for instance, the champions of free speech tend to belittle the importance of listening to the other, even though listening is the only context in which speech has any value. And yet, if those keen to exercise their freedom of speech took the trouble to listen well to those at whom their criticisms are aimed, another picture would emerge. The western adventures into largely Muslim countries over the last decade have left a trail of violence and suffering which – despite the freedom of the press – has been hideously under-reported to those within the household. The victims and witnesses of such violence see more clearly that anti-Muslim propaganda is not a freedom, but rather the unselfconscious dictates of a vicious ideological machine. Once Mars has stomped across a region, Venus is free to urinate over it. Harris himself helps to make the link clear as he concludes his article, casting the privileged and powerful members of an aggressive society as poor victims and seeing violence only in his enemies. As ever, he keenly recommends a violent response:

> The freedom to think out loud on certain topics, without fear of being hounded into hiding or killed, *has already been lost*. And the only forces on earth that can recover it are strong, secular governments that will face down charges of blasphemy with scorn. No apologies necessary. Muslims must learn that if they make belligerent and fanatical claims upon the tolerance of free societies, they will meet the limits of that tolerance.[15]

By Harris' logic, 'free speech' entitles us to abuse the other, and if they react violently to our provocation we are obliged to crush them. The ability to treat the other as an other is lost by those who insist upon terming abusive speech as free speech. Aristotle diagnosed the 'free speech' demanded by Harris and co as 'incontinence',[16] the inability to govern one's own expression, be it through ignorance, lack of reflection, over-excitement, mental disturbance, or the absence of reason.

Curiosity

Finally, from a different perspective, the capacity for openness is brought much closer to home in a character trait widely regarded as charming, admirable and worthwhile, namely, curiosity. Curious people are deemed interesting because they are open to the wonder of the world around them, and interested in the people they encounter.

Heidegger, however, went to great lengths to expose the chasm between a particular and widespread conception of curiosity and genuine wonder, describing curiosity as one of the key elements of human fallenness. Those trying to emulate this trivial form of curiosity, for instance, are likely to find themselves celebrating the latest 'must-read' book or 'must-see' movie, and would dare not miss 'the news'. This is not simply an interest in trivia. Curious people can engage in the deeper questions of philosophy and theology, the most socially pressing concerns of the day, or marvel at scientific or technological breakthrough. This mentality is not merely a character trait, an aspect of certain individuals' person- ality. For Heidegger, it represents a deep-seated unwritten social demand that affects the way in which modern people understand themselves in relation to others and the world around them. In its crudest form, it underlies the cultural mentality suggesting the 40 things to do, the 40 books to read and the 40 places to see . . . before you die. (All of which, of course, keep the capi- talist machine running smoothly, and endorse the worldview required by Venus.) Those who have completed their 40 tasks, it is supposed, are likely to be 'interesting' people with 'meaningful' lives. This looks like the desperate postmodern scramble to grasp some form of 'meaning' from an otherwise meaningless life before it is spent. The whole attempt to ascribe a 'meaning' to life (itself a very modern concern) would, for Heidegger, serve as a distraction from addressing the underlying question of what it means to be truly alive. When people are attuned to themselves, to others and to the universe, the whole desire for meaning evaporates in the intensity of radical, real-life encounter.

So disturbing is such an enterprise, so costly is the genuine wonder and fear, the disruption and joy, insecurity and harmony, all of which constitute part of encountering otherness, that it proves too difficult a task. Much easier to lose oneself in the herd mentality, seeking some form of meaning for life in great adven- tures, epic journeys, and sets of 40 things to do as laid down by Venus. These are not conscious goals, but ways of being that shape

our own being ever more deeply and imprison us ever more
hopelessly. Hence, beneath the veil of what Heidegger refers to as
'curiosity', the personal barrier against otherness remains impregnable. Curiosity kills all wonder.

This is by no means the only way to conceive curiosity. However,
this negative portrayal demonstrates that, in and of itself, curiosity
is simply a general, universal human instinct. The real questions
about curiosity concern the things about which we are curious:
the universe beyond our short and sheltered world, alternative
ways of life, the wellbeing of the other; or shoes, technological
gadgets, life-insurance, football results? These are all thoroughly
valid objects of curiosity, but, as argued above, the range of a
modern consumer's curiosity is likely to be confined within the
given limits of a prevailing worldview.

The critiques offered here are not intended to turn secular
values into vices. It is entirely possible to embody each of the
cultural values offered above in such a way as to remain genuinely open to the other. The point here is rather to show how it is
perfectly plausible to treasure the above values while remaining
fundamentally closed to anything genuinely other, to genuflect
in the direction of open-mindedness with all the hypocrisy of a
televangelist. These secular values can serve as articles of faith for
the worship of Mars and Venus, brainwashing their unreflective
worshippers with the delusion that the closed-minded refusal to
encounter otherness is in fact an open-minded, enlightened, civilized way of being. Nevertheless, the values listed above are no
less sacrosanct among most secularists than Christian practices
are for the most evangelical believers. Ironically, those Christian
practices – when rooted in their scriptural context – are far more
consistent with the philosophies of secular liberalism.

Genuine Encounter

Before launching into a discussion of Christian practices arising
from the Bible, it is crucial to abandon all language of both
values and virtues. Values are external to me, abstract, timeless
moral principles to which I may or may not measure up. Christian values, whatever they may be and however commendable

they are for society, have little to do with the genuine encounter with otherness so fundamental to Christian belief. Alternatively, virtues tend to refer to some inner quality I must strive to display. In classical philosophy, chief virtues tend to be character traits such as temperance, prudence, courage and justice. The language of virtue tends to sever the individual from otherness, suggesting self-sufficient qualities or weaknesses with which a person is forever blessed or doomed.

Neither values nor virtues have any warrant in Christian Scripture. Here there are no deeply seated natural virtues simply waiting to find expression in daily life, and individuals are not expected to strive to measure up to any form of external or ideal value or virtue. Instead, Christians are called to relate with God in worship and with others in community. This dynamic is subsequently manifest in what Scripture calls 'fruits', i.e. the consequences that grow out of engaging with cosmic and interpersonal otherness. The attempt to embody these fruits merely as virtues or values might well be an exercise in attaching artificial fruit to a rootless tree, seeking to display correct behaviour without rooting oneself in genuine otherness. The qualities outlined below emphasize the roots of Christian social and political practice and are cultivated through the rugged experience of relating well to otherness.

Humility

Humility is an aggressive, confrontational practice which, as the primal Christian virtue, is widely and deeply misunderstood. For some, it is precisely the same as modesty: the refusal to take pride in your own achievements, or the readiness to allow others to walk all over you. For others, humility is the willingness to accept our place within the natural hierarchy of the universe – a reading thoroughly consistent with the demands of Christendom and perfectly expressed by the omitted verse of the hymn, 'All Things Bright and Beautiful':

> The rich man in his castle,
> The poor man at his gate,
> He made them, high or lowly,
> And ordered their estate.[17]

From the Christendom perspective, humility is the willingness to be content and not rock the boat. Seeking to reinterpret humility from a secular human perspective, Erik Wielenberg maintains precisely the same logic by casting humility as the admission that, since we are who we are only by remarkable cosmological, biological and sociological accident, we should recognize our proper place in the universe.[18]

This is a long way from biblical notions of humility, which are neither passive nor static, but active, and presuppose confrontation. Throughout Scripture, humility is the capacity to be transformed by one's encounter with otherness. It presupposes that a person or a situation con-fronts us (comes together to stand over against us), and describes the openness of character that such a confrontation may forge. Without a context of dynamic encounter, humility is impossible. It is no abstract character trait or state of being; it is the dynamic, forceful struggle of relating well to otherness. But does the apparent powerlessness of humility condemn us to accepting defeat in the quest to enlarge the household?

Hope

'The message of Christianity,' says Wielenberg, 'is essentially one of hope, but it is important to realize that what it offers primarily is hope with respect to what lies *beyond* this world.'[19] For Christendom patterns of belief, Wielenberg's claim is accurate. However, although post-Christendom belief is structured around hope '*beyond* this world', the world here is not merely earth as opposed to heaven, but those within the *oikos* (world, household) as opposed to those excluded from it. The reality lying *beyond* our familiar world then becomes ambiguous – the residence both of the disposable humans and the Almighty God. While the Scriptures say precious little about the other world of heaven, the gospels speak repeatedly of God's dwelling place being among the *anawim*, the throwaway outcasts beyond the outposts of our comfortable world. The Spirit of the Lord locates Christ (the heavenly human being) among the poor, the prisoners, the blind and the oppressed.

Christian hope is raw active energy, residing in the belief that the God of Scripture invites us to encounter him by encountering the outsider, that the God of the universe is not merely allied with, but *one of* those excluded from the household. Regardless of whether that household was the Roman Empire or the privileged religious in-crowd, this is the burden of Jesus' preaching from start to finish. Hope for the world (and doom for oppressive regimes) is that divine power is to be found in a place and in a manner that keeps it beyond the grasp of the oppressor.

Peace

If humility and hope are both dynamic virtues, the same is no less true of peace. Again, peace here is to be distinguished between that desired by the oppressor and that sought by the oppressed. Those at the hierarchical centre seek a peace (such as the *pax Romana*) that will keep *everything running smoothly*. Those on the outside, who suffer from that regime, seek a peace from the smooth-running machine that obliterates their wellbeing.

When Jesus said, 'I have not come to bring peace, but a sword', the sword to which he referred was the sword wielded by oppressors, by 'governors and kings'. In other words, those who follow Jesus will inevitably threaten the stability of the household, and will – for that reason – face the wrath of the household. This is why, as Jesus continues, he declares to this patriarchal world, 'A man's enemies shall be of his own household.' When Jesus presented a manifesto which locates divine approval outside the household, he preaches a gospel that will bring the sword – but not a sword he wields in his own hand. To follow Jesus and defy the household, by loving those outside it, is to defy Venus and inevitably to bring down upon oneself the sword of Mars. This – as chapter 1 argued – is precisely what happened to the followers of Jesus. To plant your footsteps in the path of Jesus' journey is to place your neck in the path of Mars' sword.

Jesus certainly did not proclaim the stability-defending peace of the oppressor, the *pax Romana*, the peace required to keep the empire's economy running smoothly. The peace celebrated in Scripture has an entirely different structure. This biblical peace is an actively violent virtue because it entails profound disturbance in one's inner being. Engaging with otherness is always a violent activity with perceivable effects in one's personal, social and political life. This is reflected in the practice of baptism, which entails a mini-death and resurrection in the life of the believer. Peace, in this sense, is the violent turbulence of encountering the other rather than conquering, abusing, or ignoring the other.

Joy

Few theologians articulate the nature of joy as clearly as Monbiot. Concluding his own 'manifesto for a new world order', Monbiot recognizes both the sheer necessity and the lack of any rational motive for members of the privileged household to act on behalf of those beyond it:

> But while the proposals in this manifesto offer little by way of material self-advancement to activists in the rich world, there is, in collective revolutionary action, something which appears to be missing from almost every other enterprise in modern secular life. It arises, I think, from the intensity of relationships forged in a collective purpose concentrated by adversity. It is the exultation which Christians call 'joy', but which, in the dry discourse of secular politics, has no recognized equivalent.[20]

Joy, as Monbiot conceives it, is part of the relational practice of seeking justice. In Jewish thought, peace (*shalom*) is the fertile ground from which justice (righteousness) flourishes – and joy is the experience of that 'flourishing'. According to one New Testament document, this joy is precisely what enabled Jesus to endure the agonized humiliation of crucifixion.

This, of course, is a long way from the Christendom version of joy: the depoliticized, spiritualized psychological warmth of feeling experienced by worshippers whose own Christ exists not to announce the coming of God's kingdom (thereby reordering who is 'in' and who is 'out' of my privileged household) but exists instead to provide coping mechanisms for the already-privileged members of the household to improve their status still further by also becoming spiritually privileged. Post-Christendom joy is as active and interpersonal, as politically charged, and as radically subversive as humility, hope and peace.

Holiness

The word 'holy' is widely regarded as a synonym for 'pious', 'right-eous', 'blameless' etc. Christian preachers will often point out that to be holy is to be 'set apart', separate, different from the world, unpolluted by sin, unaffected by normal passions, uncontaminated by worldly pleasure. Christians are then encouraged to manifest holiness by striving to achieve this impossible, unnatural, external standard of perfection. As above, such an approach views holiness as an external standard, a principle to which I must measure up.

Holiness has its roots, however, in the notion of God himself as 'wholly other', a phrase coined (and later repudiated) by the Swiss theologian Karl Barth (1886–1968). The earlier Barth sought to emphasize the sheer otherness of God, his 'unknowableness', to those who tried to reason their way through the natural world to discover his divine character. Later in his life, however, Barth wanted to emphasize the sheer humanity of this God, leaving him unsatis-fied with a 'wholly other' deity – as though God could be utterly distinct from human life. It is a tension with which theologians have long wrestled: between the immanence (the terrible closeness) and the transcendence (unfathomable, distant separateness) of God.

The notion of holiness as wholly otherness, however, does get to the roots of the biblical concept, accounting for the language of sepa-rateness, distinctness, being set apart etc. Otherness, as this book has described it, articulates the sheer, cosmic distance embodied even in my *neighbours*, the monstrous threat they pose to my way of being, the daunting challenge their very existence offers to my own worldview. Holiness, in biblical terms, is the capacity to engage with this otherness – since no one embodies such profound otherness as God himself. In this light, holiness is simply the biblical version of existentialism as described in chapter 3. Remembering that to ek-sist is literally to 'stand out', to be holy is to have the capacity to *stand out* from a regime or community, a culture or worldview, in order to listen well to those who do not belong to it.

Grace

In its Greek form, 'grace' is simply the word for a gift. However, the western practice of giving and receiving gifts seems to obliterate any notion of grace. Jacques Derrida wrestles with the problematic nature of the gift, arguing that what we often regard as a gift is, in fact, simply a transaction. Convention dictates that, on receiving a gift, we are obliged to purchase one of equivalent value and offer it to the giver in order to balance the books.

The genuine nature of gift-giving quickly becomes a set of habits, of exchanging presents of similar value, what we might call an 'economy' (a law of the household) – and any notion of 'grace' falls out of the normal practice. Derrida, however, keeps the language of economy, the routine practices that shape our relationships, and likens the genuine gift to a counterfeit coin. When counterfeit currency enters an economy, it causes disruption. It moves around the economy, but cannot finally be assimilated by it. A genuine gift, says Derrida, can – in theory – enter into our world from beyond, but never really fits with our understanding of how the world works.

Derrida helps to make clear the biblical notion of grace/gift. To receive grace is to undergo radical disturbance at the hands of another. Grace enters into our world from *beyond* it, but has an impact upon who I am *within* this world. It denotes the glorious but disruptive, the liberating but unwelcome disturbance that enters, not into our routine as a mere spiritual transaction, but into our being as a radical means of reorientation. As with every other biblical fruit, grace is a manifestation of engaging well with otherness.

Faith

For Sam Harris, faith is 'generally nothing more than the permission religious people give to one another to believe things strongly without evidence.'[21] Christopher Hitchens goes further, suggesting that:

> Faith is the surrender of the mind; it's the surrender of reason, it's the surrender of the only thing that makes us different from other mammals. It's our need to believe, and to surrender our scepticism and our reason, our yearning to discard that and put all our trust or faith in someone or something, that is the sinister thing to me. Of all the supposed virtues, faith must be the most overrated.[22]

Such a view, as it is now commonplace to note, is at odds with any belief in scientific progress.[23] Against Hitchens, faith is not a religious virtue, but an essential aspect of what it means to be human. Even according to Scripture, faith is what we show when we act on the strength of unproven convictions, in the hope that such action will be justified by the outcome. It hardly needs stating that any scientist seeking evidence does not have that evidence before they seek it (although any research scientist submitting a grant application may be forgiven for thinking otherwise). They act upon the strength of conviction, thereby displaying faith. The religious virtue of faith is embodied supremely in the person of Abraham.

As discussed in chapter 3 above, faith for Abraham was not the anti-rational capacity to perform the mental gymnastics necessary to make himself believe what he knew in his bones to be false. It was rather his ability to endure the radical insecurity of the present on the conviction that God would honour his promise. Faith does not reject, but seeks, evidence. It is the name for the tension between the action of the present and the outcome to which it leads, in the belief that the preliminary evidence will vindicate the action. This is true of the bank that puts faith in a customer to honour a *credit* (literally, a *faith*) agreement. It is true of the scientist who devotes energy and time to testing a hypothesis, in the hope that those efforts will prove worthwhile. It is true of the campaigner who invests time and effort in a cause, against hopeless odds, in the hope of governments coming to change their policy. It is true of the Christian who seeks to worship the Christ they have encountered in Scripture rather than the gods of the age who demand compliance, in the hope that any hardship they may face as a result will be vindicated by joy. This joy (described above) is not simply an emotional experience for the individual worshipper, but the lived experience of those outside the household, among whom – after all – the Jesus of Scripture locates himself. Christian faith is the conviction that God is creditworthy, that he can be trusted to honour the risk required of those who covenant with him.

Love

Widely regarded as the chief of Christian virtues is love. Unfortunately, English has only one word for love and as such it remains a notoriously ambiguous and elusive virtue. At the very least, love involves encounter with another. Further, this encounter is no mere sentimental or dutiful transaction, but an encounter that reaches to the roots of one's identity. Love, however we wish to define it, is radical encounter with an other. Of course, in the modern era (in which individuals seek to construct the world around themselves) the notion of self-love was able to take root. Such attempts to boost one's psychological self-perception, however, are at odds with any biblical description of love. Here we find the injunction, central to Jewish and Christian conviction, for believers to love God with heart, soul, mind and strength, and love their neighbours as themselves. Since this latter command is often used to justify self-love, it is worth showing a political example of how this works in practice.

The prophet Jeremiah wrote letters to his fellow Israelites who had been led into captivity a thousand miles away from their homeland. Since many of his compatriots were naturally hostile towards their captors, since some were speaking of rebelling against their enemies and returning home from exile, Jeremiah unburdened himself of the following prophecy: 'Seek the wellbeing of the city where I have sent you in exile, and pray to Yahweh on its behalf, for in its wellbeing you will find your wellbeing.' To love is to find one's own wellbeing in seeking that of another. To seek the welfare of an enemy city is unpatriotic, a rejection of the gods of the state (including Mars and Venus), and yet fundamental to Christian and Jewish identity.

To love the stranger obviously does not require a lengthy sentimental interaction. One example is found in the actions of French peasant fishermen during the Nazi occupation of the Second World War. To offer any assistance to British soldiers meant execution, but when a small fishing party in Bordeaux came across members of British special forces starving, isolated and hunted by Nazi soldiers, though having little food themselves, they gave the very best of it to these helpless soldiers. Recalling the experience years later, one French woman declared, 'We were as pleased to give it as they were to receive it.'[24] Without any hint of duty or begrudging, such action embodies precisely the kind of political love in action in which Scripture roots human identity. This is as true in personal terms as it is in political. If I love another person well, then I invest my welfare in theirs; I see myself in terms of the other; I receive myself back from that other as a different person. To love well is to encounter in one's own-most being the ugliness and beauty, the calm and the terror of the otherness of the other.

Conclusion

After Christendom, Christian dynamics of engaging with otherness are able to surface more clearly from the pages of Scripture. This chapter has argued that we live in an era that seeks genuine ways of encounter, of living in tension with the other. Traditional secular attempts to do so have been unable to break the stranglehold of the prevailing capitalist worldview, but when understood well, certain biblical practices offer a more realistic means of radical encounter.

At root, the readiness to engage the other is the surest means towards ensuring that the benefit of those who belong to the household does not cause the suffering of those who do not. This is by no means to argue for the 'expanding circle', to transform humanity into one single, homogenous community, thus destroying the reality of the other by turning every 'them' into an 'us'. It is rather the attempt to hear the voice of the outsider – whether that outsider is within or beyond the household.

Christianity, in its pre-Christendom manifestations, pursued just this concern. According to the Christian gospel, regardless of the individual's place within the social hierarchy of the Roman Empire, every peasant, every sinner, every outcast, foreigner and enemy was granted direct access to an authority who could hear you and determine your plight. Though such authority was officially mediated only through the ultimate head of the household (the emperor), with the advent of Christianity it is declared universally accessible through ways of being and relating in which human life flourishes. All humans are thus declared 'sons of God', a title officially reserved for the emperor. Zizek is right to see that Christianity introduced to the smooth running of the world:

> a principle totally foreign to it, a principle that, measured by the standards of the pagan cosmology, cannot but appear as a mon-

strous distortion: the principle according to which each individual
has an immediate access to universality (of the Holy Spirit, or, today,
of human rights and freedoms) – I can participate in this universal
dimension directly, irrespective of my special place within the global
social order.[25]

When Christianity preached universal access to this dimension, it
undermined the social structures of nationalism (for certain Jews)
and of the empire (for privileged Romans.) It defies the dictates of
Venus and invites the wrath of Mars. It undermines the structures
of neoliberal capitalism, and calls humanity beyond the *given
limits* of culture, empire, and ideology, exposing human beings to
an otherness that allows their humanity to flourish.

Conclusion:

The Radical Atheist's Prayer

Radical atheism entails the political subversion of the gods of one's own age, which in turn requires the capacity to see beyond the given limits of the familiar and into an alternative (that is, a 'holy') world. As we have seen, even the highest moral virtues of secularism protect the comforts of the privileged rather than inspire serious engagement with the other. Similarly, the explosive Christian practices listed in the previous chapter, though designed to awaken believers' commitment to the other, have, by and large, stagnated into docile religious virtues. History has shown how quickly and easily virtues devolve into generalized high-sounding, free-floating values that may be incorporated into any secular or religious creed. As I have argued, it is not a community's creed but a community's life that expresses its belief. A creed is largely an articulation of how the community would like to be perceived, i.e. a public relations exercise. The Jesus who is the subject of Christianity's dominant creeds did not give his own followers a creed. He gave them a prayer. The 'Lord's Prayer' was community-defining, committing those who prayed it to a particular way of being. As such, it expresses the sentiment and hope of radical atheism and forms the substructure of the argument I have presented in this book. The brief overview I offer here will follow the traditional version from the Book of Common Prayer in showing that the Lord's Prayer is a manifesto for atheism.

Our Father

The Roman Empire's hierarchy was literally *patriarchal*, in that
the father's authority over his household was universal, from the
marble corridors of Rome to the flea-ridden streets of the provinces. From the emperor himself to the lowliest peasant, the structure of Roman society relied upon the rule of the father whose
status was recognized in law. In this context, to pray to a God
deemed to be 'our father' is to short-circuit the imperial hierarchy.
Jesus had authorized his followers to appeal for justice directly
to a Cosmic Father, with scant regard for the recognized imperial
procedure. In so doing, they reject the gods of the age as embodied
in the world's senior father, the emperor. Jesus' followers thus
root their identity in a genuinely alternative, social, political, ideological mindset, as outlined in chapter 1 above. Those studying
this prayer in the twenty-first century may establish the identity
and existence of the Cosmic Father himself only by praying (and
therefore, living out) the prayer as a lifelong pursuit. In so doing,
the community that prays 'Our Father' thereby assumes its status
as the Father's offspring, his representative on earth, a communal
embodiment of the Son of God, whose priorities and characteristics are revealed in the details of the prayer itself.

Who Art in Heaven

Whatever Christians believe about the imagery of heaven, its
observable reference point (and its literal meaning) is simply the
sky. In both Greek and Hebrew, 'heaven' is principally a word
for the sky over our head. Any notion of heaven that does not
follow this signpost is destined to stray off into the pagan fanta-
sies so frequently associated with the Christian heaven. Geological research suggests that ancient agricultural people groups
tended to worship a god of the soil, the ground beneath their
feet, which yielded all that was needed for survival. On the other
hand, nomadic peoples, even today, affirm the identity of a god
whose domain is the sky. Nomads are not rooted in the soil of any
promised 'land', because theirs is a god who is present wherever
their fate carries them. By praying to a God 'who art in heaven'

the followers of Jesus reveal a strong, nomadic element of their identity, with all the fragility and vulnerability such a way of life entails. Those who worship him, though no longer nomads in a literal sense, identify themselves instead as resident aliens, whose very presence in the land is revolutionary – the aspect of atheism taken up in chapter 2 above. Theirs is not the god of conquered territories, upholding the rulers and conquerors of the day. The fate and the power of the God in heaven transcend the community's immediate context and circumstances.

Hallowed Be Thy Name

According to Judeo-Christian scriptures, God's name is either sanctified (hallowed) or shamed by the behaviour of those who represent him. Anyone addressing Yahweh as 'father' thereby claims for themselves the status of God's representative, with the capacity to drag his name through the dirt or to sanctify his name by their lives. To request that Yahweh's name be made holy is to commit oneself to a life of holiness. As I argued in chapter 3, holiness is first and foremost the readiness to engage with the other.

To pray, 'hallowed be thy name', is firstly to recognize that God does not simply identify himself *with* the outsider, but *is* the outsider. This is not a god who visits the humble planet earth as the mythical Queen Victoria visited the humble homes of nineteenth-century London, in the tradition of a monarch whose royalty is disguised. The majesty of God is not disguised but expressed by the intolerable humility of the powerless Christ. The divine being is not concealed but revealed by the presence of an unremarkable, voiceless, working-class 'chav' known as Jesus of Nazareth. This is God the outsider, the nobody, whose name is Other. None of this is by any means to deny the greatness, power and authority of the biblical portrait of God, but serves rather as a radical redefinition of what these divine attributes are, what they look like and how they function. In this prayer, the followers of Jesus root their own identity in their relationship with this undesirable, mysterious, unfathomable outsider – the other.

Thy Kingdom Come

Anyone in the Roman Empire seeking an alternative kingdom is inviting trouble. Any deity demanding that its adherents pray for a new kingdom (and thereby, of course, a new king) is inciting sedition against the present order. To pray 'thy kingdom come', is to seek regime change. During Christendom, rebellion against the dominant order remained a punishable offence, and the Lord's Prayer had to be defused of its politically explosive charge. How is this achieved? By turning the kingdom of God into an abstract, idealized, otherworldly plane of existence characterized by post-mortem bliss: heaven. In Christendom, only at the end of the space-time order, when God draws human history to a close, will justice and fairness become a final and permanent reality. The hope of justice is thus stolen from this world and smuggled into the afterlife. Jesus is banished from the present to sit on the distant horizon of the future with welcome arms.

Chapter 4 outlined the Jewish and Christian struggle to embody divine otherness recounted throughout Christian scriptures. Various movements throughout the narrative of Scripture sought to bring about the kingdom of God by military means, but the Christ of Scripture offered an alternative. Far from spiritualizing justice away from the practical concerns of daily life, Jesus of Nazareth fostered among his followers a radically attentive disposition to the ultimate other – the Father. Those who identify themselves with this prayer, similarly, seek the coming of the Father's kingdom in the practice of striving to be consciously attentive to the other. To do so, however, is no passive cop-out for those who will not lay their lives on the line, nor is it to turn a blind eye to the injustices of the present order, nor even to combat oppressive power with some vague form of 'anti-power'. The kingdom of God arrived (and continues to arrive) in the person of Christ, but not in the way his followers or enemies expected.

Thy Will Be Done

The Father in heaven, it seems, does not necessarily get his own way on earth. Those who pray this prayer, as representatives of the Father, offer themselves as a means by which his will is put into effect. The interlude at the centre of this book explained this commitment in terms of resurrection. Did the historical Jesus fail to live up to his own political manifesto? Did his execution demonstrate that his ideals were admirable but ineffectual? Did his death show that the kingdom of God had been conquered by the powers that be? The answer to each is, of course, a resounding 'yes'. The resurrection, however, vindicates this Christ by undermining the certainties of political belief: that cold imperial power has the final word; that love has nothing to do with politics; that the divine will can only be put into effect with brutal, coercive force. Resurrection power, I argued, is both the most effective form of political power *and*, by its very nature, useless to any human authority seeking to wield it. The 'abuse-proof' nature of this power, however, comes at a cost. To pray 'thy will be done' is to give oneself to the other, a dangerous endeavour whose actual outcome is unpredictable. The second half of the prayer (and the second half of this book) explores the practical consequences of this hope.

On Earth as It Is in Heaven

This is not a god whose action is entirely otherworldly, but whose being extends throughout the 'earth/land/soil'. This prayer yearns for the convergence of earth with heaven, of the familiar with the strange, of the here with the beyond. This, as I argued in chapter 5, is a concern shared by contemporary scientists. Not that scientists simply go mining for facts from a universe of mystery. I have described scientists rather as explorers, who uncover new expanses of mystery. No longer is space 'the final frontier'. The plain rock in your hand contains an infinity of unknowns, and the reason for its existence continues to evade the grasp of the scientist who holds it. I also suggested in chapter 5 that an otherworldly God might exert influence on earth through an ontological dimension: universally available to those engaging well with otherness, inaccessible to those who would abuse it, incomprehensible to modern (but perhaps not future) science. Is this the kind of deity whose influence is to be welcomed? The rest of the prayer betrays his character.

Give Us This Day Our Daily Bread

Given the phenomenally widespread use of this prayer throughout western history, the unheard dimension of this sentence is breath-taking. It contains undoubtedly the most abused 'us' in the history of literature. This petition is not merely a demand that God cater for our basic needs. This prayer defines and locates the Christian community, thrusting them into the midst of hunger and poverty. 'The poor' are not distant objects of sympathy or charity. To pray for 'our daily bread' is to position ourselves with those who hunger. This is not merely a request, but a commitment of radical solidarity with those who hunger, so that their hunger is no longer *theirs* but *ours*. The moment we pray 'for' the poor we have distanced ourselves from them, but in asking for 'our' daily bread we identify with those who do not have it. This is the only location from which the prayer can be made. Chapter 6 addressed ethical questions thrown up by this aspect of the prayer, arguing that the Christ of Scripture is encountered in those excluded from the benefits of the household. This marginalized, powerless, outsider-Christ reveals the true nature of God's own character and power.

Forgive Us Our Trespasses, as We Forgive Those Who Trespass against Us

While we are accustomed to regard this request as clearing one's moral slate before a supernatural mind-reading Judge, the root idea is economic and is best rendered, 'Forgive us our debts, as we also have forgiven our debtors.' In a pre-capitalist society like ancient Israel, debts cannot be abstracted away from personal relationships, and forgiveness of debt is a counter-cultural social dynamic.

People in the Roman Empire who seek to be treated as equals, as citizens and as fully fledged human beings must first honour all debts, including those with which they might have been unfairly burdened. Countless slaves, for instance, were born and died in a state of inescapable debt because of the practices of others. To recognize forgiveness as a practice linking the worship of God

with the treatment of others is to make a virtue of debt-cancel-
lation and thereby to undermine the social and economic structure that enables the empire to run. By making forgiveness a core
community practice, the prayer constructs an alternative understanding of human community. Chapter 7 described how, in a
capitalist economy, human beings can rapidly devolve into *Homo
economicus*, beings defined exclusively by the rational economic
self-interest of the powerful. As in the Roman Empire, so in the
most savage capitalist economy, one human being is worth more
than another. Forgiveness is not concerned with spiritual transactions designed to keep shallow-minded peasants in a state
of psychological submission to their superiors. It is a means of
radical, political, social inclusion, designed to deny the possibility
of 'superiors'.

Lead Us Not into Temptation, but Deliver Us from Evil

Throughout the Lord's Prayer, Jesus has promoted a way of being
that undermines the prevailing ideology of Roman rule. As I have
emphasized throughout these chapters, although Christ does not
make Rome his primary target, much of what he encourages will
inevitably draw Roman anger upon his followers. In order to distinguish his community from the various movements obsessed with
violent rebellion, he steers his followers away from the rebel cause
with the final line of his prayer. Temptation here is best rendered
'trial'. The stubborn refusal to abandon Israel's headlong drive
into self-destructive rebellion against Rome will inevitably bring
upon Jerusalem the worst kinds of trials imaginable. That dreaded
time of trial would come within a generation, as the Roman military machine descended upon Jerusalem to quell rebellion in AD 70.
Those who pray this 'Lord's Prayer', who identify themselves as
children of God and who seek for his kingly reign to begin, will
want nothing at all to do with Israel's militant but suicidal drive for
national independence. Hence the closing call to be delivered from
evil is a call to escape the consequences of the Jewish nationalists'
evils and the evils that will be inflicted upon them by the Romans.
　　The ecological and economic consequences that inevitably
await a humanity approaching the future on a course steered by

the gods of the twenty-first century are potentially no less disastrous than the destruction of Jerusalem soon after Jesus' day. To invest hope for the future in prayer to a deity may be offensive to modern sensibilities, but we may respond that, firstly, to pray is to experiment. It is an act of faith to establish whether committing oneself to the kind of God portrayed by this prayer is a surer means of bringing salvation to the earth than other means of defying the hidden, destructive, unstoppable gods of our age. To pray this prayer is to embody the spirit of Prometheus, defying the gods, stealing their fire, inviting their wrath, facing their vengeance, but liberating humanity. The logic of the Lord's Prayer is that those who pray it commit themselves to become the means by which it is answered. Secondly, modernity's own strategies for dealing with the concerns of the present are salvation mythologies through and through: placing faith in technological progress to avert ecological disaster; seeking 'more of the same' economic solutions to crises caused by policies of self-interest. In both cases, this is wishful thinking designed to protect the comforts of the familiar for those within the household, rather than seek the wellbeing of those excluded from it. This is the concern taken up in chapter 8, which outlined alternative ways of en-countering otherness beyond the confines of the given limits imposed upon modernity by the currently dominant brands of capitalism.

For Thine Is the Kingdom, the Power and the Glory, for Ever and Ever

These words, generally referred to as the Doxology, are not original to the biblical texts from which the Lord's Prayer is translated. Throughout history, notions of divine authority, power and glory have often been attributed to the gods in order to uphold the luxuries, comforts and splendour of a ruling power. In Christian scriptures, however, these images are drastically reconfigured: authority is perfectly embodied in a peasant from a remote province; power is exerted through human weakness and has all the hallmarks of failure; glory is expressed ultimately in the torture and execution of a failed rebel leader. This reconfigured, alternative way of life is vindicated by the resurrection of Israel's Messiah.

Christendom, I have argued, failed to remain attentive to this central dimension of Jesus' ministry. Though comprised largely of virtues distilled from the dynamic of Christian faith, Christendom was by no means a faithful (and certainly not the only possible) means of embodying the social, political and worshipful dimensions of Christian belief. While it is impossible to assess whether Christendom was a force for good in the world, its more regrettable and lamentable heritages have been well publicized by atheists throughout history. Among them is Bertrand Russell who, although deeply critical of the faith engendered by Christendom, nevertheless accepted the validity of an alternative form of religion. As such, the manner of post-Christendom belief advanced in this book runs in deep harmony with Russell's own hopes for religion. He regarded as his clearest statement on religion a chapter written in 1916. Having lamented the negative impact of institutional Christianity, he continues:

> If a religious view of life and the world is ever to reconquer the thoughts and feelings of free-minded men and women, much that we are accustomed to associate with religion will have to be discarded. The first and greatest change that is required is to establish a morality of initiative, not a morality of submission, a morality of hope rather than fear, of things to be done rather than of things to be left undone. It is not the whole duty of man to slip through the world so as to   escape the wrath of God. The world is *our* world, and it rests with us to make it a heaven or a hell. The power is ours, and the kingdom and the glory would be ours also if we had courage and insight to create them. The religious life that we must seek will not be one of occasional solemnity and superstitious prohibitions, it will not be sad or ascetic, it will concern itself little with rules of conduct. It will be inspired by a vision of what human life may be, and will be happy with the joy of creation, living in a large free world of initiative and hope. It will love mankind, not for what they are to the outward eye, but for what imagination shows that they have it in them to become. It will not readily condemn, but it will give praise to positive achievement rather than negative sinlessness, to the joy of life, the quick affection, the creative insight, by which the world may grow young and beautiful and filled with vigour.[1]

All of this is profoundly consistent with the Christianity engendered in a post-Christendom reading of the Lord's Prayer. Even Russell's claim that power, kingdom and authority are 'ours' can – properly interpreted – awaken in humanity Scripture's own call to recognize our God-given place in the world, to take responsibility for it, and to use the powers at our disposal. The interpretation of the prayer offered above is by no means exhaustive and does not deny its 'spiritual' component. It does, however, root whatever spirituality may blossom from it in the prior, earthy, practical realities of the world as it is, aligning Christian practice with the ethical passions of radical atheism.

To be Christian, after all, is to embrace the bitter recognition of what human life really is. A human is an assembly of subatomic particles, which – for a tragically minuscule nano-fragment of time – have taken the form of carnal matter. We are comprised exclusively of shrapnel from the big bang, born in violence and propelled towards death, headless chickens, human wreckage, briefly animated corpses whose proudest achievements appear as involuntary twitches and jerks brought on by electronic impulses. The entire life span of our race, the greatest heights of our civilization and the profoundest depths of our love occupy no more than a hideously insignificant splinter of history. Floating through a dark corner of time and space, lonely amid the unfathomable expanse of infinite void, humanity will soon be engulfed in the cold shadow of eternal silence. How do we en-counter this implausible but inescapable reality? By placing our fingers in our ears and singing our hymns more loudly? By scrambling to capture some kind of meaning from an otherwise meaningless life? Or by facing this reality full on, divested of all optimism and gloom, unflinching, refusing to avert our gaze but ever searching, probing, exploring, seeking to penetrate the darkness?

If we gaze through a telescope, we are reminded that an eternal record of all activity is streaming live from every point in space and time. (Any being in the Andromeda galaxy, furnished with a powerful enough telescope, could point it at planet earth today and witness, as live events, our pre-human ancestors crafting the earliest stone tools 2.5 million years ago.) Hurtling across space at the speed of light is the unbroken, everlasting imprint of every nanosecond we live. Every detail of every moment of every life will far outlast the life span of our planet, to survive at least as long as the universe itself. Not a religious fantasy, nor philosophical wishful thinking, but the closest thing humanity has to hard, rational, modern scientific fact: the surety that every heartbeat will endure for all eternity. Our every action and experience is packed with cosmic significance, broadcast on waves of light rippling through the infinite reaches of space and time. Nothing is forgotten.

If we gaze through a microscope, we are reminded of the impenetrable depths of any object in our hand, the bottomless mystery of how it holds together as an object, and the cruel limitations of human perception. The most powerful microscope in the world is currently the Large Hadron Collider (LHC) in Switzerland, a monument to humanity's thirst for knowledge and phenomenal ability to understand the world around us. This feat of human knowledge is a worthy object of wonder in and of itself. And yet, even the LHC has a limited depth of sight. Growing numbers of physicists seeking a Unified Theory of Everything concede that 'physics will not be complete until it can explain how space and time emerge from something more fundamental.'[2] The microscope reveals that the ground beneath our feet is a swirling vortex of energy particles, behaving in ways that we can now identify and even influence, but still not understand. We have even learned that the space between two people, like the space between two galaxies, is far from empty. If nothing else, the microscope has taught us that there is no such thing as 'nothing'.

If we gaze into the eyes of another being, a whole new world opens up, and we might see all manner of things. In the modern era, I have argued, the first thing we are likely to see is our own reflection. As Narcissus stared into the pool and became besotted with himself, so the modernist must strain every moral sinew to look at the TV, the smart phone or the computer screen and see beyond their own reflection. Modern humans have been ideologically modified to see little beyond their own projected self, submerging the presence of the other beneath the overwhelming tide of ultimate self-interest. Sure, we can see the children in need, the pitiable eyes of the charity appeal, the other whose life we can save by flicking digital loose change at the computer. This is the fragile other, the object of charity who exists to confirm our moral and cultural superiority. But what about the others who will not be trampled upon, who organize themselves to stand against the status quo from which we benefit, the others we might hastily label communists or terrorists, trailer trash or chavs? What about the other whose stare we cannot hold, and from whose eyes we must avert our gaze?

In the early years of the new millennium, the dust cloud of an obliterated Christendom is beginning to clear, and the ancient Christ appears more starkly in the form of the other. The gods of our age, however, have almost demolished the human appetite, capacity and courage to engage with otherness. After Christendom, Venus and Mars have flourished to exert their genius and power in our secular, postmodern world, where they are worshipped unwittingly and obeyed unswervingly. To be radically atheist and to be radically Christian is to defy these gods, demonstrating contempt for them by seeking an alternative world, summoning up the nerve, the patience and the faith to pursue this dangerous quest to encounter the genuinely other:

Come, my friends,
'Tis not too late to seek a newer world . . .
To sail beyond the sunset, and the baths
Of all the western stars, until I die.
It may be that the gulfs will wash us down:
It may be we shall touch the Happy Isles,
And see the great Achilles, whom we knew.
Though much is taken, much abides; and though
We are not now that strength which in old days
Moved earth and heaven, that which we are, we are;
One equal temper of heroic hearts,
Made weak by time and fate, but strong in will
To strive, to seek, to find, and not to yield.[3]

Select Bibliography

Alfody, G. 'Subject and Ruler, Subjects and Methods: An Attempt at a Conclusion.' Pages 254–61 in *Subject and Ruler: The Cult of the Ruling Power in Classical Antiquity, Journal of Roman Archaeology*, Supplemental Series 17 (ed. A. Small; Ann Arbor, MI: n.p., 1996).

Aristotle. *Nicomachean Ethics* (trans. Roger Crisp; Cambridge: Cambridge University Press, 2002).

Augustine. *The City of God against the Pagans* (trans. R.W. Dyson; Cambridge: Cambridge University Press, 1998).

Baggini, Julian. *Atheism: A Very Short Introduction* (Oxford: Oxford University Press, 2003).

Barnes, J. *A History of the World in 10 ½ Chapters* (London: Vintage, 2009).

Barth, K. *The Word of God and the Word of Man* (trans. S.A. Weston; New York: Pilgrim Press, 1928).

Bauckham, Richard. *The Theology of the Book of Revelation* (Cambridge: Cambridge University Press, 1993).

Baudelaire, Charles. *Le Spleen de Paris* (Paris: Flammarion, 2012).

Boyd, Ian. 'Making Science Count in Government.' *Elife Sciences*, eLife 2013;2:e01061 (2 July 2013) http://elife.elifesciences.org/content/2/e01061 (accessed 4 December 2013).

Buckley, Michael J. *At the Origins of Modern Atheism* (Yale: Yale University Press, 1990).

Caputo, John D. *The Prayers and Tears of Jacques Derrida: Religion without Religion* (Bloomington and Indianapolis: Indiana University Press, 1997).

Cavanaugh, William T. *The Myth of Religious Violence: Secular Ideology and the Roots of Modern Conflict* (Oxford: Oxford University Press, 2009).

Chomsky, Noam. *Class Warfare: Interviews with David Barsamian* (New York: Pluto, 1995).

Conzelmann, H. *The Theology of Saint Luke* (trans. Geoffrey Buswell; London: Faber & Faber, 1960 [1953]).

Cox, Harvey, 'The Market as God: Living in the New Dispensation'. *The Atlantic* (1 March 1999).

Dawkins, Richard. *The Selfish Gene* (Oxford: Oxford University Press, 1989).

— *The God Delusion* (London: Bantam, 2006).

Derrida, Jacques. *Of Grammatology* (trans. Gayatri Chakravorty Spivak; Baltimore and London: Johns Hopkins University Press, 1976).

— *Given Time, vol. 1: Counterfeit Money* (trans. P. Kamuf; Chicago: University of Chicago Press, 1991).

— *The Gift of Death* (trans. David Willis; Chicago: Chicago University Press, 1995).

— *On the Name* (ed. T. Dutoit; trans. D. Wood, John P. Leavey Jr, Ian Macleod; Stanford: Stanford University Press, 1995).

— *The Animal That Therefore I Am* (trans. David Wills; New York: Fordham University Press, 2008).

Droge, A.J. 'The Graeco-Roman World.' Pages 230–44 in the *Cambridge History of Christianity*, vol. 1 (ed. Margaret M. Mitchel and Frances M. Young; Cambridge: Cambridge University Press, 2006).

Descartes, René. *Meditations on First Philosophy* (trans. John Cottingham; Cambridge: Cambridge University Press, 1996).

Eagleton, Terry. 'The Estate Agent: The Trouble with Principle by Stanley Fish'. *London Review of Books* 22.5 (2000): pp. 10–11.

— *Reason, Faith and Revolution: Reflections on the God Debate* (New Haven: Yale University Press, 2009).

Eusebius. *The History of the Church from Christ to Constantine* (trans. G.A. Williamson; London: Penguin, 1989).

Fara, P. *Newton: The Making of Genius* (London: Macmillan, 2003).

Fiddes, Paul. *Seeing the World and Knowing God: Hebrew Wisdom and Christian Doctrine in a Late-Modern Context* (Oxford: Oxford University Press, 2013).

Firestein, Stuart. *Ignorance: How It Drives Science* (Oxford: Oxford University Press, 2012).

Fish, Stanley. *Doing What Comes Naturally* (Oxford: Clarendon Press, 1989).

— *There's No Such Thing as Free Speech: And It's a Good Thing Too* (Oxford: Oxford University Press, 1994).

— 'Atheism and Evidence.' *New York Times* (17 June 2007) http://opinionator.blogs.nytimes.com/2007/06/17/atheism-and-evidence/?_r=0 (accessed 14 September 2013).

Flynn, James, R. *What Is Intelligence?* (Cambridge: Cambridge University Press, 2007).

France, Peter. *Diderot* (Oxford: Oxford University Press, 1983).

Friedman, T. *The Lexus and the Olive Tree* (London: HarperCollins, 2000).

Goudzwaard, Bob. *Capitalism and Progress: A Diagnosis of Western Society* (Milton Keynes: Paternoster Press, 1997).

Graeber, David. *Debt: The First 5000 Years* (New York: Melville House, 2011).

Grayling, A.C. *To Set Prometheus Free: Essays on Religion, Reason and Humanity* (London: Oberon Books, 2010).

Harbour, Daniel. *An Intelligent Person's Guide to Atheism* (London: Duckworth, 2001).

Harris, Sam. *The End of Faith: Religion, Terror and the Future of Reason* (London: Simon & Schuster, 2006).

— *Letter to a Christian Nation: A Challenge to Faith* (London: Bantam, 2006).

— 'On the Freedom to Offend an Imaginary God' (19 September 2012) http://www.samharris.org/blog/item/on-the-freedom-to-offend-an-imaginary-god (accessed 19 September 2012).

Hart, David Bentley. *Atheist Delusions: The Christian Revolution and Its Fashionable Enemies* (Yale: Yale University Press, 2009).

Hartshorne, Charles. *Omnipotence and Other Theological Mistakes* (Albany, NY: State of New York University Press, 1984).

Hauerwas, Stanley. *After Christendom* (Nashville: Abingdon Press, 1991).

Hawking, Stephen. *The Grand Design* (New York: Bantam, 2010).

Hayek, Friedrich. *The Road to Serfdom* (Chicago: University of Chicago Press, 1944).

Hedges, Chris. *When Atheism Becomes a Religion* (London: Free Press, 2009).

— *The World as It Is: Dispatches on the Myth of Human Progress* (New York: Nation Books, 2010).

Hegel, G.W.F. *Phenomenology of Spirit* (trans. A.V. Miller; Oxford: Oxford University Press, 1977).

Heidegger, M. *Being and Time: A Translation of Sein und Zeit* (trans. J. Stambaugh; Albany, NY: State University of New York Press, 1996).

Herring, George. *Christianity: From the Early Church to the Enlightenment* (London: Continuum, 2006).

Heschel, Abraham Joshua. *The Sabbath: Its Meaning for Modern Man* (London: Farrar, Straus & Giroux, 2005).

Hitchens, Christopher. *God Is Not Great* (London: Atlantic, 2007).

Hobbes, Thomas. *Leviathan* (ed. J.C.A. Gaskin; Oxford: Oxford University Press, 1996).

Hughes, Bettany. *The Hemlock Cup: Socrates, Athens and the Search for the Good Life* (London: Jonathan Cape, 2010).

Hunter, Michael and David Wootton, eds. *Atheism from the Reformation to the Enlightenment* (Oxford: Oxford University Press, 1992).

Huxley, Aldous, *Point Counter Point* (London: Penguin, 1955).

Hyman, Gavin. *A Short History of Atheism* (London: I.B. Tauris, 2010).

Johnson, Luke Timothy. *The Creed: What Christians Believe and Why It Matters* (New York: Image, 2004).

Jones, Owen. *Chavs: The Demonization of the Working Class* (London: Verso, 2011).

— 'Not in Our Name: Dawkins Dresses Up Bigotry as Non-Belief – He Cannot Be Left to Represent Atheists'. *The Independent* (9 August 2013).

Josephus, Flavius. *The Jewish War* (trans. G.A. Williamson; London: Penguin, 1959).

Justin Martyr. *The Writings of Justin Martyr* (ed. Alexander Roberts and James Donaldson; London: Apocrophile, 2007).

Kee, Alistair. *Constantine versus Christ: The Triumph of Ideology* (London: SCM Press, 1982).

Kellum, Barbara. 'Concealing/Revealing: Gender and the Play of Meaning in the Monuments of Augustan Rome.' Pages

158–81 in *The Roman Cultural Revolution* (ed. Thomas Habinek and Alessandro Schiesaro; Cambridge: Cambridge University Press, 1997).

Keynes, John Maynard. 'Newton the Man.' Lecture manuscript (1946) http://www-history.mcs.st-and.ac.uk/Extras/Keynes_Newton.html (accessed 10 December 2013).

— *Essays in Persuasion* (New York: W.W. Norton & Co., 1963).

— *The General Theory of Employment, Interest and Money* (New York: Classic House, 2008).

Kierkegaard, S. Concluding Unscientific Postscript (trans. D.F. Swenson and W. Lowrie; Princeton: Princeton University Press, 1968 [1846]).

— *Fear and Trembling* (trans. Alastair Hannay; London: Penguin, 1985).

Kimball, Charles. *When Religion Becomes Evil* (New York: Harper-Collins, 2002).

Klein, Naomi. *Shock Doctrine: The Rise of Disaster Capitalism* (London: Penguin, 2008).

Kreider, Alan. *The Change of Conversion and the Origin of Christendom* (Harrisburg, PA: Trinity Press, 1999).

Kreider, A. and Kreider E. *Worship and Mission after Christendom* (Milton Keynes: Paternoster Press, 2009).

Lactantius. *De Mortibus Persecutorum* (trans. Anthony Bowen and Peter Garnsey; Liverpool: Liverpool University Press, 2003).

Lewis, C.S. *The Lion, the Witch and the Wardrobe* (London: Harper-Collins, 1980).

Macmullen, Ramsay. *Christianizing the Roman Empire*, A.D. *100–400* (New Haven and London: Yale University Press, 1984).

McGrath, Alister. *Why God Won't Go Away: Engaging with the New Atheism* (London: SPCK, 2011).

Merali, Zeeya. 'Theoretical Physics: The Origins of Space and Time'. *Nature* (28 August 2013): pp. 516–19.

Mirowski, Philip. *Never Let a Serious Crisis Go to Waste: How Neoliberalism Survived the Financial Meltdown* (New York: Verso, 2013).

Monbiot, George. *Captive State: The Corporate Takeover of Britain* (London: Pan, 2001).

— *The Age of Consent: A Manifesto for a New World Order* (London: HarperCollins, 2004).

— 'Clearing Up This Mess.' *The Guardian* (18 November 2008).

— 'The Holocaust We Will Not See.' *The Guardian* (11 January 2010).

— 'Bang Goes the Theory.' *The Guardian* (14 January 2013).

— 'Age of Unreason.' *The Guardian* (30 September 2013).

— 'Career Advice'
http://www.monbiot.com/career-advice/ (accessed 10 December 2013).

Montaigne, Michel de. *The Essays: A Selection* (trans. M.A. Screech; London: Penguin, 2004).

Murray, Stuart. *Post Christendom* (Milton Keynes: Paternoster Press, 2004).

— *Church after Christendom* (Milton Keynes: Paternoster Press, 2005).

Nietzsche, Friedrich. *The Portable Nietzsche* (ed. Walter Kaufmann; London: Penguin, 1954).

— *Twilight of the Idols/The Anti-Christ* (trans. R.J. Hollingdale; Aylesbury: Penguin, 1968).

— *The Will to Power* (trans. Walter Kaufmann and R.J. Hollingdale; New York: Vintage, 1968).

Onfray, Michel. *In Defence of Atheism: The Case against Christianity, Judaism and Islam* (trans. Jeremy Leggatt; London: Serpent's Tail, 2005).

Origen, *Contra Celsum* (trans. Henry Chadwick; Cambridge: Cambridge University Press, 1953).

Packard, Vance. *The Hidden Persuaders* (London: Penguin, 1957).

Phillipps, J.B. *The New Testament in Modern English* (London: Collins, 2009).

Perry, Simon. *All Who Came Before* (Eugene, OR: Cascade, 2011).

— *Resurrecting Interpretation: Technology, Hermeneutics and the Parable of the Rich Man and Lazarus (Luke 16:19–31)* (Eugene, OR: Wipf & Stock, 2012).

Petronius. *The Satyricon* (trans. P.G. Walsh; Oxford: Oxford University Press, 2009).

Philo. *Philo: Volume X, On the Embassy to Gaius. General Indexes* (trans. F.H. Colson; Cambridge: Harvard University Press, 1962).

Pietersen, Lloyd. *Reading the Bible after Christendom* (Milton Keynes: Paternoster Press, 2011).

Pinker, Steven. *The Better Angels of our Nature* (London: Penguin, 2011).

Plantinga, A. 'The Dawkins Confusion'. *Christianity Today* (March/April 2007) http://www.booksandculture.com/articles/2007/marapr/1.21.html (accessed 24 March 2014).

Plato. 'Phaedrus.' Pages 405–679 in *Plato*, vol. I (trans. H.N. Fowler; Cambridge: Harvard University Press, 1914).

— *Plato II: Laches-Protagoras-Meno-Euthydemus* (trans. W.R.M. Lamb; Cambridge: Harvard University Press, 1924).

— 'Timaeus.' Pages 1–253 in *Plato*, vol. VII (trans. R.G. Bury; Cambridge: Harvard University Press, 1929).

Postman, Neil. *Amusing Ourselves to Death* (London: Methuen, 1987).

Price, S.R.F. *Rituals and Power: The Roman Imperial Cult in Asia Minor* (Cambridge: Cambridge University Press, 1984).

Quiggin, John. *Zombie Economics: How Dead Ideas Still Walk among Us* (Princeton: Princeton University Press, 2012).

Rand, Ayn. *Atlas Shrugged* (London: Penguin, 1957).

Retallack, Gregory J. 'Rocks, Views, Soils and Plants at the Temples of Ancient Greece'. *Antiquity* 8.317 (2008): pp. 640–57.

Robinson, Richard. *Plato's Earlier Dialectic* (Oxford: Clarendon Press, 1962).

Rose, Gillian. *Love's Work: A Reckoning with Life* (London: Schocken, 1996).

Russell, B. *A History of Western Philosophy* (London: Simon & Schuster, 1957).

— *Principles of Social Reconstruction* (London: George Allen & Unwin, 1971).

Sartre, Jean-Paul. *Huis Clos* (Paris: Gallimard, 2000).

Sherk, Robert Kenneth. *Roman Documents from the Greek East: Senatus Consulta and Epistulae to the Age of Augustus* (Baltimore: Johns Hopkins University Press, 1969).

Singer, Peter. *The Expanding Circle: Ethics and Sociobiology* (New York: Farrar, Straus & Giroux, 1981).

— *The Life You Can Save* (London: Random House, 2010).

— *Practical Ethics* (Cambridge: Cambridge University Press, 2011).

Smiley, T. and West C. *The Rich and the Rest of Us: A Poverty Manifesto* (Los Angeles: Smiley Books, 2012).

Stiglitz, Joseph. *Making Globalization Work* (London: W.W. Norton & Co., 2006).

Suetonius, C. Tranquillus. *The Lives of Twelve Caesars* (trans. Robert Graves; London: Penguin, 1957).

Tacitus. *Annals, Histories, Agricola, Germania* (trans. A.J. Church and W.J. Brodribb; London: Everyman, 2009).

Taibbi, Matt. *Griftopia: A Story of Bankers, Politicians, and the Most Audacious Power Grab in American History* (New York: Spiegel & Grau, 2010).

Taylor, Mark C. 'Financialization of Art'. *Capitalism and Society* 6.2, article 3 (2011) http://capitalism.columbia.edu/files/ccs/Mark%20C.%20Taylor.pdf (accessed 30 December 2013).

Tennyson, Alfred, Lord. *Selected Poems* (ed. C. Ricks; London: Penguin, 2007).

Tertullian. *The Apology of Tertullian* (trans. W.M. Reeve; London: Newbury House, 1889).

— *Apology. De Speculis* (trans. T.R. Glover; Cambridge: Loeb, 1989).

Thrower, James. *Western Atheism: A Short History* (London: Prometheus, 1999).

Trudgill, Steve. *The Terrestrial Biosphere: Environmental Change, Ecosystem Science, Attitudes and Values* (London: Prentice, 2000).

Wade, Ira O. *The Structure and Form of the French Enlightenment* (Princeton: Princeton University Press, 1977).

Wallace, David Foster. *Oblivion: Stories* (Boston: Black Bay, 2004).

Weinberg, Steven. 'A Designer Universe?' (1999) http://www.physlink.com/Education/essay_weinberg.cfm (accessed 12 December 2013).

Wielenberg, Erik J. *Value and Virtue in a Godless Universe* (Cambridge: Cambridge University Press, 2005).

Wink, Walter. *Naming the Powers: The Language of Power in the New Testament* (Philadelphia: Fortress Press, 1984).

— *Unmasking the Powers: The Invisible Forces That Determine Human Existence* (Philadelphia: Fortress Press, 1986).

— *Engaging the Powers: Discernment and Resistance in a World of Domination* (Minneapolis: Fortress Press, 1992).

Wolin, Sheldon S. *Politics and Vision: Continuity and Innovation in Western Political Thought* (Princeton: Princeton University Press, 2006).

— *Democracy Incorporated: Managed Democracy and the Specter of Inverted Totalitarianism* (Princeton: Princeton University Press, 2010).

Wright, N.T. *Jesus and the Victory of God* (London: SPCK, 1996).
— *The Resurrection of the Son of God* (London: SPCK, 2003).
Zizek, Slavoj. 'Avatar: Return of the Natives'. *New Statesman* (4 March 2010): pp. 5–7.
— *Living in the End Times* (New York: Verso, 2010).
Zizek, S. and B. Gunjevik, *God in Pain: Inversions of Apocalypse* (New York: Seven Stories, 2012).

TV Documentaries

Face to Face. Interview with Bertrand Russell (BBC, 1959).
The Other 9/11 (BBC 4, 2003).
Light Fantastic: The Light of Reason (BBC 4, 2004).
What We Still Don't Know: Are We Real? Martin Rees (Channel 4, 2004).
Timewatch: The Most Daring Raid of World War II (BBC, 2011).

Endnotes

Introduction: Atheism in an Age of Encounter

[1] Stuart Murray in Alan Kreider and Ellie Kreider, *Worship and Mission After Christendom* (Milton Keynes: Paternoster, 2009), series preface, p. 15.

[2] See Owen Jones, *Chavs: The Demonization of the Working Class* (London: Verso, 2011).

1. Atheism before Modernity

[1] G. Alfody, 'Subject and Ruler, Subjects and Methods: An Attempt at a Conclusion', in *Subject and Ruler: The Cult of the Ruling Power in Classical Antiquity, Journal of Roman Archaeology Supplemental Series* 17 (ed. Alastair Small; Ann Arbor, MI: n.p., 1996), p. 255.

[2] Simon Price, *Rituals and Power: The Roman Imperial Cult in Asia Minor* (Cambridge: CUP, 1984), p. 248.

[3] Paulus Fabius Maximus, cited in Robert Kenneth Sherk, *Roman Documents from the Greek East: Senatus Consulta and Epistulae to the Age of Augustus* (Baltimore: Johns Hopkins University Press, 1969), p. 334.

[4] Price, *Rituals and Power*, p. 3.

[5] A.J. Droge, 'The Graeco-Roman World', in the *Cambridge History of Christianity*, vol. 1 (ed. Margaret M. Mitchel and Frances M. Young; Cambridge: CUP, 2006) p. 242.

[6] Origen, *Contra Celsum* (trans. Henry Chadwick; Cambridge: CUP, 1953), p. 25.

[7] Barbara Kellum, 'Concealing/Revealing: Gender and the Play of Meaning in the Monuments of Augustan Rome', in *The Roman*

Cultural Revolution (ed. Thomas Habinek and Alessandro Schiesaro; Cambridge: CUP, 1997), p. 178.

8 G. Herring, *Christianity: From the Early Church to the Enlightenment* (London: Continuum, 2006), p. 54.

9 Nothing in the written Christian creeds of Christendom was at odds with the natural order expressed in this deeper, subconscious, universal creed – at least once Mars and Venus are kept back-stage. In Christendom, the gentle Christ can play the role of Venus, the victorious Christ can play Mars, and the emperor is his elected representative on earth.

10 Eusebius, *The History of the Church from Christ to Constantine* (trans. G.A. Williamson; London: Penguin, 1989), 8.2.4, p. 44.

11 Richard Bauckham, *The Theology of the Book of Revelation* (Cambridge: CUP, 1993), p. 38.

12 Justin Martyr, *First Apology, The Writings of Justin Martyr* (ed. Alexander Roberts and James Donaldson; London: Apocrophile, 2007), p. 214.

13 Justin Martyr, *First Apology*, p. 178.

14 Bettany Hughes, *The Hemlock Cup* (London: Jonathan Cape, 2010), p. 114.

15 Although precisely what morality means for Rome is a complex question. Tacitus, for instance, criticizes the Jews' morality because 'it is a crime among them to kill any newly-born infant'. Tacitus, *Annals, Histories, Agricola, Germania* (trans. A.J. Church and W.J. Brodribb; London: Everyman, 2009), 5.5, p. 55. Morality here is not concerned with making people good but with keeping people obedient, with deeply rooted conformity to the prevailing social rules that kept the empire running smoothly.

16 Tertullian, *The Apology of Tertullian* (trans. W.M. Reeve; London: Newbury House, 1889), p. 144.

17 Eusebius, *History of the Church*, p. 92.

18 Alistair Kee, *Constantine versus Christ* (London: SCM, 1982), p. 158.

19 Kee, *Constantine versus Christ*, p. 154.

20 Luke Timothy Johnson, *The Creed: What Christians Believe and Why It Matters* (New York: Image, 2004), pp. 60–61.

21 Stuart Murray, *Post Christendom* (Milton Keynes: Paternoster, 2004), p. 132.

22 Murray, *Post Christendom*, p. 144.

23 Singer's work here is easily misrepresented. His endorsement of infanticide is based upon a particular view of what it is to be human.

That same view of humanity drives a deep humanitarian concern for others, manifest in Singer's own commitments to alleviate poverty – commitments which expose the majority of western Christians as unwittingly indifferent to the suffering of others.

2. Revolutionary Atheism

[1] Of course, Descartes was not the only thinker in this tradition. Others have recognized in the defiance of the great German reformer Martin Luther (1483–1546) the tendency to relocate the centre of moral gravity from a god in heaven to the individual's conscience.

[2] This well-known aphorism is attributed to Protagoras in Plato's dialogue of the same name. In its original context, the aphorism is best interpreted as emphasizing human finitude, highlighting how we can only guess at what is *universal* from our own *particular* experience. However, its more favoured use is to celebrate humanity barging Christendom's god off centre-stage in accounting for the universe. In neither case is there good reason to interpret the phrase negatively.

[3] John Maynard Keynes, 'Newton the Man', lecture manuscript (1946) http://www-history.mcs.st-and.ac.uk/Extras/Keynes_Newton.html (accessed 10 Dec. 2013).

[4] Martin Rees, *Max Tegmark, What We Still Don't Know: Are We Real?* (Channel 4, 2004); Simon Schaffer, Light Fantastic: The Light of Reason (BBC, 2004).

[5] See especially the Wisdom Literature of the Hebrew Bible, notably Psalm 8; Job 38; Proverbs 30.

[6] Peter France, *Diderot* (Oxford: OUP), p. 9.

[7] Michael J. Buckley, *At the Origins of Modern Atheism* (Yale: Yale University Press, 1990), p. 249.

[8] France, *Diderot*, p. 37.

[9] James Thrower, *Western Atheism: A Short History* (London: Prometheus, 1999), p. 100.

[10] Michel Onfray attributes this honour to Jean Meslier (1664–1729), a Catholic priest who, upon his death, was discovered to have penned a manuscript advocating the brand of atheism familiar to the modern mind.

[11] Thrower, *Western Atheism*, p. 107.

12 Ira O. Wade, *The Structure and Form of the French Enlightenment* (Princeton: Princeton University Press, 1977), p. 310.

13 Wade, *French Enlightenment*, p. 319.

14 Gavin Hyman, *A Short History of Atheism* (London: I.B. Tauris, 2010), pp. 11–12.

15 Bertrand Russell, *Face to Face* (BBC, 1959).

16 Michael Hunter and David Wootton, eds, *Atheism from the Reformation to the Enlightenment* (Oxford: OUP, 1992), p. 127.

17 Quoted by A. Plantinga in 'The Dawkins Confusion', *Christianity Today* (March/April 2007) http://www.booksandculture.com/articles/2007/marapr/1.21.html (accessed 24 March 2014).

18 Plantinga, 'The Dawkins Confusion'.

19 Richard Dawkins, *The God Delusion* (London: Bantam, 2006), p. 12.

20 The USA (with over 800 bases located in 150 countries) spends as much money on military as the rest of the world put together. Under the protection of Mars, US citizens such as Harris and Dennett can afford to be courageous about their beliefs.

21 Terry Eagleton, *Reason, Faith and Revolution* (New Haven: Yale University Press, 2009), p. 13.

22 Steven Weinberg, 'A Designer Universe?' (1999) http://www.physlink.com/Education/essay_weinberg.cfm (accessed 12 Dec. 2013).

23 Charles Kimball, *When Religion Becomes Evil* (New York: HarperCollins, 2002), p. 1.

24 Dawkins, *God Delusion*, p. 44.

25 William T. Cavanaugh, *The Myth of Religious Violence* (Oxford: OUP, 2009).

26 Cavanaugh, *Myth of Religious Violence*, p. 13.

27 Cavanaugh, *Myth of Religious Violence*, p. 59.

28 Not least by Karl Barth.

3. Philosophical Traditions and Otherness

1 For this reason, I have omitted to discuss several schools of thought that arise from the larger influences I have identified. Utilitarianism, for instance, along with idealism and realism, empiricism and scepticism, I believe are surface ripples of the deeper currents identified below.

2 Bertrand Russell, *The History of Western Philosophy* (London: Simon & Schuster), p. 300.

³ Russell, *History of Western Philosophy,* pp. 362–63.

⁴ J.B. Phillips' translation of Paul's letter to Romans offers the clearest example of New Testament existentialism: 'Don't let the world squeeze you into its own mould, but be transformed by the renewing of your mind' (Rom. 12:2).

⁵ Originally, 'l'enfer, c'est les autres', Jean-Paul Sartre, *Huis Clos* (Paris: Gallimard, 2000), p. 14, translated into English as *No Exit.* Such an insight is not to be taken negatively, but rather as the recognition of the sheer trauma that genuine encounter with another can create for the individual.

⁶ The advertisers' appeal requires the target audience to be compliant with the very technological mindset from which Heidegger invested his energies trying to liberate his readers.

⁷ Terry Eagleton, 'The Estate Agent: The Trouble with Principle by Stanley Fish', *London Review of Books* 22.5 (2000): pp. 10–11.

⁸ Jacques Derrida, *The Animal That Therefore I Am* (trans. David Wills; New York: Fordham University Press, 2008).

⁹ John D. Caputo, *Prayers and Tears of Jacques Derrida* (Bloomington and Indianapolis: Indiana University Press, 1997), p. 78.

4. The Otherness of Scripture

¹ Lloyd Pietersen, *Reading the Bible after Christendom* (Milton Keynes: Paternoster, 2011), p. 97.

² Abraham showed hospitality to three strangers in the hottest part of the day, rushing around to offer them the very best of his goods. As it turned out, they happened to be agents through whom Yahweh was implementing his promise to Abraham.

³ Richard Dawkins, *The God Delusion* (London: Bantam, 2006), p. 51.

⁴ Pietersen, *Reading the Bible,* p. 93.

⁵ Augustine was the first to make use of this image in his *City of God;* see *The City of God against the Pagans* (trans. R.W. Dyson; Cambridge: CUP, 1998), book 4, ch. 10, p. 155. It was then taken up and expounded at length by Luther.

⁶ Michel de Montaigne, The Essays: A Selection (trans. M.A. Screech; London: Penguin, 2004), pp. 17–36.

Interlude: Resurrection

1 Gillian Rose, *Love's Work: A Reckoning with Life* (London: Schocken, 1996), p. 105.
2 G.W.F. Hegel, *Phenomenology of Spirit* (trans. A.V. Miller; Oxford: OUP, 1977), p. 805.
3 Terry Eagleton, *Reason, Faith and Revolution* (New Haven: Yale University Press, 2009), p. 33.
4 Eagleton, *Reason, Faith and Revolution*, p. 23.
5 Eagleton, *Reason, Faith and Revolution*, p. 27.
6 Eagleton, *Reason, Faith and Revolution*, pp. 37–8.
7 These words form the opening line of a hymn penned in 1773 by William Cowper, shortly before his attempted suicide.
8 See further below.
9 Abraham Joshua Heschel, *The Sabbath: Its Meaning for Modern Man* (London: Farrar, Straus & Giroux, 2005), p. 4.
10 The German title of Hanz Conzelmann's commentary of the Gospel of Saint Luke was *Die Mitte der Zeit*.

5. Science and Miracles

1 Peter Atkins in debate with William Lane Craig, 'Does God Exist?', University of Manchester, 26 October 2011.
2 Stephen Hawking, *The Grand Design* (New York: Bantam, 2010), p. 2.
3 Julian Baggini, *Atheism: A Very Short Introduction* (Oxford: OUP, 2003), p. 16.
4 Stuart Firestein, *Ignorance: How It Drives Science* (Oxford: OUP, 2012), p. 1.
5 Firestein, *Ignorance*, p. 2.
6 Firestein, *Ignorance*, p. 2.
7 Or 'Particle Accelerator'.
8 Christopher Hitchens, *God Is Not Great* (London: Atlantic, 2007), p. 5.
9 Terry Eagleton, *Reason, Faith and Revolution* (New Haven: Yale University Press, 2009), p. 125.
10 It is noteworthy that in the gospels the most widely reported reaction to Jesus' miracles is not to conclude that he is God, but to ask questions, namely, 'Who is this man?' The only folk to announce publicly that he was the Son of God were those possessed by demons!

[11] This highlights a recurring theme of this book, namely that most modern atheists have their cannons turned upon Christendom, not upon Christianity. The irksome thing about belief, for atheists like Dawkins, Russell and Baggini, is not so much belief in the miraculous, but the authority upon which we are encouraged to believe in the supposedly miraculous. A repressive church once compelled belief, but a crumbling Christendom has had to adopt a more humble approach: sometimes it claims that we need Christianity in order to be moral; sometimes it employs dubious reasoning in the attempt to prove the existence of God; sometimes it appeals to pseudo-science to claim that God is necessary for human existence. Atheists who obliterate such views thereby do great service for the church.

[12] Humans possess more than five senses, the most obvious being heat, movement and time.

[13] Julian Barnes, *A History of the World in 10½ Chapters* (London: Vintage, 2009), p. 241.

[14] Quoted by Steve Trudgill in *The Terrestrial Biosphere: Environmental Change, Ecosystem Science, Attitudes and Values* (London: Prentice, 2000), p. 54.

[15] See pp. 86–87 for a fuller discussion of metanoia.

[16] Lloyd Pietersen, *Reading the Bible after Christendom* (Milton Keynes: Paternoster, 2011), p. 76.

[17] Pietersen, *Reading the Bible*, pp. 76–7.

6. Sources of Ethics

[1] Charles Hartshorne, *Omnipotence and Other Theological Mistakes* (Albany: State of New York University Press, 1984), p. 11.

[2] Simon Perry, *All Who Came Before* (Eugene, OR: Cascade, 2011).

[3] Peter Singer, *The Expanding Circle: Ethics and Sociobiology* (New York: Farrar, Straus & Giroux, 1981).

[4] James R. Flynn, *What Is Intelligence?* (Cambridge: CUP, 2007).

[5] Steven Pinker, *The Better Angels of Our Nature* (London: Penguin, 2011).

[6] Pinker, *Better Angels*, p. 287.

[7] Pinker states explicitly (Pinker, *Better Angels*, p. 658) that our 'recent ancestors' are 'morally retarded'.

[8] C.S. Lewis, *The Lion, the Witch and the Wardrobe* (London: HarperCollins, 1980), pp. 142–51.

9 With perhaps the exception of Dawkins, who did oppose the war – but supported the Islamaphobia that made it morally doable. See Owen Jones, 'Not in Our Name: Dawkins Dresses Up Bigotry as Non-Belief – He Cannot Be Left to Represent Atheists', *The Independent* (9 August 2013).

10 Sam Harris, *The End of Faith* (London: Simon & Schuster, 2006), p. 129.

11 Harris, *End of Faith*, p. 147, although he adds an endnote concluding with the contradictory claim: 'Intentions matter, but they are not all that matter' (p. 255).

12 Richard Dawkins, *The God Delusion* (London: Bantam, 2006), p. 51.

7. Economics, Venus and the Whore

1 T. Friedman, *The Lexus and the Olive Tree* (London: HarperCollins, 2000).

2 As worship is defined in chapter 2.

3 John Maynard Keynes, *The General Theory of Employment, Interest and Money* (New York: Classic House), p. 383.

4 In particular, the Gramm-Leach-Bliley Act (GLB) of 1999, which removed safeguards established after the Great Depression of 1929. This allowed the merger of investment banks with commercial banks and insurance companies, creating businesses that were 'too big to fail', too big to jail and ensuring that, when they did fail, the cost was not shouldered by those who had caused the failure.

5 This was the logic both of Friedman and the Chicago Boys when their plan failed in Chile, and of Alan Greenspan after the crisis of 2008.

6 The 'Homeowner Affordability and Stability Plan'.

7 Owen Jones, *Chavs: The Demonization of the Working Class* (London: Verso, 2011), p. 257.

8 As any reading of Ayn Rand clearly demonstrates. Rand's writings, particularly her *Atlas Shrugged*, have steadily grown in popularity over the last generation, and show the inevitable convergence of modern atheism and the neoliberal capitalism that favours the wealthy and incriminates the poor.

9 Harvey Cox, 'The Market as God: Living in the New Dispensation', *The Atlantic* (1 March 1999). Cox offers an incisive and, as it turned out, a prescient reading of what the market is and how it functions.

[10] Philip Mirowski, *Never Let a Serious Crisis Go to Waste: How Neoliberalism Survived the Financial Meltdown* (New York: Verso, 2013).

[11] Mirowski, *Crisis*, p. 14.

[12] In the US, Barack Obama won advertising awards for his first election campaign. The magazine *Ad Age* grants an annual award to those whose marketing strategies are most impressive. In recent years it has gone to Taco Bell (2013), Chrysler Motor Group (2012), Coca Cola (2011), Ford Motor Co. (2010), and Hyundai (2009). The fact that the 2008 award went to Barack Obama at least raises the question of precisely what implications this has for democracy.

[13] Mirowski, *Crisis*, pp. 165–77.

[14] See Mirowski, *Crisis*, pp. 165–7.

[15] 'When art is not only commodified and corporatized but also financialized, it loses its critical function and ends up reinforcing the very structures and systems it ought to be questioning. With crises – financial, political, military, environmental, educational – proliferating faster than our ability to understand or respond to them, art might seem to be a luxury we no longer can afford. This is, however, a mistake: indeed, at this pivotal moment we need art more than ever. If art can once again find its way, perhaps we can begin to imagine alternative realities upon which a viable future depends.' Mark C. Taylor, 'Financialization of Art', *Capitalism and Society* 6.2, article 3 (2011), p. 17 http://capitalism.columbia.edu/files/ccs/Mark%20C.%20Taylor.pdf (accessed 30 Dec. 2013).

[16] Chris Hedges, *The World as It Is: Dispatches on the Myth of Human Progress* (New York: Nation Books, 2010), p. xi.

[17] Monbiot, 'Career Advice' http://www.monbiot.com/career-advice/ (accessed 10 Dec. 2013).

[18] Hedges, *World as It Is*, pp. xi–xii.

[19] Ian Boyd, 'Making Science Count in Government', Elife Sciences, eLife 2013;2:e01061 (2 July 2013) http://elife.elifesciences.org/content/2/e01061 (accessed 4 Dec. 2013).

[20] George Monbiot, 'Age of Unreason', *The Guardian* (30 September 2013).

[21] Jones, *Chavs*, p. 167, quoted by Mirowski, Crisis, p. 118.

[22] Mirowski, *Crisis*, p. 117 (italics Mirowski's).

[23] Charles Baudelaire: 'La plus belle des ruses du diable est de vous persuader qu'il n'existe pas.' *Le Spleen de Paris* (Paris: Flammarion, 2012), p. 62.

24 See T. Smiley and C. West, *The Rich and the Rest of Us: A Poverty Manifesto* (Los Angeles: Smiley Books, 2012).

25 Richard Robinson, *Plato's Earlier Dialectic* (Oxford: Clarendon, 1962), pp. 67–9.

26 All too frequently, neoliberals demand that we outline a viable alternative as a prerequisite for opposing the movement as a whole, before claiming, 'It wouldn't work.' The obvious response is that our current system is not working. No doubt, the same economists who failed to predict the 2008 crisis will fail to predict the next which will inevitably follow if we simply continue with 'more of the same'. If you are witness to a murder, and have the ability to stop it, you are not required to offer the murderer a detailed plan for the rest of the victim's life before intervening.

8. The Age of Encounter

1 '. . . A tongue-in-cheek pseudo-behind-the-scenes story designed to appeal to urban or younger consumers' self-imagined savvy about marketing tactics and objective data and to flatter their sense that in this age of metatistic spin and trend and the complete commercialization of every last thing in their world they were unprecedentedly ad-savvy and discerning and canny and well-nigh impossible to manipulate.' D.F. Wallace, *Oblivion: Stories* (Boston: Black Bay, 2004), p. 61.

2 Hitchens never acknowledges the source of this sound bite. In Greville's poem 'Mustapha', the poet laments, 'Oh wearisome condition of humanity!/Born under one law, to another bound,/Vainly begot and yet forbidden vanity,/Created sick, commanded to be sound.' The citation was popularized by Aldous Huxley's novel *Point Counter Point* (London: Penguin, 1955), p. 1.

3 David Graeber, *Debt: The First 5000 Years* (New York: Melville House, 2011), p. 382.

4 Neil Postman, *Amusing Ourselves to Death* (London: Methuen, 1987), p. 14.

5 The differences between Tweedledum and Tweedledee are real enough, but the political short-termism required of all who would be in power deters major candidates from any course of action that may jeopardize election results. Choice is more severely restricted than election campaigns suggest.

6 Petronius, *The Satyricon* (trans. P.G. Walsh; Oxford: OUP, 2009), p. 254.

7 A point recognized by George Monbiot in 'The Holocaust We Will Not See', *The Guardian* (11 January 2010).

8 For instance, the inhabitants of Senegal, Mauritania and Guinea-Bissau (who lost their fishing rights to multinational corporations) are deprived of their resources, their incomes and their homes. In fact, the world is full of the victims of economic violence who, being deprived of a voice, are kept off the moral radar (and the conscience) of most westerners.

9 Slavoj Zizek, 'Avatar: Return of the Natives', *New Statesman* (4 March 2010), p. 6.

10 Peter Singer, *The Life You Can Save* (London: Random House, 2010).

11 Slavoj Zizek, *Living in the End Times* (New York: Verso, 2010), p. 120.

12 Despite the wide currency of this pious saying, it is interesting to note that no one offered themselves up for martyrdom when the cleric Abu Hamza was extradited from the UK to the US for preaching hatred.

13 Slavoj Zizek, *End Times*, p. 144.

14 Sam Harris, 'On the Freedom to Offend an Imaginary God' (19 September 2012) http://www.samharris.org/blog/item/on-the-freedom-to-offend-an-imaginary-god (accessed 19 Sept. 2012).

15 Harris, 'On the Freedom to Offend an Imaginary God'.

16 Aristotle, *Nicomachean Ethics* (trans. Roger Crisp; Cambridge: CUP, 2002), book 7.

17 Cecil Frances Alexander (1818–95).

18 Erik J. Wielenberg, *Value and Virtue in a Godless Universe* (Cambridge: CUP, 2005), pp. 110–14.

19 Wielenberg, *Value and Virtue*, p. 139 (italics Wielenberg's).

20 George Monbiot, *The Age of Consent: A Manifesto for a New World Order* (London: HarperCollins, 2004), p. 251.

21 Sam Harris, *Letter to a Christian Nation: A Challenge to Faith* (London: Bantam, 2006), p. 24.

22 Christopher Hitchens, *God Is Not Great* (London: Atlantic, 2007), p. 43.

23 Stanley Fish unveils the faith-based demands of Dawkins and Harris in an insightful article. See 'Atheism and Evidence', *New York Times* (17 June 2007) http://opinionator.blogs.nytimes.com/2007/06/17/atheism-and-evidence/?_r=0 (accessed 14 Sept. 2013).

24 *The Most Daring Raid of World War II*, documentary about a Special Boat Squadron mission behind enemy lines.

25 Zizek, *End Times*, p. 105.

Conclusion: The Radical Atheist's Prayer

[1] Bertrand Russell, *Principles of Social Reconstruction* (London: George Allen & Unwin, 1971), pp. 203–4.

[2] Zeeya Merali, 'Theoretical Physics: The Origins of Space and Time', *Nature* (28 August 2013): p. 516.

[3] Alfred, Lord Tennyson, *Selected Poems* (ed. C. Ricks; London: Penguin, 2007), pp. 15–16.